ACHIEVING VICTORY IN IRAQ

Countering an Insurgency

Col. Dominic J. Caraccilo

and

Lt. Col. Andrea L. Thompson

Foreword by Bing West

STACKPOLE BOOKS

0 11557 00388 8

Published by
STACKPOLE BOOKS
5067 Ritter Road
Mechanicsburg, PA 17055
www.stackpolebooks.com

The ideas and opinions expressed in this book are those of the authors and do not
represent official policies of any governmental agency or the U.S. Army.

10 9 8 7 6 5 4 3 2 1

Library of Congress Cataloging-in-Publication Data

Caraccilo, Dominic J. (Dominic Joseph), 1962-
  Achieving victory in Iraq : countering an insurgency / Dominic J. Caraccilo and
Andrea L. Thompson. — 1st ed.
    p. cm.
  Includes bibliographical references and index.
  ISBN 978-0-8117-0388-8
  1. Iraq War, 2003- 2. Counterinsurgency—Iraq. I. Thompson., Andrea L. II. Title.
DS79.76.C362 2008
  956.7044'34—dc22
2008008153

CONTENTS

FOREWORD

I first met Dominic Caraccilo in a precinct station in Kirkuk in January of 2004, after a testy night. I was returning from patrol with one of his combined units—three American soldiers and six Iraqi police, or *shurtas*. On the main street, we had walked by several roadside stands aglow in strings of red and green lights that reminded me of Christmas. The troops were pointing out several black holes in the macadam from previous IEDs (improvised explosive devices) when an Iraqi Army patrol sidled by—with no American advisers. After the Iraqis exchanged guarded greetings, we walked on.

I did notice there was no warmth between the two groups, but thought nothing of it until Caraccilo showed up the next morning. He knew I was writing a piece for the *New York Times* and had been a member of a combined-action platoon in Vietnam. One point against me and one point in my favor, I guess. Ignoring my presence, Caraccilo lit into an Iraqi Army lieutenant colonel. Another IED had gone off near the barren marketplace, and two vendors were complaining that their stores had been ransacked. The IED was insurgent work, but burglaries pointed in another direction—Iraqi police or army. The lieutenant colonel complained that he couldn't watch every patrol. Okay, Caraccilo said, we join forces. From now on, every patrol—police or army—is joint.

Four years later, when I visited Kirkuk, the marketplace was thriving, and people were jamming the streets. The Iraqi brigade commander, Col. Malik Khder, briefed his operations in a way that sounded familiar. "Cooperation with the coalition," Malik said, "is responsible for the development of my brigade."

When I pressed him about his tactics, he described that when he took his first command, an American battalion commander had taken him under his wing and counseled him every day. Malik was the commander I had seen with Caraccilo in 2004.

In 2008, I again caught up with Colonel Caraccilo, who was commanding the 3rd Brigade of the 101st Air Assault Division that was occupying the Triangle of Death twenty miles southwest of Baghdad. The prior unit, the 2nd Brigade of the 10th Mountain Division, had lost sixty-nine killed, but had done such a thorough job under the command of Col. Mike Kershaw that Caraccilo had lost only one soldier since taking over in November of 2007. Caraccilo heaped praise on Kershaw. Caraccilo's men did the same thing, quick to praise the 10th Mountain that had preceded them.

On his third tour in Iraq, Caraccilo had dispersed his brigade in twenty-four battle positions across 300 square kilometers holding half a million Sunnis. Along the road next to the Euphrates where the prior battalion had encountered an IED everyday and lost twenty-nine killed, Caraccilo had set up two patrol bases. One base, called Kemple, was in the hamlet of Owesat, where two American soldiers kidnapped in May of 2007 were last seen. An al Qaeda leader, labeled MKI in intelligence files, had taken a boat across from Owesat and reconnoitered the road where humvees were strung out in guard positions several hundred meters apart. The next night, MKI returned and pitched grenades into two humvees, killing six Americans and returning to Owesat with two captives. Equipment belonging to the two soldiers was later found north of Baghdad. The soldiers were never found, and MKI was on the run, hunted by special teams.

The tragedy illustrated the need never to lower one's guard. In the entire war, there were only three soldiers listed as missing, while over 4,000 had died. Compared to all prior wars, this indicated extraordinary care.

By 2008, there were no known insurgents inside the village of Owesat, where Combat Outpost Kemple was manned by 50 Americans and 500 Sunni volunteers called Concerned Local Citizens, each paid $300 a month by Caraccilo.

"The CLC see us as providing security and money," Lt. Col. Andrew Rohling, commanding the battalion in Yusufiah, said. "We have to shift those tasks to the Iraqi government before the CLC become disillusioned."

With security improved, the soldiers of the 101st were trying to jump-start the economy. Caraccilo's rifle companies were processing 2,500 micro-grants, each with a ceiling of $2,500, for residents to buy seed, fertilizer, and basic goods. Frustrated that a frozen chicken from Argentina cost less than a local chicken, Caraccilo was studying the economics of poultry farming.

Caraccilo's brigade was typical of all eleven I visited in two trips in 2008. Each was heavily involved in economic projects, advised by EPRTs, or Embedded Provincial Reconstruction Teams, comprised of five to ten contractors and civilians from the State Department, USAID, and other government agencies.

While all brigades followed the same basics set forth in the counterinsurgency field manual, there was no equivalent manual for economic development. The U.S. military had complained for years about carrying the burden unassisted, and the EPRTs were a relatively new organization. Some EPRTs emphasized micro-loans, while others favored micro-grants. Larger projects depended on local conditions.

Caraccilo praised his EPRT. Americans, though, could never work their way out of reconstructing Iraq, because an economy is forever expanding. There was always a requirement for additional projects, whether in Des Moines or in Yusufiah. It was unclear how dollops of American aid weaned the population from supporting insurgents—the U.S. wasn't going to pay eight million unemployed Iraqis—or for how long Americans could substitute for Iraqi officials.

"The problem," Caraccilo said, "is that districts like Yusufiah have no connection to the provincial government. The Iraqi bureaucrats don't give a damn. I can't win this for them. I can train good Iraqi battalions and let them carry on the mission for themselves."

Inside a patrol base in Yusufiah, Colonel Caraccilo introduced me to the Iraqi unit he was training to take over in the Triangle of Death. The Iraqi operations officer, Major Kais, had spoken without embarrassment or flourish.

"The American soldiers and my soldiers have given their blood to feed these fields," Kais said, "and now we harvest the good crops."

Caraccilo was the real deal. He could lead, motivate, fight, train, empathize, and even master the economics of the poultry market. Above all, he understood that he and his American soldiers could not win the war. He could not eradicate the insurgency inside his battlespace. He could, though, set the conditions for the Iraqis to step forward.

That's what makes fighting an insurgency so frustrating. American soldiers, by instinct and training, focus on winning decisive battles, while American society is impatient and less than understanding of long, seemingly interminable wars. In this book, Caraccilo and Lt. Col. Andrea Thompson lay out principles of performance that they learned over the course of multiple tours. As pertinent, the authors discuss the process of learning and how to approach an insurgency.

In this book, Caraccilo and Thompson lay out the precepts necessary for operating successfully in counterinsurgency. The complexity—and the frustration—stems from the lack of control. No matter how skilled the American unit, it is nevertheless operating inside a sovereign nation whose leaders do not have to adhere to the prescriptions or advice of Americans. If the leaders in the host nation were competent, there wouldn't be a need for American soldiers in the first place.

Therein lies the dilemma for professionals like Caraccilo and Thompson. They can do everything right and not affect the outcome. Caraccilo and Thompson cite several brigade commanders as examples of leaders who knew how to operate under chaotic conditions. The colonels whom they name have proved their adaptability. Some may be selected for general officer; others will not. The correlation between advancement in rank and performance in an insurgency such as Iraq is imperfect at best, due to the lack of objective measures of accomplishment.

Looking back with hindsight, it is clear the war went through distinct stages. In the summer and fall of 2003, the Sunnis decided they had been disenfranchised. Ambassador Paul Bremer, the president's envoy, had purged the Iraqi government of high- and mid-level Baathists. His edict affected many functionaries like schoolteachers who had joined the Baathist Party for employment reasons. He also disbanded the Iraqi Army and assumed that an ill-trained and corrupt police organization could restore order.

No chance of that happening. Inside the Sunni Triangle, those who wanted to rebel—disgruntled former army soldiers, sly Baathists, former regime elements, and a few jihadist extremists—faced no indigenous opposition. The Iraqis chosen by Bremer to represent their country stayed safe inside the Green Zone.

The U.S. military quickly grew to resent Bremer and his organization, called the Coalition Provision Authority, or CPA—Can't Provide Anything. The senior U.S. commander in Iraq was the most junior three-star general in the U.S. Army. He was out of his depth. Five American divisions adopted five different styles to combat the growing insurgency. Too much time and effort were spent chasing tiny insurgent gangs, and rough tactics led to Sunni resentment and recruits for the insurgency.

2004 was a messy year of major combat with no resolution. In April of 2004, Iraq almost flew apart as the Sunnis in Fallujah resisted fiercely when the White House ordered the Marines, over their objections, to seize the city. At the same time, Bremer moved against the seditious Shiite leader, Moqtada Sadr, who responded by calling his followers into the streets. When the White House reacted by ordering the Marines to pull back from Fallujah, the arch terrorist Zarqawi moved into the city. Sadr too was trapped and permitted to escape. The year ended with U.S. forces again attacking and seizing Fallujah.

2005 was a year of false progress. Bremer had departed, with sovereignty returned to an elected Iraqi government that was inept and sectarian. Two sets of elections resulted in solidifying political power in the hands of Shiite politicians who owed their posts to a national religious party and not to local constituencies. The U.S. military concentrated on building up a new Iraqi Army, while the police languished under the inept management of the U.S. Department of State (for decades congressional legislation had restricted the U.S.

military's role in training and advising police dedicated to internal law and order tasks). Senior American generals believed they could turn most responsibility for quelling the insurgency over to Iraqi battalions by the end of 2006. U.S. forces in and around Baghdad gradually pulled back to giant forward operating bases (FOBs) because most senior generals believed that American soldiers were an irritant and a cause of the violence.

Instead of showing progress, 2006 became the year of civil war. Three years of suicide bombings by the Sunni-based al Qaeda extremists culminated in the destruction in February of a sacred Shiite mosque north of Baghdad. Shiite death squads, comprised of militias and police elements inside the dodgy Ministry of Interior, reacted by systematically killing Sunnis and driving them from Baghdad. Prime Minister Nouri al-Maliki was unable to employ the feckless police or to redeploy sufficient Iraqi Army battalions. U.S. soldiers would clear an area in the city, only to have death squads and al Qaeda cells reappear.

However, by the fall of 2006, when the war seemed at its worst as seen from Washington and inside Baghdad, the Sunni tribes in Anbar province to the west rebelled against the brutal excesses of al Qaeda and swung to the American side. The key to the turnaround on the western front was bottom-up partnership between local leaders and U.S. battalion commanders. The locals identified al Qaeda; the Americans brought the hammer. By the fall of 2006, such local partnerships were springing up across the west.

In 2007, the turnaround on the eastern front followed. The same bottom-up partnerships eventually emerged, shaped by three decisions at the top. First, President Bush sent 30,000 more troops, mainly to control Baghdad. Second, Lt. Gen. Raymond Odierno, the corps commander, chose to deploy most of them in belts around the capitol in order to crush al Qaeda countrywide. Third, inside Baghdad, Gen. David Petraeus moved his soldiers off the large bases and into neighborhoods, especially along the fault lines where the Sunnis were being driven out or where al Qaeda was in control.

Petraeus was impressed that thousands of Sunnis were joining tribal units in Anbar, with many accepted into the police or the army. He authorized battalion commanders across Iraq to recruit similar irregular forces, the Concerned Local Citizens. By 2008, U.S. battalions were paying 90,000 Iraqis, mostly Sunnis, who had volunteered for neighborhood watch groups. Al Qaeda fled, and Shiite death squad attacks greatly diminished. These bottom-up partnerships placed Americans in daily contact with local leaders who complained about poor services. In turn, the Americans pressured the government to respond to local needs.

In Shiite areas under militia control like Sadr City, the population didn't dare to accept American protection. In 2007, Petraeus left those areas to Maliki to deal with. By mid-2008, Maliki was seriously trying to break the power of Sadr's militia.

In sum, on both the western and eastern fronts, bottom-up partnerships caused the war to turn around. The antecedent was a change in attitude of the Sunni population that had experienced al Qaeda's whip hand.

Caraccilo, as a brigade commander, was assigned a vast swath of farmlands—mainly Sunni—a dozen miles southwest of Baghdad. Before his arrival, the 10th Mountain Division had organized numerous CLC units. Caraccilo recruited more, and in 2008 he added economic projects via an EPRT. Like most brigade commanders, Caraccilo in essence was acting like the governor of a medium-size state—with plenipotentiary powers a governor could only dream of.

The problem was that the Sunnis had aligned with the Americans, who in turn became their ombudsmen in pressuring marginally competent and highly sectarian district and provincial officials to deliver basic services. The provinces in turn complained that the ministries in Baghdad were impossible to deal with. There was substantial truth in that, and commanders like Caraccilo spent at least half their time dealing with stubborn, sectarian, and often incompetent Iraqi politicians and officials.

But hey, if it were easy, we wouldn't need a U.S. Army that can shoot, maneuver, destroy, heal, rebuild, protect, bargain, cajole, advise, threaten, motivate, and manipulate to achieve the objective, no matter how hard. In less than three years, two giant institutions steeped in 200 years of tradition—the U.S. Army and Marines—adopted new doctrine and turned around a losing war. This was equivalent to General Electric and Ford starting afresh in new business lines and turning a profit in three years.

Shortly after he took over as Chief of Staff of the Army, I asked Gen. George W. Casey what basic lesson he took away from Iraq.

"I used to believe if we soldiers could do conventional war," Casey said, "we could do anything. That's not true. In conventional battle, we maneuver to avoid the civilian population. In future wars, we have to prevail among the people. That changes everything."

Drawing upon a combined five tours in Iraq, Colonel Caraccilo and Lieutenant Colonel Thompson have written a handbook that focuses upon how to prevail among the people. This is the type of ground war that will be fought in the future.

Bing West
June 2008

INTRODUCTION

"If you concentrate exclusively on victory, with no thought for the after effect, you may be too exhausted to profit by the peace, while it is almost certain that the peace will be a bad one, containing the germs of another war."

Capt. Sir Basil Liddell Hart
Thoughts on War, 1944

In April 2007, just over four years since the beginning of the liberation of Iraq, Gen. David H. Petraeus took command of Multi-National Force-Iraq (MNF-I). By his own admission in a briefing to the Senate Armed Services Committee during his nomination hearing, Petraeus defined the character of an Iraqi majority as people who "confront life-or-death, stay-or-leave decisions on a daily basis."[1] Though not an epiphany, it is an extremely important observation, as it set the stage for the employment of the U.S.-led coalition under Petraeus's tenure.

His statement reflects the views of many senior leaders in Iraq, acknowledging that the Iraqis understand their dire situation and the actions of the U.S.-led coalition security force should follow suit. Unfortunately, over the past four years, the coalition has performed its mission contrary to this premise. In a great number of situations where an Iraqi force, army or police, was attacked or a crisis occurred, the coalition came to the rescue and intervened, regardless of the capability of the indigenous force to stand the ground.[2]

This scenario is seen repeatedly across the provinces of Iraq on a daily basis. It is what U.S. Army officers are trained to do: solve problems and not accept failure. Therefore, when a U.S. leader sees a coalition partner failing, the natural reaction is to run to the sound of the guns and fix the problem. In most cases, this tactical intervention occurs with absolutely good intentions.

Good intentions, however, are not enough. We maintain that if the U.S.-led coalition will hold firm to the vision of an indigenous Iraqi security force capable of standing ground even in, as Petraeus put it, a defined "life-or-death, stay-or-leave" environment, then victory can be achieved in Iraq. More specifically, this book will show that the decisive operation for the war in Iraq is a dedicated plan to train Iraqi Security Forces (ISF) capable of operating autonomously.

Unfortunately, that effort will take time. The longer the United States stays in Iraq, the more agitated the critics become. Criticism and impatience result in a grassroots opposition to the war, and with it a litany of ad hoc remedies such as proposed timelines, notions to immediately pull American forces from the theater, and knee-jerk tactical solutions.

During the U.S. tenure in Iraq, the plan to turn over areas of operations to the ISF became the main effort in Operation Iraqi Freedom (OIF) and is therefore the main effort of this book. In late summer 2007, MNF-I, under the command of Gen. David Petraeus, gathered the results of the Joint Strategic Assessment Team and assembled an initiatives group to design a joint campaign plan (JCP). On the team, among others, were Col. H. R. McMaster, hero of the battle of 73 Eastings in Operation Desert Storm and the former commander of the 3rd Armor Cavalry Regiment in Baghdad and Tal Afar in 2005 to 2006; Col. Randy George, a former battalion commander in the strategic oil center of Bayji in 2005 to 2006; and

David Kilcullen, an Australian counterinsurgency expert who is on Petraeus's advisory panel. Together they decided on a new approach reflecting the counterinsurgency precepts that protecting the population is the best way to isolate insurgents, encouraging political accommodations is a key requirement for success, and gaining intelligence on numerous threats is possible given the framework they proposed. The core assumption for this plan is that American troops cannot impose a military solution, but that the United States can use force to create the conditions in which political reconciliation is possible.[3] Therefore, there is and always really was a plan for achieving victory in Iraq—we just need to follow the plan.

BENCHMARK FOR SUCCESS IN IRAQ

The litmus test for success in Iraq, as defined by the Task Force Band of Brothers' commander, Maj. Gen. Thomas R. Turner, was to put an Iraqi element in the lead.[4] To be in the lead meant to be in charge of security in a particular area of Iraq, with the coalition forces in that area in a supporting role.

In early December 2005, at a place called Udaim, a village of about 150 homes in Diyala Province seventy miles north of Baghdad, the Iraqi Ministry of Defense (MOD) felt it was critical to exercise its autonomy for the first time since OIF began. This decision caused much consternation, especially with the American military and political leaders. After all, the Iraqi force being introduced to the area was clearly not up to U.S. standards. We believe it is this flawed attitude and Western influenced metric that are slowing progress and contributing to the obstacles preventing an acceptable conclusion.

Turner's concept was to establish a partnership with the newly introduced Iraqi Army Force. In this scenario, the force being introduced included portions of the 5th Iraqi Army, which was being transferred north from Wassit province to fill a security gap in the volatile northwest portion of the ethnically diverse Diyala province.

Initially, it appeared that the plan to put the Iraqis in the lead for the first time did not go well. As reported by the Reuters news

PROVINCES OF IRAQ

agency, insurgents ambushed an Iraqi Army patrol as it was taking the lead along a road north of Baghdad on December 3, 2005, killing nineteen Iraqi soldiers in a well-planned attack. The report noted further that the Iraqi soldiers were traveling in a five-vehicle patrol near Baqubah, sixty kilometers (forty miles) north of Baghdad, when they were hit by a roadside bomb. Immediately afterward, gunmen opened fire in what Iraqi police described as a well-planned assault.[5]

In fact, after visiting the Iraqi compound at Udaim, named Camp Hadar, it was clear that this attack was more than just an ambush. It was a deliberate attack with rocket-propelled grenades (RPGs) and machine-gun engagements on the ISF compound. Media and political pundits labeled it as a destroyed camp with a demoralized Iraqi Army. But that was the American view assessing the episode through the lens of Western society. Also, this type of violence usually led to the U.S. force in close proximity rushing to the Iraqis' aid and taking control of the situation, for it would not be acceptable in some coalition leaders' eyes to allow the Iraqis to fail on their watch.

The attack on Camp Hadar at Udaim had broader implications because of its location, the timing, and the ethnic makeup of the forces. The nineteen soldiers killed were characterized as Shi'ite Muslims, which added a sectarian element to the attack. The deaths also came amid a rise in insurgent violence preceding the elections set for December 15, as well as growing tensions between Iraq's Muslim sects. Finally, in a move that could have aggravated those tensions, the country's top Shi'ite cleric immediately urged Shi'ites to turn out and vote for their religious candidates on election day, further stirring up an already troublesome province.

The most important part of the Reuters report, however, was subtly defined this way: "Saturday's ambush on the Iraqi troops occurred in Udaim, a volatile town near Baquba, and is the latest in a series of attacks to target Iraq's fledgling police and army forces." The report continued to imply that the insurgency saw the newfound police force and Iraqi Army as a critical vulnerability in the coalition's efforts to bolster the stability in the region. But this "fledgling" police force did not drop its weapons and run away. Instead, it stood its ground, even after a second major attack just weeks later, when insurgents fired on military checkpoints immediately following the December 15 elections. This, one would argue, was success.

The normal recourse for an attack on Iraqi Security Forces, and usually a default decision for most coalition commanders in the theater, was to conduct tactical intervention to "save the day." Tom Turner, however, saw this as an opportunity to show the Iraqi theater of operations, if not the world, that the ISF would stand their ground regardless of whose measure of proficiency they were being graded against. The bottom line is, they didn't flee.

To this day, the ISF still occupy areas of Udaim, and few to no attacks occur in the region. We believe this example should be used as a benchmark for success. If the United States had intervened, it is our premise that Udaim and the area surrounding that once-hazardous route would be foci of attention for the insurgency. We will show in later chapters that many of the coalition leaders and staff did not share the same vision of "picking up and dusting off" our Iraqi counterparts.

The actions by the coalition in the city of Baghdad in the ensuing months counter this example. In the spring of 2006, the U.S.-led coalition developed a plan to surge forces into Baghdad. This operation was code-named Operation Together Forward. It included a wide array of autonomous operations that all but ignored the partnership requirements seen elsewhere in the theater. Arguably, this large-scale tactical intervention has had a lasting effect on the inability and credibility of the ISF in Baghdad.

BACKGROUND AND CONTEXT

In an effort to "right" the world and rid it of tyrannical leaders such as Saddam Hussein, the United States in conjunction with its coalition partners decided in early 2003 to remove the Baath Party from power.[6] More notably, the decision was made to remove Saddam from his self-appointed dictatorial position as president of Iraq.

Many question the validity of removing Saddam Hussein from power. After a period of time, this question became all the more amplified, with some saying Iraq might have been better off under Saddam. To counter that thought are the following facts:

- Since the fall of Saddam, Iraq has had a democratically elected and representative government (a review of how truly representative this government is appears later in this book) and is poised to conduct its second set of national elections by the end of 2008, this time including local and provincial elections.
- The populace now enjoys free speech and a free press. A flood of satellite dish imports is a great example of the enjoyment of these newfound freedoms.
- Iraq now has a free-market economy rather than strictly state-owned industries.
- Health services have improved, with a 25 percent increase in immunizations and a 90 percent reduction in cases of the measles.
- Before March 2003, most of Iraq had four to eight hours of electricity daily, while Baghdad had sixteen to twenty-four. Now it is more evenly distributed, with most of the country getting eight to ten hours, and the demand for electricity, based on the newfound freedoms, has increased 70 percent.
- The U.S. Army Corps of Engineers has assisted in completing more than 4,000 projects in an attempt to overcome twenty-five years of neglect to the infrastructure.[7]

Regardless, the critics continue to question the validity of the decision to invade. More than four years later, we were left with an insurgency and a war termination strategy that caught many by surprise. It appears that few in the group responsible for planning this operation at the strategic level thought the initial phase of the war would be followed by a robust insurgency capable of unraveling initial coalition successes.[8] The introduction of an evolving insurgency in Iraq brought with it new challenges, such as dealing with the number-one killer of troops, the lethal improvised explosive devices

(IEDs), and the reality of Al Qaeda in Iraq (AQIZ). For more than five years, the coalition has been struggling to "win" the fight.

And make no mistake, we are supposed to win. Arguably, the ultimate act of humanity in the War on Terror is indeed to win, to prevent continued bloodshed and atrocities that habitually generate from terrorist safe havens. To achieve success in this endeavor, we must adhere to two simple rules:

1. We must kill our enemies wherever we encounter them.
2. We must see to it that anyone who commits an act of terror forfeits every right he or she once possessed.

Unfortunately, these simple rules were lost in the fog of war as the conflict evolved from a high-intensity fight to battles for neighborhoods. Instead of worrying over trumped-up atrocities in Iraq (the media give credence to any claim made by terrorists), perhaps we should stop apologizing and take a stand. That means firm rules for the battlefield, not, as Ralph Peters puts it, "Gumby-speak intended to please critics who'll never be satisfied by anything America does."[9]

It is apparent that the coalition knows it needs credible and capable ISF in order to relinquish security of Iraq. But the military forces continue to get sidetracked with ancillary missions, such as government oversight and a wide array of economic initiatives, and the political rhetoric covered in detail by the media masks the reporting of successful ISF actions and muddies efforts to achieve success.

Methodical planning sessions and drawn-out doctrinal discussions are practically nonexistent in the Iraqi culture and its military organizations. Still, we attempt to superimpose our Western-modeled processes and systems on those we support militarily, hoping that over the course of a few disjointed years, we can inculcate our ways and, even more unlikely, that the processes will be acceptable to them.

Additionally, *ending* the war is perhaps the wrong focus in discussions by politicians, pundits, and military leaders. Arguably, insurgencies never really do *end;* they just fade away or lose their appeal.

But the war in Iraq isn't fading away or losing its appeal. It has evolved to become a war against a mixed insurgency supported by various terrorist cells. Now that we're fighting a War on Terror on foreign soil, how to achieve success has become more complicated. Ask ten different people how to fight the war, and you will get ten different answers. Many believe that if the coalition left, then the Al Qaeda based and fueled insurgency would also move on, leaving the fledging Iraqi government to evolve on its own in an effort to defeat former regime and Saddam loyalists, resolve the sectarian issues, and tame the political power struggle.[10] Some argue that this is what it takes to gain a foothold into democracy.

As in all insurgent-based conflicts, identifying the actual enemy and determining his intentions are always a struggle. With our recognized shortcomings in cultural awareness, we may be using terms that are inappropriate and thereby fueling the insurgency. In a June 2006 article titled "Loosely Interpreted Arabic Terms Can Promote Enemy Ideology," Jim Garamone writes that "American leaders misuse language to such a degree that they unintentionally wind up promoting the ideology of the groups the United States is fighting."

A case in point is the term *jihadist*. Many leaders, Garamone writes, use *jihadist* as a synonym for Islamic extremist. He goes on to state that "calling our enemies *jihadis* and their movement a global *jihad* thus indicates that we recognize their doctrines and actions as being in the path of God and, for Muslims, legitimate." Even calling our Al Qaeda enemies *mujahideen,* or holy warriors, reinforces success in their eyes, because essentially we are legitimizing their effort; instead, we should use *mufsidun,* meaning evil or corrupt person. The associated insurgent activities are actually what the Muslim ideologist would call a *hirabah,* or a war against society where radicals are killing defenseless and innocent Muslims.[11]

Therefore, not only do we tend not to understand the battlefield for which we fight, but we also don't grasp the cultural norms that are interwoven into that framework—a significant obstacle to overcome. Condition-based armies, on the other hand, change the environment to discredit and discourage insurgencies, in hopes that they will become less powerful and dissolve back into the populace. Few times in history has an insurgency been defeated outright with offensive operations. Our National Command Authority (NCA) has recognized this challenge and has therefore formulated a plan to turn over the security of Iraq to the Iraqis, essentially giving them the fight. Apply Iraqi forces to fight and win on their own battlefield with their own cultural norms.

FOCUS AND PURPOSE OF THE BOOK

In writing a book about an ongoing operation, we run the risk of sending to print already obsolete thoughts, techniques, solutions, and procedures. It is not lost on us that the war in Iraq is unpredictable, with ever-changing conditions. Sending this to final print a year before it is published runs the risk of its contents becoming irrelevant. But we have put in place checks and balances on the validity of what we write. Over the course of the year from late 2007 to late 2008, one of us will be deployed in Iraq and the other will be a military assistant to the army chief of staff at the Pentagon—the hub of all plans and policy development, particularly with the war on terrorism.

Using experiences, past precedents, and a multitude of studies, we have attempted to focus this book on exploring the true nature of the main effort and decisive operation for the fight in Iraq, which we believe to be conducting a battle handoff to the ISF. In doing so, we often use as a backdrop the period from September 2005 to September 2006, when Task Force Band of Brothers commanded and controlled Multi-National Division-North at Contingency Operating Base (COB) Speicher in Tikrit. Throughout the book, we equate victory with the transition of security to Iraqi control.

To help the reader understand the true nature of the war in Iraq, the book gives a detailed overview of how we got where we are today in the conflict and provides a brief analysis of the dichotomous discussion on whether we should be arguing the just nature of the war or focusing more on its prosecution. It also looks at how difficult it has been for many leaders to step back and not lead the fight, so the ISF can learn to operate autonomously. Soldiers and marines tend to feel more comfortable with the "kicking in the door" aspects of their mission. This book explores the challenges our troops and their leaders face sticking with the plan to train capable ISF in order to turn over the area of operations to them.

It is our strong belief that the soldiers, sailors, marines, airmen, and in many cases the civilian participants and counterparts, both coalition and Iraqi, have served valiantly in the war. We also firmly believe it is the same groups of individuals who will seek to find a remedy to stabilize the insurgency and establish a democratic Iraq that is at peace with its neighbors and an active member of the international community. Therefore, while we, without reproach, support our leaders from the national level on down, it is not lost on us that it took the American-led invasion and occupation of Iraq, and perhaps the mismanagement of the country by both the Coalition Provisional Authority (CPA) and new Iraqi governments, to bring matters to this dire situation.

In sha' Allah, "God willing," the war will end soon. Though hope is not typically a mindset in the employment of the U.S. military, it is indeed a way of life for the Iraqis, and therefore it is inherent within their culture for people to have patience and let the divine nature of the situation take form.

It may be difficult for us to understand the Iraqi perspective on this. Is it that faith in divine providencel is crucial in guiding the people of struggling nations like Iraq? Or is it that a deep-seated faith is truly an anchor in a seriously devout Muslim nation? And is it the reliance on tribal affiliations, with religion as a supporting role that provides the framework for the situation in Iraq today?

Whatever the case, it seems that this well-established faith coupled with years of oppression has resulted in a people unwilling to take an active role in their future. A quest for democracy is unimportant to the Iraqis, even though the U.S.-led coalition makes it a focal point for success. This reluctance may also have to do with a lack of understanding of how a democracy works. Regardless, there exists a lack of ambition among the Iraqis to take responsibility for their future, which is a Western measure of success.

To put this all in perspective, one must understand how the Islamic world views their faith. The true, faithful Muslim believes in a whole host of principal articles that are summarized in what is known as the Five Pillars of Faith, which includes the belief in One God (or Allah), Supreme and Eternal, Infinite and Mighty, Merciful and Compassionate, Creator and Provider.[12] This belief, in order to be effective, requires complete trust and hope in God, submission to his will, and reliance on his aid. According to the Muslim faith, it secures man's dignity and saves him from fear and despair, from guilt and confusion. This uncompromising and exacting faith is based upon the holy book of the Islamic world, the Qur'an.[13]

An Iraqi once told us that to understand an Arab's faith in Allah, one has to understand that Muslims do not read the Qur'an and then conclude it as divine; instead, they believe it to be divine and then they read it. This speaks volumes to how the Muslim mind works. Having a fundamental understanding of how the host nation people (friend and foe) think is at times lost on those who occupy a land. Obviously this understanding is of the utmost importance when operating in a country under Muslim control—a blinding flash of the obvious that is often ignored when making decisions.

Thomas Ricks writes in *Fiasco* that "there was no plan for the aftermath of the conventional war in Iraq."[14] Our argument is that there was and is a plan, in the form of conducting a battle handoff to the Iraqi Security Forces. Good, bad, or indifferent, that was the plan. Some areas of operation and task forces did it better than others, for a variety of reasons. This book is about the war termination strategy that indeed was defined, and the struggle to maintain that focus.

While some argue that success is winning over the people and others argue it's destroying the enemy, we propose it isn't either: It is turning the problem over to a capable security force and an established Iraqi government as defined by the Iraqis.

An abundance of written work on this subject from various perspectives, by soldiers, historians, pundits, and journalists, already exists. After having served in Iraq as primary staff officers with the

101st Airborne Division, we wanted to give a holistic look from a divisional staff position that is privy to both the strategic and tactical levels of war, while working hard at the operational level of conflict to "win the war." Given the changing conditions and an onslaught of bureaucracy, we thought that this type of study at this point in the war would be beneficial to both historians and those mid- to senior-level officials who remain in government service after this fight, especially now that we are seating a new U.S. president with an expected vision for the Middle East but saddled with the same old challenges.

There is no doubt this work will be controversial. We acknowledge this risk but also feel strongly that a fresh view of where we are in this fight, a critical self-assessment militarily, and options and insights for a way ahead are needed. This was a duty we didn't take lightly, and we hope our views serve as a catalyst for change.

CHAPTER 1

From Euphoria to Complacency

"To be a successful soldier you must know history. Read it objectively—dates and even the minute details of tactics are useless. What you must know is how man reacts. Weapons change but man who uses them changes not at all. To win battles, you do not beat weapons—you beat the soul of man, of the enemy man."

Gen. George S. Patton, Jr.,
to his son in 1944

On May 1, 2003, President George W. Bush announced an end of major combat operations in Iraq.[1] In the years following this announcement, many have criticized the president, citing that combat obviously had not concluded that May. But the president was right in announcing that "major combat operations" in the form of high-intensity conflict had ceased. What had happened, and is often misunderstood, was that the high-intensity conflict had ceased, and in the ensuing months, a new form of combat began. What this new conflict was has been the topic for much discussion. Most think that the war that evolved in Iraq is an insurgency, for it has a number of characteristics associated with a classic insurgency.[2]

The war progressed from a euphoric state, where all affected seemed satisfied with the most likely outcome—victory—to a state of complacency as our military continued to struggle in its quest to engage the then-popular War on Terrorism. Former Iraqi dissident Ali Allawi says it best in his book, *The Occupation of Iraq:* "The euphoria that accompanied this effortless victory quickly gave way to increasing bewilderment as to what to do with the 'prize,' as the occupiers came face to face with the realities of post–Saddam Hussein Iraq and the mysteries of this most complex of countries. . . . Nothing . . . could have prepared the Coalition . . . for what they actually found."[3]

Today the United States is at odds with the plight of the American involvement in Iraq. At this writing, more than 4,000 servicemen and women have paid the ultimate sacrifice in the war in Iraq. It is our desire to have others understand the nature of this war that has claimed so many.

The coalition in Iraq transitioned from closing with and destroying the enemy, which is the objective of a high-intensity conflict (HIC), to placing a major emphasis on nonkinetic mission sets, including those associated with low-intensity conflict (LIC), where the coalition forces are engaged with a complex and ambiguous enemy. The coalition made some missteps during the transition from HIC to LIC in an effort to bring stability to a war-torn nation without its own security force while also developing Iraqi government agencies capable of providing the public with essential services. This abrupt transition and the effects of it in the following years left our soldiers and their leaders confused as to what they were chartered to perform and feeling as though they were walking on eggshells every time they went out to conduct an operation.

A WAR IN TRANSITION

Our military and nation were elated over our successes in Iraq at the beginning of the war, when the coalition was undoubtedly winning each battle. Combat parachute assaults, air strikes, classic gunfights, and deliberate attacks all defined the common battlefield framework for the early stages of the war.[4] But the ending of major combat operations meant a transition to another type of fight, as the war shifted to fighting an insurgency. In essence, it became a forward operating base defense plan and a main supply route (MSR) sustainment operation, with the force becoming languid and complacent, fixed in an effort just to maintain. What ensued was the U.S. Army's attempt to "unfix" itself. Instead of defining the insurgency and predicting associated enemy activities and then employing a force, much like Gen. David Petraeus and Lt. Gen. Ray Odierno (the Multi-National Corps Iraq commander from 2006 to 2007) did in 2007, the coalition put the majority of its effort into retooling the landscape, with base closures, forward operating base management, and other bureaucracies associated with the garrisoning of large U.S. formations.

As soldiers and leaders on the ground during the initial deployment to Iraq, we could sense the transitions in not only the enemy tactics, but also the coalition responses. After the initial insurgent attacks attempting to physically destroy the Iraqi Army, the coalition seemed to have a sense of overconfidence. At the same time, a downgrade in uniform requirements, in an effort to show that the situation had changed from lethal to nonlethal or less dangerous, revealed a sense of complacent ignorance. Coalition leaders throughout Iraq in mid-2003 talked of removing Kevlar helmets and body armor and donning soft caps to portray a kindler and gentler image, perhaps more like the British approach in Northern Ireland.

What we didn't grasp early on, however, was that the enemy was becoming more lethal and more creative, as well as adaptive. Instead, the coalition focused more on the establishment of rules and the development of a garrison, developing an occupation type of mindset.

In late 2003 and early 2004, we saw the signs of a new type of war. The signature of this type of fight was what is commonly known as the improvised explosive device (IED), a makeshift roadside bomb that could be detonated in a variety of ways. It was readily apparent, both during ground operations and through intelligence reporting, that this enemy was not going to stand his ground and fight our formations. Instead, he was going to inflict damage on men and equipment with low-grade technology. Author Ralph Peters has written that suicide bombers are nearly impossible to defeat—"impassioned faith still trumps microchips."[5] Once proven successful, IEDs became the insurgents' method, albeit to Westerners a cowardly means, for fighting the pro-Iraqi establishment.

To put the enemy's shift in perspective, in September 2003 the very first IED was used in the city of Kirkuk, causing the death of Spc. Kyle Thomas (A Company, 2nd Battalion, 503rd Airborne of the 173rd Airborne Brigade, stationed in Vicenza, Italy). Since that time, the proliferation of IEDs in that and all other provinces has grown exponentially, to hundreds and sometimes almost a thousand per month.

But the coalition didn't immediately recognize this shift in enemy tactics, and it underestimated and perhaps underprepared for the potential of the evolution of an insurgency. Only over time has it come to a slow and unfocused realization of how the threat in Iraq had evolved. In practical terms, in mid to late 2003, the coalition forces introduced to destroy a standing army needed to identify the change in enemy tactics and then transition their actions from a high-intensity fight to that of defeating an insurgency. Instead of switching to an unconventional approach for defeating the insurgency, however, the coalition maintained a conventional style in most of its engagements, all the while building bureaucratic systems to emulate garrison activities found on installations in the United States and other military compounds throughout the world. Meanwhile, what was supposed to be a straightforward process of overthrowing a dictatorship and replacing it with a liberal-leaning, secular democracy under the benign tutelage of the United States instead turned into an existential battle for identity, power, and legitimacy that is affecting not only Iraq, but the entire volatile state system in the Middle East.

Before we offer solutions, it is critical to identify the oversights and miscalculations that led to the situation in Iraq today.

AN IRAQI VIEW

The Iraqi minister of finance and senior advisor to the prime minister, Ali A. Allawi, who in 2004 was named the first postwar minister of defense, writes in a recently published book that "more perceptive people knew instinctively that the invasion of Iraq would open up the great fissures in Iraqi society."[6] According to Allawi, what followed was the "rank amateurism and swaggering arrogance" of the occupation, under L. Paul Bremer's Coalition Provisional Authority (CPA), which took big steps with little consultation with any Iraqis—steps Allawi and many others see as blunders. Among Allawi's criticisms are the following:

- The Americans disbanded Iraq's army, which Allawi said could have helped quell a rising insurgency in 2003. Instead, when the army was disbanded, hundreds of thousands of angry demobilized men became a recruiting pool for the resistance. We also note that though the coalition was quick to disband the army, it was reluctant to outlaw, disband, or even marginalize, in some cases, the many militia elements sprouting up in the area of operation (AO).

- Purging tens of thousands of members of toppled President Saddam Hussein's Baath party from government, school faculties, and elsewhere left Iraq short on experienced hands at a crucial time. It also left those disenfranchised citizens, albeit former Saddam sympathizers (if one believes being in the Baath party is a litmus test for being a Saddam supporter), without hope for their future. The insurgency, especially the Al Qaeda elements in Iraq, fed on the deep resentment Sunni Arabs felt at their loss of power and prestige. Their feeling of hopelessness has been aggravated by the fact that the force that overthrew Saddam seemingly achieved the impossible—the dethronement of the community from centuries of power—in favor of, as they saw it, an unruly mob led by pro-Iranian

clerics. The Sunni Arabs' refusal to tolerate any serious engagement with the new political order has effectively pushed them
into a corner and played into the hands of their most determined enemies. It has taken more than four years for the
coalition to realize that a reconciliation plan was necessary to
reduce the violence associated with the sectarian conflict.

- An order consolidating decentralized bank accounts at the
  Finance Ministry bogged down operations of Iraq's many
  state-owned enterprises.
- The CPA's focus on private enterprise allowed the "commer-
  cial gangs" of Saddam's day to monopolize business.
- The new government's free-trade policy allowed looted Iraqi
  capital equipment to be shipped away across international
  borders.
- The CPA perpetuated Saddam's fuel subsidies, selling gasoline
  at giveaway prices and draining the budget.[7]

OTHER FACTORS

In short, we concur with Allawi's observations, though we admit that
it is neither our focus nor in our area of expertise to give an assessment outside the security arena, where our talents and experiences
lie. Coupling what has been presented by Allawi and adding our own
input to the reasons why the new Iraq is, at best, struggling for survival at this point will help better explain our blueprint for success as
presented in this book.

We also believe that other factors contributed greatly to the
struggles for success in Iraq. Creating an Iraqi Army before the establishment of law and order, in the form of an organized police force
and its accompanying justice-serving capabilities, was perhaps the single greatest error in judgment in this war. Today there is much discussion on the disbandment of the Iraqi Army but little analysis on
what effort should have been taken to establish a bona fide police
force first.

The initial entry forces in Iraq, however, focused solely on the establishment of the Iraqi police forces. This was evident in the initial deployment to the city of Kirkuk, which sits on the edge of what is known as the Green Line, the unofficial border between Kurdistan and the central Arab state. In 2003, the mission of the 2nd Battalion, 503rd Infantry (Airborne) was to establish a functional police force in the ethnically divided and diverse city of Kirkuk, which has a population of 800,000. After the initial push into Kirkuk alongside the 10th Special Forces Group and the *peshmerga* from the north, the focus was on stabilizing the city.[8] It was obvious that Kirkuk needed a police force, so the airborne battalion set up a police headquarters, seven substations, a city jail, a traffic police headquarters, a local police academy, and an emergency services unit. By the end of the year, 2-503 Airborne had hundreds of police, from all ethnicities, on hand in Kirkuk, capable of transport by SUV and communications by handheld radio, all tied into a joint command-and-control headquarters that integrated the city's emergency services. This was done with little to no guidance from above the division level.

Today the Kirkuk Police Force is a model to emulate for the rest of the country. The police force and the Iraqi Army in that region do not compete for power, since the initial security force established was indeed the Iraqi Police Service (IPS).[9]

As identified in *The Iraq Study Group Report,* the following urgently need to be done to establish law and order in Iraq:

- Give the Iraqi Police greater responsibility and training to conduct criminal investigations.
- Identify that the sole authority to pay police salaries and disburse financial support to local police should be the Iraqi Ministry of Interior (MOI), and it should be delegated to the provincial level to execute.
- Identify, register, and control the Force Protection Services (FPS).
- Bolster the training of the national and border police.

- Expand the current major crime unit's capability and reach, and give it more authority over local police forces, to ensure that the work being done by the police is not for naught because of the lack of a judicial system.
- And finally, train judges, prosecutors, and investigators, and create supported and funded institutions and practices to fight corruption.[10]

Tying together the IPS and the judicial systems is an absolute must to gain some measure of stability in the urban parts of Iraq. With this need comes the incredible challenge to man, equip, and fund the IPS while simultaneously developing, at the time, a ten-division army. These conflicting security requirements leave the police forces and the Iraqi Army in a major battle for resources.

Another major factor that contributed to the troubled state of the coalition in the first part of the war, and continues to challenge commanders, soldiers, and civilian leaders at all levels today, is a structural flaw: There are too many headquarters in the Iraqi theater of operations. These multiple headquarters at times appear in conflict or competition with each other, especially when it comes to the division of a finite set of resources for both the Iraqis and coalition forces.

For instance, one of the four-star commands in Iraq is the Multi-National Force-Iraq (MNF-I), also known as the coalition. MNF-I is the organization of nations whose governments have military personnel in Iraq as part of the American-led war effort. The media normally use the term "U.S.-led coalition" to describe this force, since nearly 92 percent of the troops are from the United States. But the majority of nations that did deploy troops either confined their soldiers to their bases because of widespread violence or issued specific orders to avoid hostile engagement.[11] Thus the term "U.S.-led coalition," when used in the context of combat operations, can be considered inaccurate, as the United Kingdom is the only partnered nation engaged in consistent military operations, in the form of raids.

In November 2002, President George W. Bush, visiting Europe for a NATO summit, declared that "should Iraqi President Saddam

ORIGINAL COALITION MEMBERS FOR OPERATION IRAQI FREEDOM

The following are the original coalition members involved in Iraq. Their contributions to various extents, including direct military participation, logistical and intelligence support, specialized chemical-biological response teams, overflight rights, humanitarian and reconstruction aid, and political support.

Afghanistan	Honduras	Poland
Albania	Hungary	Portugal
Angola	Iceland	Romania
Australia	Italy	Rwanda
Azerbaijan	Japan	Singapore
Bulgaria	Kuwait	Slovakia
Colombia	Latvia	Solomon Islands
Costa Rica	Lithuania	South Korea
Czech Republic	Macedonia	Spain
Denmark	Marshall Islands	Tonga
Dominican	Micronesia	Turkey
Republic	Mongolia	Uganda
El Salvador	Netherlands	Ukraine
Eritrea	Nicaragua	United Kingdom
Estonia	Palau	United States
Ethiopia	Panama	Uzbekistan
Georgia	Philippines	

Hussein choose not to disarm, the United States will lead a coalition of the willing to disarm him."[12] Thereafter, the Bush administration briefly used the term "Coalition of the Willing" to refer to the countries who supported, militarily or verbally, the 2003 invasion of Iraq and subsequent occupation of postinvasion Iraq.

Ironically, though President Bush is oftentimes criticized for taking on the fight in Iraq, there was unilateral acceptance from a great
majority across the globe, at least in the form of verbal support. The
original list prepared in March 2003 included forty-nine members in
the coalition. Of the forty-nine, only four in addition to the United
States contributed troops to the invasion force: the United Kingdom,
Australia, Poland, and Denmark. Thirty-three provided some number
of troops to support the occupation after the invasion; of these, at least
six have no military. More than forty nations provide contract support
of some sort. As of 2007, there were 129,000 contractors: 21,000 from
the United States, 43,000 third-country nationals, and 65,000 host-
nation Iraqis.[13] As the war unfolded in 2003, it was apparent that it
was very unpopular among the citizens of most of the coalition
countries except the United States. In September 2004, Costa Rica,
which has no armed forces, requested that it no longer be considered
a member. As of today, the official White House list of the coalition
shows forty-eight member states; although the inclusion of several of
these members on the list has been questioned. Additionally, there
have been five UN Security Council resolutions in support of Operation Iraqi Freedom since the beginning of the war.[14]

TOO MANY CHIEFS

Here is a brief description of the various levels of command as they
affect or relate to the Middle Eastern theater of operations.

U.S. Central Command (CENTCOM) is a four-star headquarters. In March 2007, Adm. William J. Fallon took charge of CENT-
COM, replacing the retiring Gen. John P. Abizaid. As this book goes
to press, Gen. David Petraeus has been nominated to serve as CENT-
COM commander, replacing Admiral Fallon, who resigned in protest.

Multi-National Force-Iraq (MNF-I) is another four-star headquarters. In the spring of 2007, General Petraeus assumed command
of MNF-I from Gen. George Casey, who became the U.S. Army
chief of staff. As part of the Summer–Fall 2008 command change, Lt.
Gen. Raymond Odierno was selected to receive his fourth star and
follow Petraeus in command of MNF-I.

Multi-National Corps-Iraq (MNC-I) is a three-star headquarters. It was commanded by Lt. Gen. Raymond Odierno of 4th Infantry Division fame through late 2007, followed by Lt. Gen. Lloyd Austin, commander of the 18th Airborne Corps, through 2008. MNC-I was established on May 15, 2004, as a result of concerns that the Combined Joint Task Force 7 (CJTF-7) headquarters was not sufficient to handle the range of military operations in Iraq, which included peace support, civil military operations, and conducting strategic engagements, such as talking to the sheiks and the local political authorities. Simply put, MNF-I was established to handle strategic issues, while MNC-I was chartered to direct the daily tactical operations.

Today MNC-I conducts offensive operations to defeat remaining noncompliant forces and neutralize destabilizing influences in Iraq, in order to create a secure environment. It concurrently conducts stability operations to support the establishment of government, restoration of essential services, and economic development, in order to set the conditions for a transfer of sovereignty and operations to designated follow-on authorities. MNF-I and MNC-I are the two senior headquarters in Iraq.

Yet another headquarters, one of two three-star headquarters in the theater, is Multi-National Security Transition Command-Iraq (MNSTC-I), the branch of the MNF-I that is responsible for developing, organizing, training, equipping, and sustaining the Iraqi Security Forces (ISF), which consists of the Iraqi military and police. The stated mission of MNSTC-I is to train the ISF so that they become capable of defeating the insurgency and taking responsibility for maintaining security within Iraq. Implicitly, this should be done so that the coalition can reduce the number of troops in Iraq.

MNSTC-I is commanded by a lieutenant general and is organized into three training teams. Coalition Military Assistance Training Team (CMATT), commanded by a one-star general, organizes, trains, and equips the Iraqi Army. Civilian Police Assistance Training Team (CPATT), another one-star billet, organizes, trains, and equips the Iraqi police. The Joint Headquarters (JHQ) Advisory Support Team assists the joint headquarters of the Iraqi Army in developing a command-and-control system. It also helps in operational planning of the security forces and gives strategic advice to the Iraqi government. Many of the subordinate leaders in the theater, however, especially those who are in partnership with their Iraqi military counterparts, feel that it is the Iraqis who should be conducting the missions that CMATT and CPATT provide, especially the tactical portions.

What should be readily apparent from this effort to define the functions of the various headquarters in Iraq is that there are too many. More specifically, there are too many headquarters in Iraq vying for power and the limited resources available. A running joke in the theater among subordinate commands, when posed with the challenges of answering to multiple headquarters, is "never have so few been commanded by so many."[15] What tends to happen is that leaders at all levels default to what they know best—that level of command where the majority of their time has been spent, say a thirty-year career at the tactical level. If the commanders tend to default to directing orders at the tactical level, then not only will it cause conflict at the lowest level, but it also leaves one wondering who is militarily focused on the operational and strategic levels.

Working directly for MNC-I are seven multinational divisions in Iraq commanded by two-star generals: Central-South (Polish headquarters in Wasit), Southeast (British headquarters in Basra), Baghdad, Central (also located in Baghdad), North (Tikrit), West (Al Anbar), and Northeast (South Koreans in Irbil).

Brigade combat teams of up to six battalions are tactical commands each led by a colonel. The number of brigades in Iraq is what the coalition uses to measure how much force is on the ground at any given time. Battalion task forces are made up of multiple companies and commanded by lieutenant colonels. Companies consist of three to four platoons and are commanded by captains. Platoons are led by lieutenants and have three to four squads led by staff sergeants, and each squad has two teams led by sergeants.

To add to the complexity of this command structure, Defense Secretary Robert Gates, the "soft spoken, courteous . . . and absolutely decisive" Department of Defense leader, named the former

Joint Chiefs of Staff officer Lt. Gen. Douglas E. Lute as President George Bush's new "War Czar." This position was designed to be the chief coordinator among all government agencies for the War on Terrorism.[16]

Unfortunately, the Iraqis are copying the coalition's example of headquarters building. Already the Iraqi Ground Forces Command (IGFC) is in competition with the Iraqi Joint Headquarters (JHQ), both four-star headquarters vying for control of the Iraqi Army. This mirroring effort is taking shape even at the very senior levels. A mismatch of Iraqi Security Forces working for both the Ministry of Defense (MOD) and the Ministry of Interior (MOI) has caused great challenges for both the Iraqis and the coalition. Border Police, Iraqi Police, National Police, Iraqi Special Operations Forces, Iraqi Air Force, Strategic Infrastructure Battalions (SIBs), Iraqi Army, and Force Protection Services (FPS) all make up a labyrinth of confusion when it comes to defining what ISF element works for whom and which gets what resources. This confused assemblage of command relationships in both the coalition and Iraqi commands leaves one wondering why a more simple organization wasn't developed initially, especially since the nature of the conflict—a counterinsurgency—is complex.

The U.S. Army has transformed aggressively in the past decade to meet the demands of the contemporary operating environment, changes triggered by the end of the Cold War. One of the most significant changes is the adjustment in the sizes of the war-fighting headquarters, the brigade combat teams (BCTs), which grew from organic commands consisting of three infantry battalions each to a mix of battalions coming together into six-battalion-size formations complete with a full array of functional capabilities. Essentially the BCT grew from approximately 1,500 soldiers to nearly 4,000.

With that growth and transformation of mission sets should come a review of its level of command. Arguably the BCT is now an operational level of command with strategic implications rather than just a tactical force. This is important, because it contributes significantly to the relevance behind the number of BCTs in theater and the number of commands from which our soldiers receive their orders.

LINES OF OPERATION

Operational designs, battlefield frameworks, and operating environments are all based on the knowledge of a commander's ability to employ companies and battalions, all the while trying to give a strategic underpinning to what is required to achieve success at the political level. An example of this leadership challenge relates to lines of operation (LOOs).[17] The accompanying graph depicts the mission sets that MNF-I and MNC-I expect divisions to carry out. Divisions and their subordinate units employ their forces to accomplish these mission sets and thereby achieve a measured success in each LOO.

Many planners and commanders have reached the conclusion that our planning processes need to incorporate lines of operation. Though this is not a new concept, articles written about their use in Iraq, such as one by Lt. Gen. Peter Chiarelli, commander of MNC-I from 2005 to 2006, have renewed the debate. Lieutenant General Chiarelli used the following lines of operation to focus his forces while in command: combat operations, train and employ security forces, essential services, promote governance, and economic pluralism. Essentially he developed measures of effectiveness (MOE) and measures of performance (MOP) to guide the daily actions of his force against each line of operation. Others have suggested rule of law and information operations as appropriate additions. While working to assist the Sri Lankan government against insurgents in the 1980s, Dr. Tom Marks developed a campaign based on the following LOOs: elimination of grievances, population and resource control, and military/operational measures. The point is, lines of operation are those areas associated with activities such as stability operations where the environment is complex and the need to operate militarily across a full spectrum requires a compartmentalized focus.

A telling illustration of how LOOs work, and the importance of identifying the right areas for which we should employ combat power, is Maj. Gen. John Batiste's account of the 2004 battle for Samarra. According to Batiste, then commanding general of the 1st Infantry Division, key to the division's success was identifying four

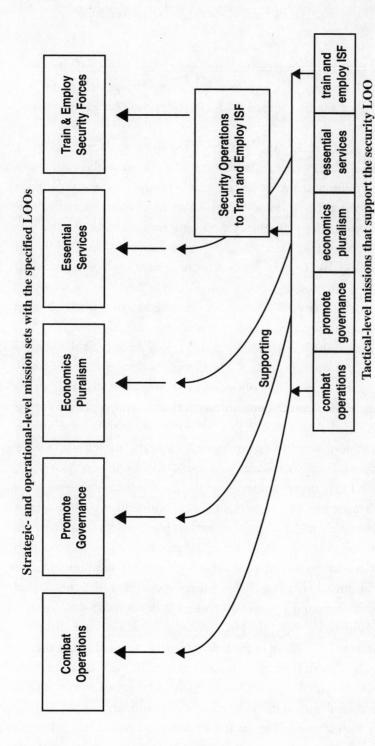

Strategic- and operational-level mission sets with the specified LOOs

| Combat Operations | Promote Governance | Economics Pluralism | Essential Services | Train & Employ Security Forces |

Security Operations to Train and Employ ISF

Supporting

Tactical-level missions that support the security LOO

| combat operations | promote governance | economics pluralism | essential services | train and employ ISF |

Lines of operation and how they relate strategically, operationally, and tactically.

lines of operation: "governance, communications, economic development, and security."[18] Only security is directly tied to traditional
military roles; the first three LOOs clearly focused on gaining popular support for the counterinsurgency.

Most commanders in the theater see the populace, or popular
support from the populace, as the center of gravity in the counterinsurgency fight, and therefore feel that employing assets to achieve
success along those lines is essential. But units of division size and
below are organized for the tactical fight and conduct mission sets
with a primary emphasis on achieving the security LOO. Though
divisions and BCTs can perform mission sets such as assisting in
establishing essential services in a region, in reality they do so just to
support the security LOO they are chartered to develop. This is an
important realization that is often lost when engaging forces.

Because units at division level and below operate at the tactical
level, they can be expected to achieve only a measured level of success along the security line of operation. This is not to say that a subordinate element cannot conduct missions, for example, to bolster the
governance of a province. All other endeavors merely exist at that
level to achieve security. For instance, a tactical force such as a BCT
operating in the city of Samarra in the Salah ad Din province north
of Baghdad may devise a plan to employ local military-age males in a
city cleanup endeavor. In actuality, the commander at that level is
focused on ensuring that those otherwise potential terrorists for hire
have employment elsewhere. He therefore wants them employed to
clean up the streets in order to support his security requirement. The
local economic benefits are a secondary result. Basically, the tactical
commander is taking a potential "trigger puller" off the street.

The difference is subtle, but that BCT is *not* working along the
essential services LOO *at its level*. What we have missed in the theater
is that when tactical-level commanders establish a plan to provide
support to the ancillary LOOs, those that are essential for success at
the operational and strategic levels of command, little is being done
to coordinate these efforts at the higher level. What we believe is

actually occurring is that commanders simply array a set of LOOs across all levels, and then superimpose their strategy onto all subordinate commands without capitalizing on the success of each level.

For example, using the scenario described above, the MNC-I level command should have a grand strategy for attaining essential services that takes into account those efforts being made at the tactical level, even if the results are a by-product of an effort to achieve the security LOO at the lower level. After all, it takes a corps-level effort to devise a national plan to provide essential services. Random engagements to achieve governance, essential services, and even economic pluralism usually fail unless a national plan is in place to nest funds, political support, and popular involvement in the effort. If we have learned nothing else as a military force these past few years in both plan development and operational execution, we do recognize that some mission sets require a grand strategy to succeed.

The street cleanup detail in Samarra perhaps is a subset of a nationwide program built and sponsored to achieve success along the essential services LOO. We can conduct all these LOOs at the tactical level, but the majority of tasks exist as shaping operations to ensure that security is achieved. Therefore, when explaining the essential services LOO at the tactical level, it may be helpful to point out that it is a supporting effort in achieving a measured success along the security LOO.

THE GROWTH OF THE BUREAUCRACIES
The lack of a capable manned, trained, and equipped police force is clearly a major issue in Iraq, and it is perhaps the single most important problem that must be solved to achieve victory. As was disbanding the army initially, not establishing a police force as a baseline defense against crime and those terrorist elements who capitalize on it was a mistake. Additionally, it is difficult to achieve victory in an already complex environment, with too many bosses and limited resources, if we have not prioritized our efforts to achieve that victory.

Our experiences in 2003 in the 173rd Airborne Brigade and 25th Infantry Division provide the background for how we view this issue. The 2nd Battalion, 503rd Airborne Infantry was part of the Northern Front assigned to the 173rd Airborne Brigade based in Vicenza, Italy. Because the government of Turkey denied the Fort Hood, Texas, 4th Infantry Division (Mechanized) passage through their country in the coalition's attempt to close a force from the northern boundary in Iraq, the coalition was forced instead to conduct a combat parachute jump onto Bashur (Harir Airfield) drop zone north of Kirkuk.[19]

At that time, the 2nd BCT of the 25th Infantry Division based in Hawaii was getting ready to replace our airborne force in the city of Kirkuk for the second Operation Iraqi Freedom (OIF 2), beginning in early 2004. As OIF 1 came to a close, there was a tendency to build bureaucracies—and in the business of conducting military operations, the growth of bureaucracies left unchecked can be detrimental to achieving victory.

The major focus of the coalition went from closing with and destroying the enemy to nonkinetic mission sets that left soldiers confused and feeling as though they were walking on eggshells every time they went out to conduct an operation. This type of attitude and command climate were results of the increase in bureaucracy.

Fundamentally speaking, the human being is a builder, and every large organization builds bureaucracies. Profit-making organizations tend to build more efficient bureaucracies with the sole purpose of making more money. Those organizations that do *not* make a profit tend to build less efficient businesses centered around the proliferation of bureaucracies. By default, the U.S. military is one of these organizations.

This inadequacy was reflected in our unit's attempt to gain support from external agencies early in the war to develop the Kirkuk Police Department. The executive officer for the 2nd Battalion, 503rd Infantry (Airborne) was Maj. Michael Fenzel. Mike is an incredibly talented officer who now commands 1st Battalion, 503rd Infantry, which is deployed to Afghanistan as of this writing, and was a White House fellow early in the decade. While working in D.C., he developed a number of ties to government officials, including Miami Police Chief John Timoney, who agreed to come to Kirkuk to provide his expertise.[20]

Having served for months in Kirkuk in an effort to inculcate the Kurds, Arabs, Turkomen, and Assyrians with police experience and a capacity to operate as part of the new IPS, and having spent thousands of dollars to restore police stations and acquire police equipment, we were at our limit of what we could do to proceed in our effort to train the police. Therefore, we asked for help from known experts who had experience forming successful police forces. It seemed like a simple request, but it became a power struggle from the outset. As in most other endeavors, Baghdad wanted to be the lead, but for reasons we couldn't understand at the time, there not only was no tangible support, but also no direction. Therefore, we were left fending for ourselves.

We were told numerous times that CJTF-7 was developing a plan to attain and train Iraqi police, but after nearly a year of unfulfilled promises, nothing had come to fruition. After informing the 4th Infantry Division commander, Maj. Gen. Ray Odierno, who supported the Kirkuk plan, the coalition force decided on its own to move forward with Timoney's support.

But at the eleventh hour, after days of coordination and numerous plans had been put in place to execute what appeared to be a supportable training plan with Timoney at the lead, he was denied entrance to country by the Department of Defense lead, Bernard Kerik.

In May 2003, Kerik was appointed by the Bush administration as the interim minister of interior of Iraq and the senior policy advisor to the U.S. presidential envoy to Iraq, L. Paul Bremer. He would be responsible for reconstituting the Iraqi Ministry of Interior, which had dissolved into the community during the U.S.-led coalition's invasion. The Iraq Interior consisted of the National Police, Intelligence Service, and Border and Customs Police.

Rajiv Chandrasekaran, an assistant managing editor at the *Washington Post*, writes in his book on Iraq, *Imperial Life in the Emerald*

City, "It didn't take long for experts to conclude that more than 6,600 foreign police advisors should be sent to Iraq immediately. The White House dispatched just one: Bernie Kerik."[21] Kerik was the police commissioner in New York on 9/11, so it was little surprise that his name carried clout with the CPA. In the end, he was said to be arrogant, incompetent, and undedicated in his position. Says Chandrasekaran: "He was the wrong guy at the wrong time . . . [he] didn't have the skills. What we needed was a chief-executive-level person. . . . Bernie came in with a street-cop mentality."[22] But no one questioned the guy who was the police chief on 9/11. And he certainly wasn't going to be trumped by another U.S. city police chief of the likes of John Timoney—even if it meant that nothing would be done for the IPS during Kerik's tenure.

George Packer also criticized Kerik in his book *The Assassins' Gate: America in Iraq:*

> He [the army lieutenant colonel in charge of Kirkuk recon-struction] was afraid that the new Kirkuk police force, which the battalion he commanded had already set up, would have to be scrapped when Bernard Kerik—the colorful former New York police chief—finally got around to announcing his national plan. Instead, Kerik spent his time in Baghdad going on raids with South African mercenaries while his house in New Jersey underwent renovation. He went home after just three months, leaving almost nothing behind, while the Lt. Colonel spent almost a year in Kirkuk.[23]

What has happened over the past few years was an economy-of-force effort to establish the police force, all the while struggling to restore the Iraqi Army and develop the multiple other arms of the ISF. The adage "trying to be strong everywhere makes one weak overall" was clearly the case in establishing the Iraqi Security Forces. Power struggles and central control were the by-products of the newfound bureaucracy growing in Iraq.

Nowhere is the bureaucracy more evident than in the way the coalition has established the transition team concept. A June 2006 article in the *Wall Street Journal* talks about U.S. Army leaders at odds with each other rather than moving toward the same goal—a goal that itself is not clearly defined by our senior leadership in the theater.[24]

Many of these issues have been rectified in the past few years. Early on, however, the coalition violated the unity of command principle of war by injecting numerous command elements into a division's area of operation without giving the on-site commander the ability to command and control those forces.[25] In layman's terms, this means that there were many subordinate commands working in another commander's area without that commander being in charge of their actions.

Retired general and former supreme allied commander of Europe George Joulwan is quoted as saying, "There are only two things that matter when it comes to running operations like Bosnia or Iraq or I don't care where it is. . . . And that is absolute unity of command and absolute clarity of instructions. . . . For the U.S. military, unity of command is nearly liturgical."[26]

Any military officer would tell you that ambiguous command relationships are a recipe for trouble. Multiple command headquarters, an ill-defined command relationship, and an inability to identify the appropriate requirements for those Iraqi Security Forces in need leave a force on the ground questioning its next move.

If the goal is to give the mission set back to the Iraqi government, army, and police, then we should have done all we could to ensure that the command-and-control lines of communication between the transition teams and the coalition forces were clean. Instead, we have built a bureaucracy with an ambiguous chain of command that leaves everyone questioning who works for whom.

This was very evident in the 1/4 BCT sector in Camp Taji, Iraq. *The Wall Street Journal* article cited earlier reports that the Coalition Force Brigade, commanded by a U.S. Army officer, was at odds with the officer's senior military transition team (MiTT) leader. Thus we

RULES OF ENGAGEMENT

The rules of engagement (ROE) are defined as "directives issued by competent military authority to delineate circumstances and limitations under which . . . naval, air and ground forces will initiate and/or continue combat engagement with other forces encountered."[27]

Commanders are generally free to make ROE more restrictive, but they must obtain approval from higher headquarters to make them more permissive. In the transition from combat-type, kinetic operations to more peacekeeping, nonkinetic operations, these types of decisions cannot be made instantaneously.

What is lost on our leaders is something that has inherently been an issue with extended conflict over the past 100-plus years: It is the struggle in defining when we need to transition from kinetic to nonkinetic operations. We have to ensure that our commanders and troops stay within a defined set of parameters by following a set of rules called ROE.

Commanders always retain the right and obligation to exercise self-defense in response to hostile acts or demonstrations of hostile intent. Self-defense includes the authority to pursue and engage forces that have committed a hostile act or demonstrated hostile intent if those forces continue to commit hostile acts or demonstrate hostile intent. The use of force in self-defense must be proportional. The amount of force used may exceed the means and intensity of the hostile act or hostile intent, but the nature, duration, and scope of force used should not exceed what is required to defeat the threat.

had two U.S. Army colonels working in one area of operation with no clear command-subordinate relationship—a recipe for friction. The MiTT leader habitually works closely with the Iraqi Army (IA) leadership, and the partnered unit conducts missions with the same

Rules of Engagement continued

"Hostile act" and "hostile intent" are two of the most important terms in the ROE and are defined as follows: A hostile act is an attack or other use of force against the United States, U.S. forces, or other designated persons or property. Hostile intent is the threat of imminent use of force against the United States, U.S. forces, or other designated persons or property. It also includes the threat of force to preclude or impede the mission or duties of Coalition Forces (CF), including the recovery of personnel or vital CF property. For commanders and soldiers, identifying a hostile act is usually easy, but determining whether something is a demonstration of hostile intent is often a judgment call based on everything known to the commander or soldier.

Another important ROE concept is the "declared hostile force." Forces may be declared hostile only by the appropriate authority. In most cases, it will be at the very highest levels of command. This is never done at the unit or soldier level. Once a force or group has been declared hostile by the appropriate authority, U.S. forces need not observe a hostile act or a demonstrated hostile intent before engaging it.

Declared hostile forces may be engaged based on their status as members of a particular group. If permitted by the ROE, facilities associated with a particular hostile force may also be engaged based on their status. As such, they are sometimes referred to as "status-based targets."

IA unit. According to the article, the MiTT leader stated that the U.S. brigade leadership at Camp Taji treats Iraqis with utter scorn and contempt. "The Iraqis may not be sophisticated but they aren't stupid. They see it."[28] In the end, the two colonels bickered so much that it left the Iraqis confused as to whom they could trust. This is just one example of how having no clear chain of command has resulted in turf fights among our leadership, when we should be focusing all of our coalition energy and resources on doing everything we can to turn over the reins to the Iraqis. The good news is that by the summer of 2007, the new Iraqi Assistant Group (IAG) commander, Brig. Gen. Jim Yarbrough, recognized the need for unity of command for the BCTs. In an unprecedented and completely selfless move, he detached all MiTT teams from the IAG's command and control to that of the land-owning commander. This clearly was a boon for all commanders across Iraq.

LACK OF TRUST IN SUBORDINATES

A defining characteristic in the Iraqi theater, at one point, appeared to be a waning ability, and in some cases desire, to trust subordinate leaders. Top cover, as we call it at the tactical level, appears to be challenged as we progress in this war. "Top cover" refers to the senior leaders' support for the subordinate commanders, with the attitude that those subordinate to you are doing the right things unless proven otherwise. But at times in Iraq, the inverse of that seems to be holding true in many cases, and it causes discontent and confusion in the lower ranks.

The military habitually has had a number of checks and balances in place, such as the rules of engagement, directives, and orders that provide direction and prevent confusion. With the progression of this war, however, too many leaders have lost confidence in their subordinates, and many of these "rules" have become clouded and confused in their presentation to the forces that execute the plans.

Some believe that this lack of confidence, which results in a command-directed investigation for just about every ambiguous act, is because today's senior leaders have not led in combat at the lower levels and therefore lack the experience to understand and subsequently trust that sergeants and lieutenants will act appropriately in accomplishing their missions. While this no doubt is true in many cases, there are notable exceptions, leaders who have had great confidence in their subordinate commanders, such as Lt. Gen. Ray Odierno, a recent MNC-I commander and former commander of the 4th Infantry Division; Lt. Gen. Lloyd Austin, the current MNC-I commander; Lt. Gen. Tom Turner, who commanded Task Force Band of Brothers in MND-N; Maj. Gen. Randy Mixon, who replaced Turner in MND-N at the end of a year deployed; Maj. Gen. Rick Lynch, a recent commander of MND-C; and Maj. Gen. Mike Oates, the current commander of MND-C. Because of that trust and confidence, they let subordinates do their jobs.

In other areas, however, the onslaught of a full array of investigations for all kinds of alleged violations often leaves junior leaders second guessing their actions—another recipe for failure to achieve victory. Bureaucracies lead to commands starved for information, which leads to mistrust of subordinate commanders and staff, which in turn leads to countless investigations and overly structured hierarchies of command.[29]

INTERIM OBJECTIVES

Free elections are no guarantee for democracy—but isn't it true that if a country has free elections, it has the beginnings of a democracy? Larry Diamond, a senior fellow at the Hoover Institution, writes in *Squandered Victory*, "Beginning in 1974, a new wave of democratic expansion began to sweep the world, and the proportion of the world's states that were democratic climbed dramatically, from a little over one-quarter in that year to about 60 percent in 1994."[30] Extrapolating from these figures, by 2008 a natural trend toward democracy across the globe should have become the norm.

It requires genuine vision and statesmanship to pull the Middle East out of its death spiral. The elements of a possible solution are there if the will exists among the majority of people to accept an alternative to the politics of fear, bigotry, and hatred. The first step is recognizing that the solution to the Iraq crisis must be generated first internally, and then at the regional level. The two are linked, and the successful resolution of one would lead to the other. Therefore, provincial elections are key at this point for victory. It would be of great value to the Iraqis if the mission sets we devise along the lines of operation would replicate those developed by the Iraqi government.

No foreign power, however, no matter how benevolent, should be allowed to dictate the terms of a possible historic and stable settlement in the Middle East. No other region of the world would tolerate such wanton interference in its affairs. The coalition's attempts to make the region mirror the Western world need to cease. Although due consideration should be given to the legitimate interests of the great powers in the area, the future of the region should not be held hostage to the design and exclusive interests of the coalition or any other outside party.

Second, any settlement must acknowledge and accommodate the forces that the invasion of Iraq unleashed. These forces, in turn, must accept limits to their demands and claims. That would apply, in particular, to the Shiites and Kurds, the two communities who seem to have gained the most out of all the Iraqi people from the invasion of Iraq.

Third, the Sunni Arab community has to become convinced that its loss of undivided power will not lead to marginalization and discrimination. There must be a mechanism in place to allow the Sunni Arabs to monitor, regulate, and if need be, correct any signs of discrimination that may emerge in the new Iraqi state. The processes of reconciliation are key to this success.

Fourth, because the existing states surrounding Iraq feel deeply threatened by the changes there, Iran and Turkey need to be introduced into a new security structure for the Middle East, with their legitimate concerns, fears, and interests taken into account. It is far better that these countries are seen as part of a stable order in the area than as outsiders who need to be confronted and challenged. These regional issues need to be recognized and dealt with in order to develop any lasting stability for Iraq and the area, a task well above the tactical level.

Finally, the Iraqi government resulting from the admittedly flawed political process must be accepted as a sovereign and responsible government. No settlement can possibly succeed if its starting point is grounded in the belief that the Iraqi government is neither legitimate nor lasting.

THE NATURE OF THE COUNTERINSURGENT FIGHT TODAY

Is it too late to take on the insurgency using the proven steps as defined by the great military theorists of our recent past? Though it may be too late to engage in all the learned steps of a theoretically and doctrinally correct counterinsurgency operation, such as those offered by David Galula in *Counterinsurgency Warfare: Theory and Practice,* in our estimate, stepping into a counterinsurgency fight after having missed a number of phases, while difficult, is not impossible. What may be more difficult at this point is to defeat, neutralize, and destroy an enemy that is embedded in the populace. What makes matters worse and the situation more complex is that we—meaning the coalition—had a hand in creating this enemy. It is believed that the majority of the insurgent forces are Sunni Arabs.[31] Though every Iraqi ethnicity has its share of the insurgency, the Sunni dominate because we made them who they are—or at least allowed their disenfranchisement under the new Iraqi government. The struggles today are about missed opportunities and the failure to learn from past mistakes to find a solution to achieve victory.

Author Thomas Ricks writes in *Fiasco* that "the 2003 U.S. invasion and occupation of Iraq can't be viewed in isolation."[32] He maintains that Operation Iraqi Freedom was an extension of a "botched" effort in Desert Storm to dislodge Iraq from Kuwait. We, on the other hand, believe that the goals of Desert Storm were met.[33] But his theory raises some questions: What were the goals for Operation Iraqi Freedom? And is it futile at this point to identify a desired end state and come up with a set of actions for achieving those goals?

CHAPTER 2

The Changing Face of Battle: Diagnosing an Insurgency

"War in Practice is never the same as War in Theory."

Gen. Wesley K. Clark
*Winning Modern Wars: Iraq, Terrorism,
and the American Empire*

The Department of Defense defines an "insurgency" as "an organized movement aimed at the overthrow of a constituted government through the use of subversion and armed conflict."[1] Simply put, an insurgency is a power struggle between a nonruling group and their ruling authority. Though it may be a stretch to deem the somewhat provisional Iraqi government an authority figure, it is nonetheless the elected body. There is also some ambiguity surrounding its governing documents, with many Iraqis and allies questioning the legitimacy of the Constitution.[2] The ruling government must ask itself whether the constitution is truly ratified at this point, for many of the articles have yet to be enacted. One of the many misconstrued decisions is that under the rule of law, authorities are required to present a warrant before entering an Iraqi home, but a declared state of emergency negates that requirement.

It is unfortunate that those entities attempting to counter the actions of those who are defying the authoritative governing body have not learned from the history of "best practices" common to successful counterinsurgencies.[3] At least fifty-three conflicts over the past 100 years have had characteristics of an insurgency, and a number of them had similarities to the war in Iraq.[4] Why then weren't these insurgencies used as models for potential resolution? Once President Bush announced the end of the high-intensity conflict on May 1, there was an obvious change to the environment, instigated either by the enemy (as was the case with the onset of the insurgency) or by the coalition, which had just announced the end of the big fight. Did the insurgency occur by happenstance? Was it a planned phase by the enemy or a last-ditch attempt at maintaining Baathist power? Few saw this type of fight on the horizon in mid-2003 as the dust settled on the euphoric state in Baghdad. Perhaps the coalition could have anticipated it by better studying history. But the United States and its allies failed to learn from the past because we forced ourselves to learn the wrong lessons—or at least an incomplete set of the right ones.

At the end of the Vietnam War, our military was in shambles; poor discipline and poor morale were widespread throughout the force. In the 1980s, President Ronald Reagan was intent on overhauling the U.S. military. One of the themes at that time was "no more Vietnams," meaning, among other things, that we would never again engage in the piecemeal introduction of forces as was done during the prolonged conflict in Southeast Asia. More important, the ensuing command-and-control structure for our military force was framed with the intention that it would not be micromanaged from afar. In the end, however, what we ended up saying was that we would never again fight in a counterinsurgency if at all possible; it was simply too hard and far too costly. But saying "no more Vietnams" doesn't guarantee that there will be no more insurgencies, and most everyone involved in both planning and executing the strategy for Iraq probably knew this.

Fighting an insurgency in Vietnam and the failures that plagued our country because of it were the catalysts for change and the driving force behind the overwhelming effort of our leaders in the 1980s to build a different kind of army. The plan was to build a cohesive fighting military with an all-volunteer force and the best technological capabilities known to mankind. In short, we needed a force that could overwhelm a uniformed enemy and destroy it. And with the way our military evolved since Vietnam also came a new way of war.

The changes proved successful in the first Gulf War and were confirmed in the Panama invasion in 1989, where overwhelming combat power was used and a set of clearly attainable objectives were defined.[5] One could also argue that the new kind of war was further validated in how the force fought in Afghanistan in 2001 and 2002, during the early stages of the War on Terrorism.[6] The United States applied the Powell Doctrine where overwhelming an enemy force would result in a quick victory, and where it didn't work, as in Somalia, we simply pulled out.

Therefore, though it took nearly a quarter of a century to shape the force that went to war in March 2003, the focus in the end, or at least how it was applied to the next big counterinsurgent fight, was misdirected. Gen. David Petraeus admits that "counterinsurgent operations generally have been neglected in broader American military doctrine and national security policies since the end of the Vietnam War over 30 years ago."[7] What was lost during the transition period was the need to define *how* to wage the full-spectrum fight, including the need to defeat a counterinsurgency correctly and not just ignore it.

To the U.S. military's credit, it had planned all along to fight a war in Iraq. The question was not whether the United States would go to war in Iraq, but when.[8] It was widely felt that the cost of going to war with Iraq on Saddam's terms was too great. Regardless of what one believes about the potential of Iraq to have weapons of mass destruction, it was universally agreed that Saddam had calamitous potential to wage war, which could include weapons of mass destruction. Most would agree that if the country has to go to war, starting the war on our terms is prudent to waging successful combat operations. Strategic planners often made the analogy to asking 1945 decision makers whether, if they had known in 1938 what they knew about Hitler in 1945, they would have allowed him to start the war on his terms.[9] Though Saddam Hussein was no Hitler (mostly because Iraq was never as powerful as Germany), most Americans agreed that war in Iraq in an effort to remove Saddam was required and therefore imminent. So why weren't we prepared for the aftermath of the high-intensity conflict?

Given the wide array and sheer number of insurgent-based conflicts in the twenty-first century alone, one would think there has to be a theoretical concept for countering defiance. Even in the effort to reengineer our military after Vietnam so that it could fight a clear and concise technologically based fight with overwhelming firepower, it seems obvious that ignoring the low-intensity conflicts was not an acceptable course of action. But even our nation's greatest strategists, and most of our official positions, tended to take an indirect approach to how our nation should react to an insurgency. During the late part of the twentieth century, counterinsurgent and guerrilla-warfare type fights were perceived as something we could use to further our purposes: "Doctrine, known as Low-Intensity Conflict, foresees aiding anti-communist guerrilla groups throughout the world as a way of confronting the Soviet Union without actually committing U.S. troops to combat."[10]

To many, this was the way we would fight a counterinsurgency: by *not* committing forces. Perhaps we hoped to emulate the 1980s example, where elements within our government covertly funded weaponry in the now infamous Iran-Contra support to the right-wing insurgency in Central America. This application of forces, albeit not U.S. forces, was the prevailing thought at the time and had a lasting effect on how the United States would get involved in low-intensity conflicts in the future.

CURRENT U.S. COUNTERINSURGENCY DOCTRINE

"Counterinsurgency" (COIN) is defined as the military, paramilitary, political, economic, psychological, and civic actions taken by a gov-

ernment to defeat insurgency.[11] Notice the two additional considerations for COIN warfare beyond those of conventional warfare: paramilitary and civic actions. The emphasis on the inclusion of multiple
nonlethal lines of operation, which habitually include the need and
use of civilian professionals, becomes especially relevant when considering lines of operation in a COIN campaign plan concept.

On the operational level, COIN doctrine as it relates to a specific
service—army, air force, marines, or navy—is somewhat general and
rudimentary in its attempts to address the preponderance of insurgent warfare in the twentieth century. Joint, or multiservice, doctrine,
however, has existed in a fairly complex and relevant context for
some time and was fairly well developed at the onset of the War on
Terrorism.

Learning from the Past

"Throughout its history, the U.S. military has had to relearn the principles of counterinsurgency (COIN) while conducting operations
against adaptive insurgent enemies."[12] This has been a challenge for
forces across time. Going back and studying the British counterinsurgency experience in 1952 in Malaya (commonly referred to as the
model for defeating an armed insurgency), where British general
Gerald Templer understood his role as that of preparing Malaya for
self-rule, one can see the similarities. Templer had the foresight during that conflict to concede that independence would not succeed
without government and military unity. In an interesting comparison
to what is occurring in Iraq today, Templer realized that to achieve
unity among the three major ethnic groups in Malaya—the Malay,
Chinese, and Indians—they all had to concede to compromises so
that the three could live in harmony. Templer achieved this by engaging the populace. In fact, he coined the popular phrase among those
attempting to counter an insurgency as "winning hearts and minds"
of the populace in order to get them to side with friendly forces
rather than the insurgency. But like most counterinsurgent efforts, his
victory in Malaya came at a cost: The British Army deployed eleven

battalions in Malaya for ten years to work with and assist 60,000 full-time Malayan police and 200,000 home guards, whereas the war in Iraq is now in its sixth year.[13]

The very foundation of the United States was built on an insurgent-counterinsurgent struggle, and the birth of the Continental Army was the result of a colonial insurgency against the British Empire. The history of the development of U.S. Army counterinsurgency doctrine is well documented in the book *U.S. Army Counterinsurgency and Contingency Operations Doctrine, 1860–1941*. This study describes how leaders of the U.S. Army, since its infancy, have made little effort to learn from the past, which would result in an effective doctrine dedicated to counterinsurgency operations.[14]

The history of U.S. warfare shows that counterinsurgency operations are merely diversions from the more important concern of classic maneuver warfare. Doctrinal studies of how to attack and defend conventionally are in abundance, whereas the knowledge of how to conduct counterinsurgency operations is mainly just "a long-standing oral history passed down from veterans to recruits."[15] Counterinsurgency doctrine has not received the same attention as conventional warfare, and it unfortunately has to be relearned each time as insurgency occurs. In the early twentieth century, the U.S. Army's counterinsurgent operations were readily apparent in the Philippines at the turn of the century and then again after World War II. Though there were some counterinsurgency operations in both World War II and the Korean War, the lessons learned from the Vietnam War had the greatest effect on our nation.

The 1940 *Small Wars Manual* still stands as the historical standard for U.S. tactical COIN operations, and one of its chapters talks of disarming a population. The citing of a 1940 field manual that appears to have answers for a war that is happening half a century later, in a country where the major conflict is an internal arms race between insurgents and pro-Iraqi government forces, is both heartening and disturbing.

Many wanted to disarm the population throughout Iraq in early 2003. It was a major goal of our units in the Kirkuk province, but without operational oversight from those at the highest levels, it was a futile effort. Both the local populace and many who have studied the culture argued that the AK-47 is somewhat of a national symbol, and that weapons have been a part of each family for generations. Bearing arms for an Iraqi is a lifestyle standard about as common as owning a second car is for an American. The idea that adults (and some apparent juveniles) carry AK-47s freely should not have been a surprise to our soldiers as we entered the towns, cities, and villages across Iraq. Unfortunately, it was. Here is what the *Small Wars Manual* has to say about disarmament as a requirement in the effort to defeat an insurgency:

> Due to the unsettled conditions ordinarily prevailing in a country requiring a neutral intervention, and the existence of many arms in the hands of the inhabitants, the disarming of the general population of that country is not only extremely important as a part of the operation of the intervening forces but also to the interests of the inhabitants themselves: It is customary in many undeveloped or unsettled communities for all of the male population upon reaching maturity, to be habitually armed, notwithstanding that such possession is generally illegal. There is a logical reason for the large number of weapons in the hands of the inhabitants. The arbitrary political methods which frequently result in revolution, and the lawlessness practiced by a large proportion of the population, is responsible for this state of affairs. The professional politicians and the revolutionary or bandit leaders, as well as their numerous cohorts, are habitually armed. Legal institutions cannot prevail against this distressing condition; persons and property are left at the mercy of unscrupulous despots, until in self-preservation the peaceful and law abiding inhabitants are forced to arm themselves.[16]

This excerpt was written more than fifty years before the beginning of Operation Iraqi Freedom. Therefore, there already existed not only in writing, but readily available in military doctrine, the concepts and precepts for exploiting a measurable foray against those forces making up the successful arm of an insurgency.

Many believe that the Vietnam War was the model and its lessons learned were the formula for defeating an insurgency. Experience alone provided those that would eventually become the senior leaders a "way ahead" for the makeup of the military in the post-Vietnam era. Not only do experience and the doctrine that ensued provide a guide for at least understanding this kind of fight, our forces also had available to them a plethora of books written by historians to help them understand how to fight an unconventional war.

The Army and Vietnam, by Andrew F. Krepinevich, Jr., does a superb job of outlining the different strategies used by the U.S. Army throughout the war. More important, it describes the institutional army's refusal to see the conflict as anything other than a conventional fight to stop North Vietnam from occupying the south. If this were true, then surely the resultant strategies would support a weak attempt to defeat insurgent operations.[17]

On Strategy: A Critical Analysis of the Vietnam War, by Col. Harry Summers, provides a good analysis of the impact of the Southeast Asian war on current thought in the post-Vietnam U.S. Army regarding counterinsurgency operations. Its focus is primarily on military operations and the inability or failure of the army to correctly apply the principles of war in those operations. So while Summers accepts the need for a strategy to defeat an insurgency, he claims that our military was incapable, to an extent, of executing it during Vietnam—an argument made by many critics of Operation Iraqi Freedom.[18]

Volumes describing the post-Vietnam military thought are in abundance. So are historian-based and think tank–compiled analyses of the Central American conflict in works such as *American Military Policy in Small Wars: The Case of El Salvador,* compiled by the Institute for Foreign Policy Analysis. This work explains how the U.S. Army has tried to develop an effective counterinsurgency doctrine in the wake of Vietnam. It notes that army decision–makers realized that many effective lessons learned from Vietnam could be applied in El Salvador; however, there still was no common effort between the military and political authorities. A lack of unity hampered decisions in all the programs in place at the time.[19]

Incorporating Lessons Learned into Doctrine

Prior to the publication of the current U.S. Army doctrine, *Field Manual (FM) 3-24: Counterinsurgency,* the most up–to–date source for counterinsurgency doctrine was *Field Manual (FM) 3-07: Stability Operations and Support Operations.* This was the governing manual that existed at the beginning of the war and presumably defined the doctrine our forces relied upon to conduct the Iraqi-based military operations in mid-2003.

FM 3-07 was written with an emphasis on "supporting friendly nations operating in or threatened with potential hostilities."[20] This manual discusses distinct characteristics of both stability and support operations, together with doctrinal foundations that facilitate their accomplishment. It amplifies the army's operations manual (a conventional doctrinal thesis), *Field Manual (FM) 3-0: Operations,* a manual used mostly for conventional-type warfare.

Prior to Petraeus's development of a sound doctrine in *FM 3-24, FM 3-07* was the basis for the military's understanding of stability and support operations, an offshoot of lessons learned in the Balkans in the late 1990s. It was a generalized concept, aiming more for a broad understanding rather than giving details of how to conduct stability and support activities to aid a host nation. This manual provided the analytical tools needed to evaluate a stability or support operation; unfortunately, and greatly misunderstood by those enamored by bureaucracies, Iraq was not the Balkans.

FM 3-07 did cover the categories of foreign internal defense (FID), a role often taken on by the special operators in an attempt to help the host nations get back on their feet. While surprisingly Special Operations Forces (SOF) weren't called upon to execute FID, the requirement to conduct the activities with foreign internal defense may still stand now that a sovereign nation exists in Iraq. The question is who will conduct those activities associated with FID. Most realize it will be conventional brigade combat teams.

The emphasis on *support* to friendly nations implies the leading role that the army expects the host nation to play. In fact, under the heading "The Role of the Army in Counterinsurgency," paragraph 3-23 states, "Generally, U.S. forces do not engage in combat. The threat to American interests does not support that degree of involvement, even if it were effective. An American combat role tends to undermine the legitimacy of the host government and risks converting the conflict into an American war."[21] Following this guidance early on would have pushed the Iraqis to the forefront faster, and there would have been an emphasis on organizing, training, manning, and equipping the Iraqi Security Forces.

The doctrine in *FM 3-07,* the manual that existed to guide our forces at the beginning of the war, is very general. It notes the importance of understanding the categories of foreign internal defense, ranging from indirect support to direct support to combat operations. It also states that it is critical to neutralize the insurgency by rendering it ineffective through political reform. And most of all, it addresses the necessity of modifying military operations for counterinsurgency to avoid alienating the population with excessive violence, saying, "Collateral damage destroys government legitimacy. The insurgents' best recruiting program is indiscriminate killing and damage by government forces."[22]

FM 3-07 recognizes that military operations are only one facet of the strategic problem: "Military operations must complement and reinforce political, social, and economic reform."[23] The doctrine does not, however, address the conduct of U.S. forces when serving as occupiers that have assumed the powers of sovereignty over a foreign nation.

Clearly by 2004, our senior leaders saw the shortcomings associated with the very document that was to define the conduct of the war. As a result, Lt. Gen. David Petraeus was charged with leading a team from Fort Leavenworth to write what may be the most important document in the War on Terrorism: *FM 3-24*.

Joint Doctrine

To account for multiservice requirements, *Joint Publication (JP) 3-07.1: Joint Tactics, Techniques, and Procedures for Foreign Internal Defense*, published in April 2004, is the standard reference to assist soldiers and leaders in this counterinsurgent fight. This manual reads much like *FM 3-07*, except that it covers all U.S. forces from every service and emphasizes the criticality of coordination and the integration of effort among various U.S. agencies.

The manual also emphasizes the importance of providing support to the host nation, stating: "The United States will normally consider FID support only if the following three conditions exist: 1) the existing or threatened internal disorder is such that action by the United States supports U.S. national strategic goals; 2) the threatened nation is capable of effectively using U.S. assistance; and 3) the threatened nation requests U.S. assistance."[24] Note that all of these prerequisites depend upon the existence of an already established government, a situation that didn't exist in Iraq when the insurgency started.

JP 3-07.1 does not address the issues of conducting foreign internal defense (FID) as an occupying force or establishing a military government. It stresses the need to conduct close coordination with the U.S. diplomatic mission and the country team within the host nation to build an effective FID program, neither of which currently functions in a great capacity in Iraq.

The manual also provides a framework for the diplomatic, economic, informational, and military elements for conducting FID and stresses connectivity among these elements for an effective FID program. Like *FM 3-07*, it focuses on the indirect and direct support operations as those that are optimal for supporting a foreign nation's internal defense.

In addressing combat operations, the joint manual states, much like the army circular, that U.S. forces will be a temporary combat force only until the host nation can stabilize the situation. Additionally, it says that the primary role for U.S. military forces in combat operations is to support, advise, and assist host nation forces through logistics, intelligence or other combat support, and service means. This allows the host nation force to concentrate on taking the offensive against hostile elements.[25] It is interesting how the joint manual talks explicitly about the temporary role of our military occupying force and the primacy of the requirement to build a host nation security force.

The manual also states that host nation forces should conduct unilateral combat operations whenever possible to increase the legitimacy of the host nation government, whereas U.S. forces, if conducting combat operations, should concentrate on force protection. According to the existing joint doctrine, it is clear that U.S. forces are not intended to take a leading role in combat operations, and when they do, they are to conduct them only insofar as required for their own protection. There is much emphasis on working with the U.S. diplomatic effort and country team to build an understanding of how and when to best employ U.S. military assets to assist in FID.

JP 3-07.1 stresses the vital importance of correctly identifying the root cause of unrest so that FID efforts will apply to a long-term solution, rather than addressing a short-term symptom. This approach works well in a scenario where a sovereign nation is threatened by an insurgent movement. Iraq doesn't necessarily fit that mold, however. It was run by a tyrant who was overthrown by an outside force—a coalition of the willing—and the vast majority of the population at the time supported it. Next came the insurgency, which existed to cause unrest before a formidable and capable government could take root. So the scenario outlined in this joint publication is not necessarily synonymous with what happened in Operation Iraqi Freedom.

Nonetheless, the joint manual does express facets relative to the fight in Iraq. It identifies human intelligence (HUMINT) as probably more important than electronic or technical intelligence for successful FID. It also states that operations should be backed up with a significant counterintelligence and operational security effort.

Further, part of the HUMINT effort will be supported through training soldiers expected to operate in a FID environment. The manual recommends an emphasis on language training as much as possible to enable soldiers to operate in the environment and to facilitate cultural awareness. Standards of conduct training—training on the Rules of Engagement, FID principles, and force protection—are emphasized also.

There are other noteworthy documents that sister services have used in some detail in defining their fight against the insurgencies. *Small Wars,* published in 2004, addresses the tactical, operational, and strategic level from a contemporary perspective. The U.S. Marine Corps' 1980 manual, *Fleet Marine Force Manual (FMFM) 8-2: Counterinsurgency Operations,* frames the insurgent problem and then applies USMC doctrine, with an emphasis on the planning and conduct of internal defense and internal development operations.

JP 3-07.1 was an adjunct to both the U.S. Army and Marine Corps field manuals, and the joint publication provided a framework to follow at the early stages of the war. Additionally, in 1990, *Field Manual (FM) 100-20/Air Force Pamphlet (AFP) 3-20: Military Operations in Low Intensity Conflict* was coauthored by the U.S. Army and the U.S. Air Force. Though not joint doctrine, it was multiservice doctrine that applied to army and air force units in joint and combined low–intensity conflict (LIC) operations. LIC operational planners and leaders could use it to develop implementing doctrine. Appendixes provide quick references on several topics, including how to analyze an insurgency, how to counter an insurgency, and a guide to counterinsurgency operations. FID was the primary means of supporting counterinsurgency, and the language and processes described easily could be construed as the precursor for the current joint doctrine for FID, *JP 3-07.1*

JP 3-07.1 describes how the United States supports the host nation's program of internal defense and internal development (IDAD) operations. These operations are the full range of measures taken by a nation to promote its growth and protect itself from subversion, lawlessness, and insurgency. IDAD focuses on building viable institutions—political, economic, social, and military—that respond to the needs of society.

Joint doctrine at the beginning of the War on Terrorism directed that the role of the military in FID was to provide a secure environment for the other instruments of national power to bolster the host nation's IDAD program. Military assistance can be applied in three different forms of operations: indirect support, direct support (not involving combat operations), and combat operations. Indirect support consists of security assistance, joint and multinational exercises, and exchange programs. Direct support (not involving combat operations) includes civil-military operations, military training to host nation forces, logistics support, and intelligence and communications sharing short of combat. It is imperative that any combat operations are conducted with the host nation government and security forces remaining in the forefront to demonstrate control and substantiate claims of legitimacy. All three of these types of military assistance are appropriate in the conduct of COIN warfare, and each type must be synchronized across all lines of operation.

The joint manual also defines two additional FID planning imperatives for operational COIN planners to consider: maintaining host nation sovereignty and legitimacy, and understanding the strategic implications of all U.S. assistance efforts. The FID program is only as successful as the host nation's IDAD program, and as such, the host nation must remain at the forefront of key decision making. Strategic implications of foreign policy are delineated in each combatant commander's theater security cooperation program (TSCP).

Security cooperation is the means by which the Department of Defense encourages and enables countries and organizations to work with the United States to achieve strategic objectives. It consists of a focused program of bilateral and multilateral defense activities conducted with foreign countries to serve mutual security interests and build defense partnerships. Security cooperation efforts also should be aligned with and support strategic communication themes, messages, and actions. The secretary of defense identifies security cooperation objectives, assesses the effectiveness of security cooperation activities, and revises goals when required to ensure continued support for U.S. interests abroad. Although they can shift over time, examples of typical security cooperation objectives include creating favorable military regional balances of power, advancing mutual defense or security arrangements, building allied and friendly military capabilities for self-defense and multinational operations, and preventing conflict and crisis.[26]

All theater campaign plans must be integrated with the aims of the security cooperation plan, and as such, they are an extension of the long-term theater strategy. The overall combatant commander's theater security cooperation program is the interpretation of this national security direction, and it is built from the foundation of a regional strategic appraisal. Theater security cooperation is executed through the TSCP, which proposes and prioritizes military activities with other countries.

TSCP activities include those defense relationships that promote specified U.S. security interests, senior official visits, personnel and unit exchange programs, foreign internal defense, security assistance programs, planned humanitarian and civic assistance activities, multinational training and exercises, multinational education, and arms control and treaty monitoring activities.

A TSCP is a deliberately developed plan covering noncombat military activities with other nations within a region. The plan implements the combatant commander's TSCP and thus is a way to shape the security environment to protect and promote U.S. interests and regional objectives. It is a joint strategic plan, part of the joint operation planning family.

Joint Publication 5-0: Joint Operation Planning describes the security operation planning process: In response to direction in the Department of Defense Security Cooperation Guidance (SCG), combatant commanders, service chiefs, and combat support agency directors prepare security cooperation strategies in accordance with SCG objectives for chairman of the Joint Staff review and secretary of defense approval, with the geographic combatant commanders as the supported entities.[27] These strategies serve as the basis for security cooperation planning. Collaboration among the combatant commands, services, and combat support agencies is essential. Equally important is close coordination with U.S. agencies that represent other instruments of national power, and particularly with the U.S. chiefs of mission (ambassadors) in the combatant commander's areas of operations.[28]

A TSCP is composed of a theater situation overview, the combatant commander's mission, how the plan will be executed, an assessment of the program to date, and the current plan's implementation. The situation section is derived from an area's regional strategic appraisal and analyzes the environment in which the TSCP will be implemented. The mission states the theater's prioritized regional objectives as derived from national strategic direction. The combatant commander gives guidance on the threats to security and stability in the theater, opportunities, assumptions, and a planning schedule to develop a TSCP.[29]

The cooperation program clearly is heavily dependent on participation by the Department of State and other agencies within our government. Thus far, however, the Iraqi theater of operations has relied heavily on the military to conduct many of the inferred and implied strategic engagements discussed as part of the overall strategic requirements necessary to meet a national plan for security cooperation.

Special Text 3.05.206: Counter Urban Insurgency Planning Guide was published in 2003 by the John F. Kennedy Special Warfare Center and School specifically for Central Command and builds on the strike and consolidation operations described in *FMFM 8-2* and *DA Pamphlet 550-104: Human Factors Considerations of Undergrounds in Insurgencies.* Though neither the special text nor the DA pamphlet is doctrinal, they are attempts by the U.S. Army to address contemporary counterinsurgency warfare.

In 1986, the U.S. Army published *FM 90-8: Counterguerrilla Operations,* and then in 2004, it expedited *Field Manual Interim (FM-I) 3-07.22: Counterinsurgency Operations* into print. *FM-I 3-07.22* was written for division-level leaders and below and is more of a "how-to" on tactics, techniques, and procedures than operational-level doctrine.[30] The final copy of the field manual was published shortly thereafter, in 2005.

Field Manual (FM) 90-8: Counterguerrilla Operations was written for leaders of units of brigade size and below and provides ample insight for counterinsurgency planning, training, and operations. Many of these manuals recommend what we believe should be the steps to follow for a counterinsurgency, based on David Galula's description of the insurgent nature. One of the accomplishments of *FM 90-8* was distinguishing between counterguerrilla and counterinsurgency operations. Counterguerrilla operations address only the military aspect of the insurgent movement, whereas counterinsurgency operations focus on internal defense and internal development programs and address all the disparate elements of an insurgency.[31] Clearly, *FM 90-8* focuses on the tactical considerations of foreign internal defense (FID). It, like *FMFM 8-2,* uses Galula's dual objectives for counterinsurgency: defeat or neutralize the guerrillas and conduct noncombat operations to provide an environment where the population can become self-sustaining.[32]

What all this means is that there was a doctrinal backbone to guide how our forces operated at the beginning of the War on Terror. In some cases, we were neither fully immersed nor educated in its contents. This lack of education and know-how was arguably due to failings in our universal military and government education systems. In some cases, too, some chose to ignore the steps associated with conducting a rigorous counterinsurgency operation. It's a challenge for leaders to train their forces in both high-intensity combat operations and counterinsurgency. Under the shadow of the past few decades and desired changes in the post–Vietnam War era, most leaders chose the high-intensity option for their training priority. Nonetheless, there are developed counterinsurgency doctrinal guides, and Galula's model probably should have been the one followed.

THE GALULA MODEL

The service-level counterinsurgency doctrine used to frame the first six years of the War on Terrorism lacked an operational-level appreciation for the increasing number of contemporary insurgencies. Thanks to General Petraeus and a strict adherence to joint doctrine, an ample framework for planners and commanders now exists that extrapolates David Galula's counterinsurgency theory beyond the scope of quelling an internal insurgency to bringing a coalition of foreign forces and agencies to the counterinsurgency effort.

We will use the Galula theory in future discussions as the proposed preferred method for the overall execution of counterinsurgency operations. Galula's focus on a political solution seems the predominant premise used in developing joint doctrine. With a focus on foreign forces and civilian agencies assisting the host nation internal defense and internal development programs, we believe Galula's theory is the model that should have been used and may still be used to achieve victory in Iraq today.

The Galula model makes clear that in order to defeat an insurgency, a full spectrum of resources is required. The U.S.-led coalition undoubtedly had those resources, especially funding, available early in the fight, when it struggled in the initial stages of the counterinsurgency because of a lack of a service-oriented doctrine. The challenge now will face is adhering to the new doctrinal focus given a lack of resources. Today funding for the war is waning, and unfortunately the U.S. military has provided nearly all the manpower and other resources in use in the theater. These resource challenges present a complex problem to the coalition and government of Iraq.

David Galula (1919–67) was born to French parents in Tunisia and raised in Morocco, earning his baccalaureate in Casablanca and attending the military academy at Saint-Cyr. Galula graduated on the eve of World War II, and as a French officer, he immediately saw action in North Africa, Italy, and France. An officer of the marine infantry in the old colonial army, he was assigned to China and then served with the United Nations as a military observer in Greece and military attaché in Hong Kong. Colonel Galula was stationed in Algeria at the time of the revolt by the French Army. Shortly before retiring, he wrote *Counterinsurgency Warfare: Theory and Practice,* while in residence at the Center for International Affairs at Harvard University. This book has been and currently is heavily advocated by much of the U.S. military for advice on operations in the campaign in Iraq. When General Petraeus wrote the *Counterinsurgency* manual *(FM 3-24),* it is apparent that he referred quite often to Galula's book and analysis for formulating the current doctrine on the counterinsurgency fight.

Even though Galula's experience dates to the mid-twentieth century, in places like China, Greece, Hong Kong, and Algeria, there is indeed timelessness to his theories. We concur with so many others in believing that if there is a Clausewitz of counterinsurgency, Galula is it. Many believe that when formulating the right strategy to defeat an insurgency, there is no better guide than the Galula's 1964 work, *Counterinsurgency Warfare: Theory and Practice.* Relying on the work of Galula establishes a baseline understanding of the counterinsurgency fight and is key to understanding how to win.

Somewhere in the bowels of the Pentagon or Central Command there may have been a strategist who delved into the steps presented by theorists of the likes of Galula. With the inclusion of David Kilcullen as the senior counterinsurgency advisor to General Petraeus at MNF-I, perhaps we finally are fully embracing experts on the subject when it comes to fighting an insurgency.[33] Time will tell.

The coalition was blindsided by the onset of the insurgency and subsequently took an inordinate amount of time to react to it. This slow reaction allowed the insurgency to grow roots and flourish. As the insurgency came to fruition and the coalition developed courses of action to defeat it, it was obvious that this would become a unilateral fight on the part of the military. For whatever reason, our Department of State and other governmental agencies were unable to provide the appropriate civilian oversight so vitally needed by the newly flourishing government of Iraq in the counterinsurgency fight. Therefore, the government struggled early in the fight to gain a level of sovereignty. Clearly, we had not learned from counterinsurgencies of the past.

For an insurgency to flourish, a majority of the population must either support or remain indifferent to insurgent ideals or practices. To counter this fight, the Department of Defense has termed the actions taken by our government as a "counterinsurgency," meaning actions to defeat an insurgency. We contend, however, that much of the action in Iraq during the first few years of the war was not taken in an effort to defeat an insurgency. Instead, the coalition got caught up in bureaucratic checks and balances, all the while attempting to root out the enemy by hunting him down one by one—a conventional force fighting an unconventional war.

Galula writes on the perils of failure to recognize the signs of a budding insurgency, using the situation in Algeria in the late 1950s as an example: "'Ordinary banditry,' said a high-ranking government official in Algiers. . . . By the time the insurrection was finally recognized for what it was, only drastic political and military action would have reversed the tide, and slowly in any case."[34] Thus the question is whether we have been using the wrong medicine to fight a misdiagnosed disease.

Galula defines victory for the counterinsurgent as "the permanent isolation of the insurgent from the population."[35] He writes that our focus should not be on "the destruction in a given area of the insurgent force and his political organization," saying that "if one is destroyed, it will be re-created by a new fusion of insurgents from the outside."[36] Unfortunately, this is exactly how conventional forces in the Iraqi theater had been operating in the wake of the insurgency. An incredible and impressive effort to develop link charts and enemy target folders, though making us feel better by hunting down nefarious individuals, expends a vast amount of resources with little in return. There are short-term tangible results but seldom long-term gains.

While coalition forces have an intense desire to neutralize the enemy so that the Iraqi Security Forces can take the lead, unfortunately what actually happens is that our soldiers and marines fall back on what they know best: seeking out and destroying the enemy themselves in a unilateral manner. This would be fine if someone else in the theater were available to execute other facets of a counterinsurgency fight, but the military constitutes approximately 90 percent of what the United States has for committed resources to conduct counterinsurgency operations in Iraq.

Prerequisites for a Successful Insurgency

Galula describes four prerequisites for an insurgency to be successful: an attractive cause; a weakness in the counterinsurgency camp; a not-too-hostile geographic environment; and outside support in the middle and later stages of an insurgency. He further refines these prerequisites by writing that the first two are musts, geography is usually predetermined, and the last one is an asset that may become a necessity.[37]

According to Galula, the insurgent's cause must be attractive in order to draw the largest number of supporters, and it must be meaningful enough to last until the insurgent movement is established. In unconventional warfare, where intangible assets often outweigh tangible ones, an attractive ideological cause is the precursor to forming a formidable strength in the will of the population. In Iraq, that cause appears to be a desire to disrupt a potential Iraqi democracy that is heavily influenced by the Western world, particularly the United States. Most would agree that this is the goal of Al Qaeda and its localized Iraqi associates. The disenfranchised Sunnis are obviously concerned by the loss of their power base to the Shiites. And the Shiite insurgents want to ensure that the Sunnis or lesser Shiite elements don't tip the balance of power.

Once the insurgents have identified a cause, the other absolute prerequisite is a weak counterinsurgency effort. In Iraq, the perceived weakness of the coalition—as we are told time and time again by the

Iraqis themselves—is our lack of credibility. Simply put, when the coalition says it is going to do something, often it does not. A lack of funds, direction, or other resources often causes it to renege on a plan or promise. A new school, an increase of employment, even the provision of essential services such as fresh water don't come to fruition for various reasons, mostly funding. The U.S.-led coalition has a habit of not following up on its promises. To the average Iraqi, this means that the most powerful nation in the world—in fact, the world's only true superpower—simply cannot provide. It is unfathomable to them that this is the case.

Instead, the populace finds credibility in the insurgents, who are true to their word. The coalition promises services that it does not provide. The insurgents promise kidnappings, murders, and other atrocities, and they follow through. This weakness in the counterinsurgency camp is lending to the success of the insurgents, for the Iraqi people are reluctant to side with the pro-Iraqi forces and either become ready-made insurgents or remain fence-sitters.

A second part of the credibility issue is both the perceived and real credibility of the Iraqi government. This fledgling governing body must be strong in order to address the political nature of insurgent warfare. The strength of the host nation political regime will be evident as it competes for the support, allegiance, and loyalty of the population. A way to do this in Iraq today is to show the populace that the new Iraqi government can and will provide essential services. The insurgents counter this, however, by sabotaging the pipelines and power lines. To the average observer, an IED on a pipeline may appear to be a random act of violence, but to the insurgency, it is a way of ensuring that the counterinsurgency looks weak in the eyes of the populace.

This battle, as Galula puts it, is primarily a protracted political engagement waged in an unconventional manner through the use of propaganda and fear. It is usually a cheap war for the insurgents but very costly for the counterinsurgency.[38] By causing the counterinsurgent forces to overextend, the insurgency fixes them in place, meaning that they have minimal combat power to employ to meet other requirements to fight an insurgency.[39] This is clearly an attained weakness recognized by the enemy.

Counterinsurgency warfare is expensive in funding, manpower, and time, and the host nation's resolve will be tested by the protracted nature of this asymmetric form of warfare. Knowledge of counterinsurgency warfare at the Iraqi governmental national level will prove to be critical in determining objectives and assigning resources to control the population. Galula describes four instruments of control organic to the government infrastructure: the political structure; the administrative bureaucracy; the police; and the armed forces.[40]

The government's administrative bureaucracy runs the country's day-to-day operations and may or may not be directly affected by decisions and actions of the political leadership. What's more important, however, is that the loyalty and credibility of the police forces be gained and held, because they are the first level of government interaction with the people. The police are vital to the government's ability to provide security for its citizens, and possibly the most important Iraqi Security Forces asset. Similarly, loyalty or repatriation of members of the armed forces is required, as they will serve dual roles as security maintainers and ambassadors of the government among the people. The coalition effort to stand down the Iraqi Army in the first few months of the war runs counter to this corollary.

A not-too-hostile geographic environment is the third prerequisite for an insurgency. In Iraq, the insurgents have an advantage geographically, for they are predominantly an indigenous force. The Iraqi Security Forces should have the same advantage if they are operating in areas where they reside, but this potential advantage has repeatedly been stripped from the ISF as the coalition leadership continues to move Iraqi Army units and the National Police freely around the battlefield. This shifting of ISF from one province to another results in their being as unfamiliar with their geographic surrounding as their coalition partners.[41]

Galula defines eight factors that also influence the geographic advantage: location, size, configuration, international borders, terrain, climate, population, and economy. The location of Iraq places it between three countries—Iran, Syria, and Saudi Arabia—that oppose the U.S.-led coalition efforts and provide the ability for terrorists and potential insurgents to freely enter and leave the country.

The country's size is also on the side of the insurgency, as it is difficult for the coalition to cover all areas that may become safe havens for insurgent forces. For example, the area of operations of Task Force Band of Brothers, an infantry division with four brigade combat teams, was approximately 47,000 square miles, roughly the area of the state of Pennsylvania.

Configuration is a wash for both insurgent and counterinsurgent forces. Both are easily compartmentalized in areas like the canal-filled southwest Baghdad region.

The international borders clearly are in favor of the insurgency. The borders between Iraq and its neighboring countries are similar in total length to the U.S.-Mexico border. If the United States cannot prevent illegal immigrants from crossing this border freely, why would we expect the Iraqis to be able to do so in their country?

The terrain in Iraq supports the indigenous forces, both insurgent and ISF. Climate generally should favor the counterinsurgents, which tend to have better logistical and operational facilities, although one could argue that the climate in Iraq is so harsh that it favors anyone accustomed to that type of environment. Even with repeated tours, that clearly is not the U.S. coalition.

The population is truly the prize, for as the population goes, so does victory. This factor is based on what actions each side takes. Right now, it is in favor of the insurgency, which the populace deems more credible. However, in areas like South Baghdad, where more than 15,000 volunteers (mostly Sunni) are paid to stand guard, the security situation is at a level of stability when the population is now in favor of peace and therefore supportive of the CF-ISF force. The economy in Iraq supports the insurgency, for the combination of the 1990s U.S.-led sanctions and the current inability to provide security for and reengineer the country's infrastructure leaves the coalition struggling to find solutions for a failed state economy.

Thus a majority of the eight factors relating to the geographic prerequisite for success fall mostly on the side of the insurgency.

The final prerequisite is obtaining outside support, which can come in the form of moral, political, technical, financial, and military assistance. The U.S.-led coalition obviously has provided this support. Moral support is expressed by public opinion, and propaganda is the chief instrument of moral support. Political support may be direct pressure on the counterinsurgency leadership or international diplomatic action in favor of the insurgents' cause. Technical support is advice on the organization and conduct of operations. Financial and military support may come openly as well as covertly.[42]

According to Galula, an attractive cause and a weak COIN effort are the two most profound prerequisites for a successful insurgency. Geography and demographics aren't prerequisites so much as they are key enablers. Outside support may be necessary, but it is not required for the insurgents to complete their campaign.[43]

Laws and Principles of Counterinsurgency Warfare

Galula defines four laws and five principles of counterinsurgency warfare in order to develop a successful counterinsurgency strategy.[44] The first law is that the support of the population is as necessary for the counterinsurgency as it is for the insurgency. Galula recognized decades ago that "the crux of the problems for the counterinsurgent" is to keep an area clean.[45] The Petraeus-Odierno clear-hold-build strategy developed formally in Iraq in 2007 defines the need to keep our areas clean so that the coalition and ISF can operate elsewhere in the vast urban and rural areas of each multinational division. The key part of this law is the fact that it can be achieved only with the support of the population, and therefore it is the objective for both the insurgency and the counterinsurgency.

The second law is that support is gained through an active minority. Galula's premise states that the power consists in relying on the favorable minority (those that we have shown the way to become pro-Iraqi government) in order to rally the neutral minority and neutralize or eliminate the hostile opposition. Through this law, we can derive victory, as the goal is to achieve "the permanent isolation of the insurgent from the population."[46]

The third law is that the support of the population is conditional. This means that a counterinsurgency will not be able to rally the bulk of the population so long as the population is not convinced that the counterinsurgency has the will, means, and ability to win.[47] Again, credibility is an imperative in the drive to achieve victory.

The final law is that intense efforts and vast resources are essential to achieve victory. Large concentrations of effort, resources, and personnel are needed to abide by this law, an obvious challenge in Iraq today. Funding is waning, and there is a partisan tug-of-war over the length of deployments and size of deployed forces.

Galula's principles are consistent with the current counterinsurgency doctrine, *FM 3-24,* with some exceptions. The first principle, economy of force, is essential for the insurgents, for they can achieve much with few resources. The second, irreversibility, refers to that critical turning point when local leaders have everything to lose from a return of the insurgency. It is the Sisyphean nature of some wars in the form of a recurrent nightmare for the counterinsurgent. To prevent such endless futile labor, leaders such as the current MNF-I and MNC-I commanders have recognized the need to "live among the population and give it protection until the population is able to protect itself with minimal outside support."[48] Our current chief of staff of the army and former MNF-I commander, Gen. George Casey, recognized this principle when he insisted that forces remain in Samarra, thus preventing the need to retake the city each time an insurgent performed a spectacular event in order to cause unrest.[49]

Another principle is that of the objective. *FM 3-24* says that "the primary objective of any COIN operation is to foster development of effective governance by a legitimate government. Counterinsurgents achieve this objective by the balanced application of both military and nonmilitary means."[50] Galula, in our opinion, tends to oversimplify the pursuance of this objective. He states that the government should pursue an offensive counterinsurgency strategy and seize the initiative to force the insurgent to accept the challenge. The insurgent has two options: take a defensive posture or leave the area and become powerless to oppose the counterinsurgents' actions on the population.[51] *FM 3-24* clarifies this principle of initiative in its discussion of legitimate versus illegitimate government. If a government is legitimate, it rules through its initiative primarily with the consent of the governed. If a government is illegitimate, it rules through fear and coercion, much like Saddam's Baathist regime.[52]

Yet another principle is simplicity of action, which provides the necessary clarity in pursuit of the population's favor in waging war. Simplicity in concept and execution are important requirements for any counterinsurgency doctrine. Both coalition and Iraqi forces often violate this principle, however, for it is difficult to define in clear, concise, and simple terms how to achieve the goal of gaining the support of the population.[53]

Steps for a Successful Counterinsurgency

Coherently gathered into a general strategy, the principles and laws of counterinsurgency warfare laid out by Galula suggest eight tactical steps to build (or rebuild) a political machine from the population upward. Important in each step is a discussion of how propaganda—the information war—supports the insurgency, the counterinsurgency, and the population.[54]

The first step in Galula's operations for a successful counterinsurgency is to apportion and then maneuver enough armed forces to destroy or expel the main body of armed insurgents. It is important that a substantial enough force remain after the initial surge in the area to impose physical control over the population. This step sets the stage for actions to work on the population to win their hearts and minds. To expel the insurgents and then hold the area is obviously not an end in itself; however, it is the initial impression the counterinsurgency makes on the population. First impressions are lasting ones, and if a force exhibits disregard for the populace early on, or if it causes a vast amount of collateral damage, then the populace will approach the counterinsurgents warily. If this is the case, the Sisyphean task begins.

The second step is to mass static units where the population lives to provide local security as well as holding operations so the insurgents do not return. Here we switch our attention from the insurgents to the populace to show the people we are committed to providing them security. Fallujah failed early on because it was attacked violently by multiple coalition and Iraqi forces but then abandoned. It took some time before a force was living among the populace and therefore gaining a better understanding of the people's needs. The purpose in deploying a force is to establish a grid of troops so that the population and the counterinsurgent political teams are reasonably protected. In this step, resettlement actions take place, intelligence sources are attained, and fence-sitters are turned.

The third step is to make contact with and control the population. It is during this step that military operations are replaced by an increased emphasis on political operations. Building of the counterinsurgency's political arm begins ideally at the local level. For success during this step, it is imperative to establish contact with the people and control their movements to isolate them from the guerrillas. Gathering intelligence is critical as well in this step, to prevent any possible derailment when seating the local government.

The fourth step is the destruction of the local insurgent political organizations. The earlier steps provided the counterinsurgency an ability to gain and maintain contact with the populace, all the while gathering intelligence on the true nature of the insurgency in that area. The counterinsurgency now can use a mixture of leniency and restructuring of the judicial process to achieve the desired end state in this area. An example is Maj. Gen. Rick Lynch's 3rd Infantry Division's plan for reconciliation in 2007, when he went full force in trying to reconcile those fence-sitters in an effort to define the true nature of the insurgency in southwest Baghdad. Another means for success, according to Galula, is to "roll up" all the military-age males in an area to weed out insurgents hiding among the populace.

The fifth step is to hold elections and establish provisional local authorities. The goal is to place local leaders in positions of authority. The challenge is ensuring that the right local leader is placed in the right governmental position. Corruption and nepotism loom large in this step. In the sixth step, the counterinsurgency tests these new authorities and organizes self-defense units. An identity is truly defined in the seventh step, where party affiliation is now encouraged. In the last step, a final purge of the residual insurgent force takes place.[55]

It would make sense that these eight steps for offensive operations in an effort to achieve victory against an insurgency be done in sequence. If these steps were not followed sequentially—as seen throughout Iraq from 2003 to 2007—is it possible to start anew with any hope of achieving success? Can we achieve victory at this stage by "plugging in" and injecting a strategy into the process? And if the answer is no, then what can we do to mitigate the lost opportunities? In the end, we believe the answer comes in the combination of leadership, trust, and a genuine willingness to turn over the control of the fight to the Iraqis. The question remains, can the coalition do so without getting sidetracked by the intense desire to unilaterally hunt an elusive enemy and pursue a solution to the arguably unsolvable counter-IED fight?

CHAPTER 3

Just or Unjust War?
A Historical Bridge

"History will judge the war against Iraq not by the brilliance of its military execution, but by the effectiveness of the post-hostilities activities."

Lt. Gen. (ret.) Jay Garner
Appointed in 2003 as director of
reconstruction and humanitarianism
assistance for Iraq, but soon replaced
by L. Paul Bremer

As the great military thinker Carl von Clausewitz wrote hundreds of years ago, "War is simply a continuation of policy by other means."[1] Yet to the American people, war signifies a failure in policy. This is why soon after the war began, critics claimed that the war was unjust. In concert with the question of justness came the onslaught of casualties, though they're not as high as in many other wars we've engaged in during the twentieth and twenty-first centuries (see table on the following page). Those same critics began to set timelines for the withdrawal of forces.

Although the current senior commander in Iraq, Gen. David Petraeus, developed a new doctrine based on David Galula's methodology—a methodology that should have enabled our forces to defeat any insurgency—unfortunately, this doctrine was presented to our armed services some five and a half years after the War on Terrorism unfolded globally.

AVERAGE DAILY U.S. CASUALTIES IN TWENTIETH AND TWENTY-FIRST CENTURY WARS[2]

World War I:	199 killed in action per day
World War II:	301 killed in action per day
Korea:	32 killed in action per day
Vietnam:	20 killed in action per day
Iraq:	2 killed in action per day

Timing is a fundamental condition for any military operation. Regardless of the size of the force or magnitude of the decision; timing is critical. The mission could be as small as a nine-man squad moving toward an objective or as important as the president of the United States announcing the end of combat operations. In either case, whether or not the timing is right, will eventually determine the outcome of events.

Military decisions are made based on a number of factors; time is one of the most valuable resources for commanders when making important decisions. At the lowest level, soldiers take into account time as a resource, an asset, or perhaps a constraint.

Insufficient time for mission preparation often forces commanders to accept greater risk in planning, preparation, and execution of orders. To avoid or mitigate the risk associated with inadequate time for planning, leaders habitually allow subordinates two-thirds of the available planning time as a means of control. This is fundamentally understood by all soldiers in our military. Bottom line, time is a critical factor when deciding all mission sets—to deploy or not, and as in this case, when to withdraw forces.

Of all the operations of war, a withdrawal under pressure is probably the most difficult and most perilous. This is well known in the conventional world and arguably was first defined as an unlikely desired event in combat by the great Prussian general Field Marshal Helmuth Karl Bernhard von Moltke. During the Franco–Prussian War, Moltke was told that he most likely would be compared in history with the greatest of all leaders. When told, however, that the comparison might include the likes of Napoleon Bonaparte, who had retreated from Russia, the Prussian answered, "No, I am not so great, for I have never conducted a retreat." The thought of retreating or withdrawing has always had a negative connotation to most military leaders, because most soldiers see it as bordering on surrendering the fight.

Interestingly enough, Moltke implies the importance of timing when referencing the perishable nature of all military operations. He makes several comments about the need for staffs to realize that even the best-laid plans need to be reconciled at some point. No plan, Moltke once observed, could survive for long once contact with the enemy was made. Over the past few years, a number of politicians and other critics have voiced their opinions about establishing timelines for leaving Iraq. They believe, much like Moltke in his definition of time allotments to mission sets, that as the coalition has had continuous contact with the enemy over an extended period of time, it therefore has reached its limits.

In March 2007, the Democratic-controlled Senate pushed legislation for withdrawal of U.S. combat troops from Iraq by March 2008. This demand essentially set a timeline that had no measures of success associated with it. Senate Majority Leader Harry Reid, Democrat of Nevada, said the moment was at hand to "send a message to President Bush that the time has come to find a new way forward in this intractable war." The president had previously said he would veto any bill containing the timeline, saying, "This and other provisions would place freedom and democracy in Iraq at grave risk, embolden our enemies and undercut the administration's plan to develop the Iraqi economy."

Others in Congress oppose a timeline without measures of success. Republican Senator Kit Bond of Missouri has stated that "wars cannot be run from these hallowed and comfortable and sanctified chambers 10,000 miles away from the war zone." He went on to say, "How about allowing the officers, the men and the commanders in the field who are engaged daily, risking their lives to bring peace and security to Iraq, to determine when and how we can best turn over to the Iraqi security forces the critical job, the critical job of assuring security."[3] In short, what opponents to a timeline propose is following the *Iraq Study Group Report* proposals presented by Baker and Hamilton. If one looks deeper at what the current president proposes in concert with his senior military official on the ground, Gen. David Petraeus is executing what the report had laid out in the summer of 2006.

As the congressional struggles continue over the next few months and years, it is clear that a lack of patience for achieving benchmarks, and hence a desire for timelines, crosses partisan boundaries. Constituents from across the nation with a clear misunderstanding of what it takes to fight an insurgency have demanded support in Congress for immediate successes.

For instance, Republican senators John Warner of Virginia and Richard Lugar of Indiana proposed legislation in July 2007 that would have given President Bush until mid-October of that year to submit a plan to limit the military mission in Iraq to protecting borders, fighting terrorists, protecting U.S. assets, and training Iraqi forces. Clearly, there is merit to this proposal, since it narrows the focus of the coalition support to the war. The administration's national security advisor, Stephen Hadley, took stock in this proposal, but he was anxious to let Petraeus make an assessment of where we were at that point in the strategy to achieve victory.

Democrat of Michigan Carl Levin, chairman of the Senate Armed Services Committee, was more determined to direct the strategy toward a timeline for withdrawal, saying, "This is not a half-full, half-empty issue. They have made no progress in the one key area that everyone agrees must have progress or the violence will not end, and that's on the political side of things. . . . This is just a veneer and the veneer has worn away." Levin had proposed legislation that would require most troops to be out of Iraq by April 30, 2008.[4]

A hedonistic need for a short-term fulfillment of sorts is representative of the attitude of the American populace in times of war. This mindset is clearly something that has evolved in our nation, and it is, counterintuitively, a freedom our troops embrace in their effort to defend it. Pragmatically speaking, one could make this analogy: Would we abandon a cancer patient just because chemotherapy is too hard to take? Or more fitting in this case, could we feel good about attempting to treat the cancer patient appropriately after years of neglect and misdiagnosis in treatments? Simply put, should we expect success in the eleventh hour after neglecting the cancer for years?

The military uses the acronym METT-TC, which stands for mission, enemy, terrain, troops available, *time,* and civilian considerations, to manage a standardized methodology for addressing both threat- and hazard-based risk for tactical and nontactical operations and off-duty activities. These components are all part of the military decision-making process for tactical missions. The acronym helps commanders remember and prioritize what to analyze during the planning phase of any operation.

A given operational setting is described by METT-TC. The situation is the context that dominates every aspect of planning, including rules of engagement. Across the range of potential military operations, commanders can encounter situations of bewildering complexity. This complexity is reduced, at the operational and tactical levels of conflict, by applying the conceptual template of METT-TC, whose components can be defined as follows:

Mission establishes the purpose of the operation. Planners must consider the dispositions, equipment, doctrine, capabilities, and probable intentions of an *enemy*—actual and potential. The current conflict environment is increasingly characterized by shades of gray in which enemies are less apparent. Commanders also evaluate potential threats to mission success, such as disease, political instability, and misinformation. *Terrain* and weather affect mobility, concealment, observation, cover, avenues of approach, and the effectiveness of military operating systems. Commanders must consider the nature of their *troops*—their military capabilities. Troop characteristics such as numbers, mobility, protection, training, and morale influence plans for their employment. The amount of *time* available for preparation and execution of the mission is critical and can dramatically influence the scope and nature of the plan. *Civilian considerations* are a key factor of the situation across the entire range of operations. Attitudes and activities of the civilian population in the area influence the outcome of military operations. Refugees and humanitarian assistance requirements are frequent concerns, not only in stability or support operations, but also in conventional combat. Interagency operations bring to bear the civilian resources of the Department of Defense, other components of the government, and private voluntary and non-governmental organizations, thereby multiplying the effectiveness of our operations.[5]

The main resource needed by troops on the ground in order to achieve success, however, is time. Many ask our soldiers their opinions on how the war is unfolding and whether they want to continue the fight. The ones that the media and others are especially interested in are those who have deployed consecutively over a number of years. The troops on the ground clearly know that they follow without reservation the orders of the president of the United States and the officers appointed over them. In fact, those same words are in the oath of enlistment into the military service.[6] So in the end, for our soldiers, it is not a question of how long they will deploy, but whether they are given clear, concise orders and the resources to allow them to do their job. And one of the most important resources is time.

Pressuring our soldiers to get the job done is not the answer. Additionally, penalizing a force by withdrawing it at the first sign of a perceived lack of progress is just as bad as tactically intervening to assume its mission. Tactical patience is key, but in our society, people are used to fast food, fast cars, and fast Internet service. Waiting for any service nowadays is simply unacceptable. Today's generation can't relate to tactical patience, nor will they wait long for success. It seems that those who preceded us understood this concept far better, for we have been in Europe for almost seventy years, Korea for fifty-plus years, and Bosnia for more than ten. Success takes time. There is no simple formula to doing what is being asked here. And it is clear from history that if we choose impatience now, we will be passing the fight and all its associated obligations to the next generation.

"No state has ever benefited from a long war," said Sun Tzu. "Those that garner five victories will meet with disaster; those with four victories will be exhausted; those with three victories will become hegemons; those with two victories will be kings; those with one victory will become emperors."[7] But even the sage Sun Tzu would say that the art of war does not have a place for abandoning an ally in time of need.

The Iraq Study Group Report cautions against both an immediate or timed withdrawal and an open-ended commitment to Iraq. It warns that if U.S. forces withdraw too soon, circumstances may worsen and they may have to return later, and that an unstable Iraq could serve as a base for international terrorism. Instead, it looks toward a possible withdrawal of U.S. combat brigades by the first quarter of 2008, adding the caveat that this time plan is "subject to unexpected developments in the security situation on the ground."[8] This position is really not much different from the current U.S. stance that as the Iraqi Army "stands up," coalition forces will "stand down."

Calling the situation in Iraq "grave and deteriorating," and that of Baghdad and several provinces "dire" suggests that "time is running out."[9] The report nevertheless argues that "because events in Iraq have been set in motion by American decisions and actions, the United States has both a national and a moral interest in doing what it can to give Iraqis an opportunity to avert anarchy."[10] The report otherwise refrains from addressing the decision to invade and instead purports to find a bipartisan way forward in order to achieve victory.

It also accepts that the commander on the ground should be the judge of how measures are met.

Former presidential candidate and New York City mayor Rudy Giuliani said in a Radio Iowa talk show on April 3, 2007, "It is . . . very disturbing that the Congress of the United States . . . came to the conclusion that we should announce our retreat to our enemies and give them a schedule of retreat."[11] He went so far as to say that opponents to a sustained fight in Iraq have all but attempted to put the nation on the defense in the War on Terrorism.

As recently as July 14, 2007, at the height of the operational surge, Iraqi prime minister Nouri al-Maliki told the Associated Press that the Iraqi Army and Police are capable of keeping security in the country when American troops leave "any time they want." He quickly acknowledged, however, that the Iraqi Security Forces needed additional weapons and training in order to succeed, and his government needed "time and effort" to enact the political reforms sought by Washington, "particularly since the political process is facing security, economic and services pressures, as well as regional and international interference."[12]

Even the mainstream media tends to understand the challenges associated with the establishment of a withdrawal timeline for American forces in Iraq. In an article posted on May 3, 2007, on CNN.com, news analysts and other observers warn that pulling U.S. forces from Iraq could trigger catastrophe affecting not just Iraq, but also its neighbors in the Middle East, with far-reaching global implications.

It is common thought in conservative camps that sectarian violence could erupt on a scale never seen before in Iraq if coalition troops leave before the Iraqi Security Forces are ready.[13] The CNN article expresses the concern that supporters of Al Qaeda could develop an international hub of terror from which to threaten the West. From our own experiences in country, we believe that the most dangerous scenario is that civil war could draw countries like Turkey, Saudi Arabia, and Iran into a broader conflict.

CNN terrorism analyst Peter Bergen believes that a rapid with-drawal of all U.S. troops would hurt America's image and hand Al Qaeda and other terror groups a propaganda victory indicating that the United States is only a "paper tiger." He goes on to say that "it would also play into their strategy, which is to create a mini-state somewhere in the Middle East where they can reorganize along the lines of what they did in Afghanistan in the late '90s."[14] Bergen was one of the first Western journalists ever to meet with bin Laden and is considered a leading authority on Al Qaeda.

Don Shepperd, a retired air force major general and military analyst for CNN, agrees that "Sunni Muslim fighters who support al Qaeda would seek an enclave inside a lawless Iraq likely along sectarian lines into Shiite, Sunni and Kurdish regions." There would be "increasing attempts by terrorists to establish a training sanctuary in Iraq."[15]

That's one of the reasons why analysts predict that a rapid with-drawal will not occur, regardless of what politicians say. "Everyone wants the troops home—the Iraqis, the U.S., the world—but no one wants a precipitous withdrawal that produces a civil war, a bloodbath, nor a wider war in an unstable Mideast," Shepperd says, adding that the image of the United States is important too.[16]

"And we do not want a U.S that is perceived as having been badly defeated in the global war on terror or as an unreliable future ally or coalition partner." Shepperd, a veteran fighter pilot of the Vietnam War, has served as a CNN analyst of the Iraq War since it began.[17]

HISTORICAL PRECEDENCE: SOMALIA

Both military and civilian leaders can learn from history. Struggles to understand the complexities of countering an insurgency are not lost on the leaders of our nation; in fact, our recent history is rife with these types of challenges. Somalia in the early 1990s is one example we all could have learned from during the onset of the War on Terrorism.

In April 1992, the United Nations Operation in Somalia (UNO-SOM) was established to provide security for humanitarian relief efforts. Early on in that mission, conditions in Somalia deteriorated, and in December, the Security Council approved a U.S.-led multinational Unified Task Force (UNITAF) to establish a secure environment for humanitarian relief operations and prepare for the subsequent transition to UN forces.

The transition to UNOSOM II occurred on May 4, 1993, and during this phase, the majority of U.S. forces were withdrawn.[18] At this time, there were about 2,900 U.S. logistics troops assigned to the UNOSOM II force and 1,100 troops deployed as a quick-reaction force under U.S. command and not under UNOSOM II. U.S. combat forces ashore and afloat grew to about 14,000 personnel by October.

On October 3, 1993, Somalia hit the headlines when eighteen U.S. soldiers died in an attempt to capture a warlord in the capital, Mogadishu.[19] U.S. Representative John Murtha, Democrat of Pennsylvania who has been leading the fight to withdraw forces from Iraq some fifteen years later, urged President Clinton to begin a complete withdrawal of U.S. troops from the region. Concerned with public perception, and most likely with the perception drawn from the polls, President Clinton conceded to that request, and on October 7, he announced the decision to withdraw almost all U.S. troops from Somalia by March 31, 1994. The U.S. troops were part of the 50,000-strong United Nations Operation Restore Hope, which essentially ended in failure in 1995 when the UN withdrew.[20] This also included logistics troops assigned to the UN force. Department of Defense officials reported that the withdrawal was completed by March 25, 1994, just over five months after the controversial loss of American life.[21]

The impact today on the decision to hastily withdraw in the eye of a potential disaster is that Somalia has been all but abandoned to the warlords of that region. The security situation has deteriorated, with growing factional violence and almost daily attacks against Ethiopian forces and transitional federal government officials in Mogadishu, Baidoa, Kismayo, and other cities in that region. Unfortunately, civilians bear the brunt of the violence, and an estimated 1.1

million face a humanitarian crisis in the southern part of the country. In the early part of 2007, Ethiopian troops stormed Mogadishu to end the eight-month control of Somalia by the Union of Islamic Courts.[22] But the most damaging aftermath was the precedent set by the United States on the international level, that when the going got tough, our nation would retreat.

This is an illustration of what some would say is a U.S. quick-fix mentality. With the intention of reducing human suffering in the country two years after the fall of the Somalian head of state Siad Barre in 1992, the United States decided to quickly fix the situation by rushing planeloads of relief food to the country in an exercise dubbed Operation Provide Relief. Four months later, after dropping 13,000 tons of food, the United States belatedly discovered that the solution to the Somalia crisis was not food but restoration of law and order.[23]

By then, nearly half the food airlifted from the United States was rotting in stores as Somali clan warlords sabotaged distribution networks set up by relief agencies. Without any consultation, the United States came up with yet another quickie solution: soldiers and marines were dispatched to Mogadishu with instructions to restore law and order and return home as soon as possible. Two years down the line, the Somali situation had become worse, leading the United States to retreat in a hurry.[24]

What we should have learned from Somalia is that deadlines for transitions from one operation to another should be avoided. When dates are set during the transfer from one security force to another, as seen in this example where a non-UN contingent security requirement was transferred to a UN one, parties slow down and even derail the peace process until the new party takes over. This is amplified further if the mission's premise has the wrong intentions and immeasurable goals associated with it.

This is what happened in Somalia. The warlords knew when the Americans were going to leave, so they waited us out. They avoided any major confrontation with international forces, and when

UNOSOM II took over with a less powerful force, they capitalized on our weaknesses.

This was seen in Bosnia as well. The June 1998 deadline set by President Clinton for withdrawing American forces from the NATO-led Stabilization Force in Bosnia and Herzegovina raised fears that fighting would resume after that date. Other examples occurred across the globe. In Haiti, the instability of the situation at the end of the United Nations Mission to Haiti (UNMIH) mandate led the secretary general to request the creation of another UNMIH. Instead of a deadline, the fulfillment of conditions, to be evaluated by the Security Council and troop-contributing nations and organizations, would determine the date of the withdrawal.

In a striking resemblance to the coalition's goals in the conflict in Iraq, the main condition for the withdrawal of the multinational force from Haiti was the establishment of "a secure and stable environment." The determination thereof was made by the Security Council. The United States still had a decisive influence in the timing of the transition, but the "environment" condition gave more power to the United Nations in the bargaining process. The state of readiness of the follow-on UN operation also should be taken into account. Likewise, the UN force would not withdraw until a set of objectives, both political and military, had been attained. Disarmament, demobilization of troops, mine clearance, reorganization of armed forces, elections, creation of a police force, safe delivery of humanitarian aid, and repatriation of refugees were all considered.[25]

The question to go to Somalia in the first place, however, was only mildly criticized. The coercive nature of American foreign policy was exemplified in the humanitarian "rescue" of Somalia. Struck by images of starving children, Americans warmly accepted President George H. W. Bush's decision, taken unilaterally in the last days of his administration, to intervene militarily in the violence-ravaged country. The military was dispatched to quell the fratricide and ensure that relief workers were able to run the gauntlet of armed clans to reach the starving populace. Upon meeting resistance from the local warlords, the scope of the operation was gradually expanded, especially after the Clinton administration took office in January 1993. As American soldiers became targets, calls for immediate withdrawal grew—particularly from rival Republicans seeking to make political hay out of military disaster. Public support for the mission plummeted. The administration quickly abandoned the endeavor as public sentiment for humanitarian support was quickly overshadowed by the open violence against U.S. forces.[26]

Somalia is a model in failure that illustrates the perils of abandoning a struggling country to determine its own fate. More than a decade after the United States pulled out of a peacekeeping operation, the situation in western Africa has come back to haunt America. Islamic fundamentalists in Somalia allegedly having ideological affinity, if not ties, with Al Qaeda have recently taken over, forcing the world leaders to frantically summon an international conference to discuss the country's future.[27]

If only the United States and others had shown this concern a dozen plus years ago. Instead, American policy has consisted of little more than arming "secular" warlords battling Islamists for control. The failed approach of giving hundreds of thousands of dollars to these warlords has led to finger-pointing within the current administration and also those that preceded it.

It is clear that the Clinton administration started this process of administration-backed abandonment after the 1993 killing of eighteen U.S. servicemen (made famous by the book and movie *Black Hawk Down*). When the administration's mission got into hot water, it decided to ditch not only Somalia, but arguably the whole of Africa. The Somalia decision had a major part to play in Clinton's refusal to allow UN intervention to stop the Rwandan genocide in 1994. Most critics of the current administration, unfortunately, do not care to recall the dynamics of the mid-1990s.

Somalia certainly isn't the most prominent example of a country that the United States deserted and came back to worry about later. That distinction most likely belongs to Afghanistan. But even the

Taliban challenge doesn't seem to have taught the United States a basic lesson: If you disdainfully ignore a country after paying short-term attention to it, it will bedevil you as a "failed state." Most of us inherently know that the United States needs to invest in a nation-building effort in order to prevent a failed state. Efforts consisting of support for the formation of stable democratic governments, coupled with the provision of aid, are clearly the starting blocks on a path to success. But even the Somalia and Afghanistan examples won't lead to adoption of such an approach. For some reason, we seem to be incapable of learning from our mistakes.

Somalia was a huge tragedy that could have been averted. When the United States decided to withdraw after suffering a limited number of casualties at the hands of the Al Qaeda fighters, disappointment resonated throughout the military and most of the American public. Giving in to the brutality of terrorists so easily goes against American values.[28]

After the failure in Somalia, violent terrorist activities by Osama bin Laden's Al Qaeda and numerous other Islamist groups increased dramatically across the world. Somalia spiraled into a disastrous civil war, much like the country of Iraq would if we decide to pull out and leave hastily. Ironically, most believe that the long-term counterterrorism objectives can still be achieved by a concentrated U.S. investment in the Somali peace process, yet the State Department has just one full-time political officer working on the Somalia desk.

We believe, as we do for Iraq, that perseverance ultimately would have made the United States victorious, and the Somalis would have benefited. Today Somalia still has no effective central government, and it has been cited as a possible refuge for Al Qaeda operatives fleeing Afghanistan. If we abide by timelines, this is what could happen in Iraq—but on a much grander scale.

BENCHMARKS FOR SUCCESS

In the 1980s, Secretary of Defense Caspar Weinberger argued that defining our national interests in a broad and general fashion was dangerous. To counter this danger, he developed a "litmus test" consisting of six distinct independent questions that defined when forces should be employed.[29] This test gives our leaders a set of referenced queries on which to base decisions to employ combat power. It didn't take into account the evolving world environment in the post-Cold War era, however, and it also doesn't give a holistic solution. It provides a framework for entering conflict, but there is no test for withdrawing or redeploying forces once they have been employed, which is a necessity in order to fully apply the test to the decision-making process.

Weinberger's conditions that judge when to employ forces assume a bipolar world where a clearly defined threat exists and national objectives are measurable. Understanding that the world is more complex makes these conditions too general. More importantly, though they are clearly definable, these conditions are not criteria. Rather, they are initial-level objectives emanating from our security objectives. What is missing from this doctrine is a set of criteria tailorable to a particular crisis, so that the six-step Weinberger test and the follow-on set of criteria can be used to define when a mission has reached its objectives. We contend that *Primus solus* is a theory of the past, and therefore the Weinberger doctrine no longer adequately "tests the waters" for crisis response.[30]

Immediately following the Cold War, the United States had difficulty deciding if and when to deploy. Much analysis took place defining what was considered a vital interest. Since the beginning of the War on Terrorism, however, the United States has been able to replace its Soviet Union nemesis with that of "the terrorist." Therefore, it has become less difficult to define when to fight but more complex to define when to stop fighting.

The ancient Greek Thucydides wrote that a nation will fight for three reasons: security, ideology, or economics. In Iraq, one may argue that all three are root causes for the Iraqis to fight. For the United States, security is the guiding principle, but many also argue that economics plays a significant role in developing our goals and objectives.

Knowing that our goals and objectives stem from the security principle in our national security strategy allows us to determine the supporting objectives to help define our benchmarks for achieving victory.

Thus far, Iraqi leaders have failed to comply with Washington for a timetable to achieve certain benchmarks as a precondition for U.S. military and financial support. There seems to be an incredible misunderstanding as to what decision makers suggest when they talk about particular means for success. Although the president is not in favor of conveying military or political benchmarks in Baghdad in the form of time-based objectives, he said in July 2007 that "it makes sense to have benchmarks as a part of our discussion on how to go forward."[31] This should come as no surprise, for any leader has to establish goals if he expects his organization to achieve success.

Benchmarks, sometimes called milestones, refer to specific objectives. For the coalition to succeed in Iraq, the Iraqi government must meet quantifiable measures of progress toward a future goal with regard to national reconciliation, security, economic performance, and governance. The goal of setting these benchmarks is to pressure Iraq's leaders to make political progress and start taking over responsibility for security from American troops. "The purpose is to infuse a sense of urgency into the political process in Baghdad," says Andrew Exum of the Washington Institute for Near East Policy. This has been found lacking, he adds, as evidenced by Iraqi lawmakers' recent push for a two-month summer vacation.[32]

How does one define progress? Merely wanting to see people in markets or get Iraqis to clean sewage from certain city blocks is not enough. That is why it is so important that the actions taken at each level of the lines of operation are nested with an overall plan for success. Additionally, in order to measure how success is achieved in this newly formed nation, we need to first understand what the prewar conditions were under the Saddam regime.

Some lawmakers are pressing for more specific metrics to gauge whether the surge and the overall plan in Iraq are working. That is a good thing. What military leaders in the theater need is pressure to define goals, not to meet timelines, analyzing what we have won and whether we have set the Iraqi government on a path toward stabilization or reconciliation. Even polling in the form of questions such as the former chairman of the Joint Chiefs of Staff, Gen. Peter Pace, asked, "Do the people in Baghdad feel more secure today?" is a good way to measure how well things are going.[33]

Although a litany of benchmarks for Iraq does exist, we believe they can be achieved if they are nested hierarchically basis. There may be a plan, for instance, to include milestones at reaching an agreement on the status of the disputed disposition of Kirkuk, or meeting certain economic criteria such as a targeted annual growth of 10 percent, or perhaps reducing subsidies on energy and food, which cost Iraq's economy roughly $11 billion per year. But despite the existence of a number of lines of operation that all have measures of success associated with them, little appears to have been done to translate those higher-level requirements for achieving success into actionable mission sets at the lowest level.[34]

Current Benchmarks

In January 2007, President Bush outlined a clear set of benchmarks so that soldiers on the ground have a standard to work toward.[35] This current set of benchmarks includes provincial elections, the passage of an oil law that equitably distributes revenues among the country's warring factions, and a reversal of the debaathification plan, among others. Gen. David Petraeus, U.S. ambassador to Iraq Ryan Crocker, Lt. Gen. Ray Odierno, and Lt. Gen. Lloyd Austin have implemented these actions.

Holding Provincial Elections. The president called for provincial elections to be held at the earliest possible date, saying that "under the constitution, new provincial elections should have been held already. They are necessary to restore representative government." Elections obviously have an impact on the governance line of operation, where the strategic and operational requirements matter. It is also an area where a brigade combat team can realize success in providing support. In turn, successful provincial elections trigger a synergized effort felt across the theater. In short, if all provinces achieve success in this effort, then we are moving further toward victory. Because most Sunnis boycotted the December 2005 provincial elections, local governments are primarily dominated by Shiites in the south and center and Kurds in the north. The Bush administration is pushing the Shiite-led government to hold additional elections at the local level to reverse this imbalance, thus allowing a Sunni buy-in and paving the way toward greater reconciliation.[36]

Negative news associated with the Iraqi government will always receive more press than its accomplishments. Truly there has been some success along the governance line of operation, challenging the myth that the Iraqi government is completely inefficient. With the establishment of this fledgling government came key legislative accomplishments, including the convening of a regional conference of thirteen nations in March 2007, the establishment of the Prime Ministers Emergency Powers Renewal Act, the Provincial Powers Law, legislation to pass the Hydrocarbon Law by the Council of Ministers, the Constitutional Referendum, and passing the 2007 budget equivalent to $41 billion. Additionally, by spring 2007, four of the eighteen provinces were controlled officially by Iraqi governors.[37]

The government also has shown a capacity to control its military, as seen in the support of significant military actions during the 2007 and 2008 surge in the highly volatile neighborhood of Sadr City in Baghdad and in the former "Triangle of Death" in South Baghdad. This is the first time since the war started that the Iraqi government has supported, without constraints, the military intervention in a Shiite stronghold. There is no doubt that all involved have finally come to the conclusion that the military cannot "win" this war, but can only set the conditions for a political solution.[38]

Passing Oil Revenue-Sharing Law. "Oil revenues should accrue to the central government and be shared on the basis of population. No formula that gives control over revenues from future fields to the regions or gives control of oil fields to the regions is compatible with national reconciliation."[39] Disagreements over oil and revenue sharing threaten to unravel hopes for a political breakthrough and national reconciliation. A proposed oil law has left Iraq's leaders bitterly divided. It has drawn criticism from Iraq's Sunnis, who prefer a stronger role for the central government, and Kurds, who prefer a stronger role for the regional authorities. The majority Shiites have sought to mollify the Sunnis by keeping control of Iraq's oil sector in Baghdad, not the provinces. Most of Iraq's oil rests in the Kurdish north or Shiite south, not in the Sunni heartland. The role of outside investors and the classification of old versus new oil fields also remain unsettled. The oil issue has sparked some disagreement in the U.S. Congress, where there is a proposed bill calling primarily for the privatization of Iraq's oil, not the equal redistribution of revenues. Some maintain that the oil law, despite its flaws, is necessary for Iraqis to develop their untapped oil reserves and reap the profits.[40]

Reversing debaathification. This is what is meant by national reconciliation. In 2003, the Bremer-led Coalition Provisional Authority (CPA) chose to disenfranchise all Baathists from being allowed to work in areas of responsibility.[41] This caused a rift between those Sunni educators, businessmen, and other field experts and the new governing party and its goals. They essentially felt hopeless in their abilities to care for their families and saw no chance for a future. Under the Saddam regime, in order to hold certain jobs, such as a teacher, a person had to be a formal member of the Baath party. Therefore, being a Baathist didn't necessarily mean someone was a staunch Saddam supporter; in fact, in many cases the opposite was true.

The May 16, 2003, CPA decision for debaathification had a huge effect on 30,000 people, which included the Sunni elite under the Saddam regime. At the time, it was said to be "central for the plan to remake Iraq into a new democracy, and to produce a new political culture that would replace the authoritarian and nationalist models of the past,"[42] as the Baathist party seemed to be much like the Nazi party in all but the name. But in reality, debaathification is synonymous with desunnification. Unfortunately, its proponents did not consider the deep roots that the Baathists had developed in Iraq over nearly thirty-five years. Instead, they saw it as an ideological bloc that had to be removed and its influence excised.

Successful political reconciliation requires the reintegration of Baathists and Arab nationalists into the social and political Iraqi cycles of life, excluding only the leading figures of Saddam Hussein's regime. The Iraqi government must send a clear signal to Sunnis that there is a place for them in national life. The United States is already encouraging the return of qualified Iraqi professionals—Sunni or Shia, nationalist or ex-Baathist, Kurd or Turkoman, Christian or Arab—into the government.

Since early 2007, White House officials have pressed the Maliki government to reverse laws that bar tens of thousands of low- to mid-ranking former Baath party officers from government posts. This move is part of a larger effort to make constitutional concessions to minority groups such as the Sunni Arabs, but it faces intense opposition from more conservative and religious Shiite members of Iraq's parliament.

The government needs to act now to give a signal of hope. Unless Sunnis believe they can get a fair deal in Iraq through the political process, there is no prospect that the insurgency will end. To strike this fair deal, the Iraqi government and the Iraqi people must address several issues that are critical for successful national reconciliation and therefore for the future of Iraq.[43]

There is little doubt that the U.S.-led coalition carries a burden of blame for actions that led to an ambiguous set of conditions in the counterinsurgency. During the months of the U.S. transition from high-intensity operations to a counterinsurgency, there were multiple errors that continue to plague the country today. Most critically, the U.S.-led coalition forces lost momentum and the initiative they had gained early on.

Ali A. Allawi writes in *The Occupation of Iraq* in reference to Bremer's predecessor, Garner, that he "had no specific de-Baathification policy. In fact he seemed to have decided that he would avail himself of the skills and assistance of any person who would be useful and who would willingly cooperate with the new administration."[44]

Tom Ricks's *Fiasco* quotes Maj. Ike Wilson, a 101st Airborne Division combat veteran of Operation Iraqi Freedom 1, as saying that "during this calm before the next storm, the U.S. Army had its eyes turned toward the ports, while former regime loyalists (FRL) and budding insurgents had their eyes turned toward the people," which were the prize. As Wilson stated later, we have been playing catch-up ever since.[45] The bottom line is that national reconciliation among Iraq's ethnoreligious communities is a necessary precursor to stemming the country's sectarian violence. But most think the prospects look bleak.

The trial and execution of Saddam Hussein, which were originally billed as an exercise in reconciliation, instead only inflamed sectarian tensions. Iraq's factions also remain deadlocked over the distribution of oil revenues, issues of federalism, and the ethnic makeup of the Iraqi government. Prime Minister Maliki's cabinet is seen by Iraq's Sunni Arabs as a puppet state of Shiite militias, which in turn are seen as puppets of Iran. Unless efforts at national reconciliation can persuade Iraqi Sunnis to buy into a power-sharing agreement, experts expect a continuation of the current levels of internecine violence.

In order for reconciliation to be successful, the government must first establish itself as representative of the Iraqi people and prove effective at providing basic services, security, and jobs. Many things have to take place thereafter in order to make reconciliation work, but unless the government can provide basic services, the effort to reconcile is futile.[46] Thus far, however, the government has not been able to deliver these in any capacity.

Amending Iraq's Constitution. Review of Iraq's constitution is essential to achieving national reconciliation and should be pursued in concert with the turnover of control of security to the Iraqi Security Forces. Perhaps the United Nations, which has experience and the requisite expertise in this field, should play a role in this process, as recommended by *The Iraq Study Group Report*.[47] We believe that the United Nations has done all it can to avoid being physically involved in Iraq. Over the past five years, we have seen time and time again a UN element unwilling to enter parts of the country because of "security issues." There is no doubt that security is a necessity, but unless agencies like the United Nations garner the intestinal fortitude to venture into a risky situation, there will be no security for this nation. UN involvement would help stabilize the balance of power and associated sectarian power struggles.

The Sunnis favor a constitutional amendment to prohibit the formal breakup of Iraq into regional states divided along sectarian lines. They fear that the Shiites will seek a federal state in the south modeled along the lines of Iraqi Kurdistan, which would cut into the Sunnis' share of political power and revenue.

Providing Funding for Reconstruction. With a major effort under way to establish timelines, Congress has had little desire to appropriate more funds for reconstruction. Iraq obviously has a substantial need for continued reconstruction, however, and therefore funding. Serious questions remain about the capacity of the U.S. and Iraqi governments to achieve success in this area. No matter how many agencies or headquarters we strive to establish in this arena, there are no clear guidelines as to who is in charge of reconstruction. Perhaps it should be Iraqi led. Regardless, it is clear that money—American or Iraqi—can achieve a level of victory. If each company commander had been given money in 2003 to work mission sets that lined up with the operational and strategic objectives, unemployment would be down drastically, and the local and national governments would have gained a level of credibility they so desperately need today.

As resources decline, the U.S. reconstruction effort is changing in focus, shifting from infrastructure, education, and health to smaller-scale ventures that are chosen and to some degree managed by local communities. A major attempt is also being made to improve the capacity of government bureaucracies at the national, regional, and provincial levels to provide services to the population as well as to select and manage infrastructure projects. Several senior military officers commented to us that the Commander's Emergency Response

Program (CERP), which funds quick-impact projects such as the clearing of sewage and restoration of basic services, is vital. CERP was considered critical in the early stages of the war, but by September 2003, the funds associated with it withered away. That was clearly a turning point in the war. Just as the insurgency was taking root, the money to fight it dried up. It has since been reinstituted at the tactical level, but the parameters to use the funds are more cumbersome and bureaucratic.

The fiscal year 2007 war supplemental spending package signed into law by President George Bush on May 25, 2007, HR 2206, provided $456.4 million for CERP in Iraq and Afghanistan. Organizations such as the U.S. Agency for International Development (USAID) are focused on long-term economic development and capacity building. Although USAID can provide hope, funding has been slow to support these efforts, and as a result, the agency is limited in what it can do and therefore is seen as almost impotent by both the coalition military and the Iraqi government.

As of the summer of 2007, the State Department leads seven provincial reconstruction teams (PRTs) operating around the country. These teams can have a positive effect in secure areas, but not in areas where their work is hampered by significant security constraints. Additionally, although the PRTs have been in Iraq since 2005, the teams still have not been fully manned by the Department of State. In some areas, a PRT consists of only one person.[48]

An essential part of reconstruction efforts in Iraq should be greater involvement by and with international partners, who should do more than merely contribute money. They should also actively participate in the design and construction of projects.[49] One benchmark is the fair distribution across the country's provinces and various ethnic groups of $10 billion in reconstruction funds, as allocated in the Iraqi government's budget. The money is to build infrastructure, improve services, and create jobs for all Iraqis, but parliament cannot agree on how to equitably disburse the funds. Many think the easiest way to distribute aid quickly across ethnic lines is to tie it to education or home-improvement funds, but that hasn't been done in Iraq as of yet.[50]

Consequences of Failure to Meet the Benchmarks

The five significant benchmarks outlined by the president clearly represent the milestones that need to be met for us to achieve victory. But what happens if Baghdad fails to meet these benchmarks?

The consequences of failure remain unclear. Some Democratic lawmakers have pushed for a freezing of monetary aid to Iraq, while others have sought a more rapid withdrawal or a redeployment of troops. White House officials say that performance benchmarks should not be linked to troop deployments and reconstruction aid disbursements—that is, the consequences of Iraqi inaction should not include imposing limits on the ability of U.S. military leaders or the president to carry out the war. It is obvious, however, that having benchmarks means little unless there are consequences if they are not met. That is the issue: It seems clear that the Iraqis do not believe there will be serious consequences if they fail to achieve these benchmarks. After all, if they felt the pressure, why would they take vacations every few weeks while our forces are working around the clock during twelve- to fifteen-month deployments?[51]

Nonetheless, it is instructive to consider the potential impact if the coalition left without reaching measurable milestones. Leaving now would negatively impact the Iraqi people. The Brookings Institute estimates that an immediate pullout of U.S. forces would result in 750,000 casualties, much along the lines of the catastrophe seen in Rwanda when more than 800,000 Tutsis were slaughtered by the Hutus in 1994. Al Qaeda would find a safe haven in Iraq and would probably grow roots there, potentially preventing us from ever defeating the terrorist organization. In fact, Iraq could become a nation-state for Al Qaeda, as it is not strictly affiliated with any particular country. In short, Iraq would most likely become a failed state and set precedence for the failure of other efforts elsewhere in the world.[52]

FOCUSING ON THE POPULACE

In any conflict, the focus of all civil and military plans and operations—for it takes a combination of civilian and military operations
to defeat an insurgency—must be on the populace. Clausewitzians
tend to think of the center of gravity as the source of strength for the
friendly side.[53] In Iraq, the coalition derives its strength from the
populace.

Most agree that an important facet in the war in Iraq is the
country's people and their belief in and support of their government.
"Winning their hearts and minds" must be the objective of the government's efforts. "Hearts" means persuading people that their best
interests are served by the coalition success; "minds" means convincing them that you can protect them and that resisting the coalition
and the Iraqi Security Force is pointless.[54]

"If the United States is to succeed," wrote Robert C. Orr, the
Washington director of the Council on Foreign Relations in 2003,
"it must kick the entire reconstruction effort into high gear, dramatically increasing the money and manpower it is devoting to the
reconstruction" in support of the populace. Orr explained that the
United States must give priority attention to a set of key issues if it is
to "win the hearts and minds" of Iraqis and successfully return the
nation to its own people.[55]

It was immediately after the war began that Orr wrote these
things, saying that the primary lesson of past postconflict interven-
tions is that security is the sine qua non for successful reconstruction.
Orr's blueprint for success is a coincidental look at what wasn't done.
If it had, then perhaps Iraq would already be standing on its own and
enjoying its newfound sovereignty. Orr's insightful instruction was to
do the following:

> The United States must simultaneously rebuild a new army,
> reintegrate hundreds of thousands of former soldiers into
> society and create a new police force in short order. A
> second priority must be to establish Iraqi buy-in to the entire

reconstruction process. Iraqis must be given significant decision-making power and governing responsibility if they are
to have a real stake in the coalition's strategy. The newly
formed Iraqi Governing Council is a good start. Perhaps even
more important will be the CPA's efforts to provide direction
and resources to the local and provincial councils that inter-
face with the citizenry with greater frequency.[56]

Thus the coalition actually had the solution in hand in 2003 but
unfortunately did not capitalize on it. About the same time as Orr
was doing his analysis, George McGovern and William R. Polk
quoted in *Out of Iraq* what President Woodrow Wilson said at the end
of the First World War: "There is only one thing that can bind men
together, and that is common devotion to right."[57] The authors later
expanded on this thought by insisting that America respect the fundamental right of the people of Iraq by letting them determine their
own future. Our nation inherently knew that the insights offered by
these individuals were the appropriate way to get the Iraqis to take
responsibility for their actions, and therefore maintain the required
focus. We were sidetracked by other priorities, however, allowing the
war to evolve into what it is today.

Interestingly enough, Orr was one of many analysts who determined what needed to occur in the early days of the counterinsurgency. While some, like Tom Ricks, claim that the original plan was
the "worst plan in American history," the goal for COBRA II, the
ground component of the classified U.S. war plan, was actually well
thought out and organized. COBRA II's premise was to force the
collapse of the Iraqi regime with an end state for the operation as
regime change.[58] That is precisely what the coalition has been
attempting to do since March 2003 in order to establish a society run
by and for Iraqis.

Quite simply, Iraqis needed jobs. The coalition had just put thousands of Baathists and soldiers out of work. The newly unemployed

should have been put to work getting state-owned enterprises up and running, as well as in a crash program to provide electricity, water, sanitation, and a complete array of services. Both of these ventures could have ensured that the 30,000-plus former Iraqi soldiers were off the market for the insurgency.

With the successful overthrow of Saddam Hussein and his henchmen and the establishment of a new government through a legal and legitimate election process complete, another key challenge identified early on was to facilitate a change in the Iraqi mindset from one of mistrust and skepticism to one of trust and optimism. This policy objective, as directed by the country's political leaders, was to coach the Maliki government into believing in itself and help it understand that corruption was counter to good order and discipline in an established government. Also critical to the Maliki government and our policy objectives was to remind the ruling government body that the Iraqi population was the prize, and not something that should be bartered in order to make a buck. Although corruption in Iraq is not likely to go away, it's important for the country's leaders to know that the coalition is aware of the negative impact of the corruption, regardless of whether it does anything about it.

One example of winning the hearts and minds of a country's populace is what has occurred over the past few years in Colombia. The South American country's president, Alvaro Uribe, gained broad support of the populace in the struggle against the Revolutionary Armed Forces of Colombia and National Liberation Army narcoterrorists. Today his government is weakening the insurgents' hold on their traditional zones of control and threatening their financial and recruiting base.[59] This is but one model that could be followed by the Iraqi government to achieve this goal.

Bringing attention, services, and an apparent resolve to help the people by showing them that what the government is doing is being done for them will win the support of the populace. It is a credibility issue, and one of the biggest challenges in Iraq today is convincing the government at the national level that this effort is required for success. So how does a coalition in support of a counterinsurgency achieve this?

British brigadier Richard L. Clutterbuck writes about counterinsurgency that "the first reaction to guerrilla warfare must be to protect and control the population."[60] As troubling as it might be, the evidence suggests that the main lesson to be drawn from the British practice of counterinsurgency is that physical control of the contested segment of the population is essential. Physical control is a risky course of action, for it could lead to abuses in power and a multitude of international investigations. Nonetheless, analysts including Galula would support this strategy early on in an insurgency to garner support, even if it is coercive. Further, that physical control is greatly facilitated when the insurgency's support is concentrated among a small and relatively unpopular minority of the population. This thought fits well with Galula's second law, which defines that support is gained through an active minority.

Insurgents rely on members of the population for concealment, sustenance, and recruits, so as Galula wrote, they must be isolated from the people by all means possible. Among the most effective means of employing the strategy are population control measures such as vehicle and personnel checkpoints and national identity cards. In Malaya, the requirement to carry an identification card with a photo and thumbprint forced the communists to abandon their original three-phase political-military strategy and caused divisive infighting among their leaders over how to respond to this effective population control measure.

Population control, as stated by Galula, is key in conducting a counterinsurgency. While coercion and force are sometimes required, physical control of the population is also attainable by less direct means. Informational campaigns can explain what the people can do to help their government make them secure from terrorist insurgents, encourage participation in the political process by voting in local and national elections, and convince insurgents that they can best meet their personal interests and avoid the risk of imprisonment or death by reintegrating themselves into the population through amnesty, rehabilitation, or simply not fighting. The Philippine government's psychological warfare branch was able to focus its messages on individual villages and specific Huk guerrilla bands during the 1946–54 Hukbalahap Rebellion because it employed locals and surrendered insurgents on its staffs.[61]

During the rebellion, the Japanese occupation raised the cost of rural dissent, equating nonviolent with violent resistance and rapidly introducing measures to counter the emerging Hukbalahap. Japanese counterguerrilla tactics against the Huks in central Luzon, and elsewhere against U.S.-supported guerrillas, were not that different from the tactics used by the European powers in quelling colonial uprisings. Guerrillas were "bandits" outside the law and could be shot on sight. This is called status-based targeting and would be very restrictive in Iraq and other areas where U.S. forces are involved in direct action attacks.

Also during the Huk Rebellion, punitive expeditions could act on a principle of collective responsibility, holding communities as a whole responsible for actions in their vicinities. This would equate to holding the entire town of Samarra responsible for the Golden Mosque attack and ensuring that the community as a whole suffered punitive consequences. Torture was routine during the rebellion, and suspects who died under torture frequently disappeared. Tens of thousands of prisoners held in internment camps died of hunger and disease. As they should be, those methods are clearly unacceptable under the U.S. forces rules of engagement.

On Mindanao, bounties were paid for dead guerrillas. One million of the 16 million or so Filipinos at the outbreak of war with Japan are estimated to have died in the course of the occupation, a large proportion of them in the devastation of Manila and other areas in the last stages of the war. Population control measures imposed by the Japanese included issuing identity cards and a system of mandatory travel passes for movement outside local communities.

In one basic counterinsurgency measure, what the Japanese called *zona,* a strong force of Japanese troops and Filipino constabulary would surround an area and bring all of the men into a central square. Like a flash, thirty or forty troops and police would swoop down on a barrio or a section of town and surround the place. Anyone who moved or objected in any way could be shot, no questions asked. This method, championed by Galula, was used in the past in Iraq, when all military-age males were rounded up and interrogated individually for information on insurgent activities. This became a forbidden course of action under the V Corps' MNC-I command tenure.

The intent of this method is to find people who might be part of the resistance movement. Anyone whom the counterinsurgent forces suspect is hauled off and detained indefinitely. In the Philippines, suspects were frequently beaten and tortured. They were checked against population records and scanned by hooded informants to seek out potential guerrillas, spies, and sympathizers. The Japanese also established what we would call neighborhood watches today to monitor and control the movements of all inhabitants and account for their activities.

The neighborhood associations were also to be the channel for the distribution of rationed food and commodities. Although implementation of this system appears to have been imbalanced, these units formed the lowest rung of a hierarchy and reported to a section, which in turn reported to a district. Reports were complemented by spot checks by Filipino collaborators and Japanese patrols. The system was perhaps theoretically sound as a totalitarian means of population control, but it was not fully successful, as a result of administrative inattention and grassroots resistance to collaboration. The system even provided a useful cover for the civilian side of the Hukbalahap resistance in some areas of central Luzon, where the official neighborhood associations provided the framework for the Hukbalahap Barrio United Defense Corps while collecting "supplies, money and information for the guerrillas."[62]

Clearly there are examples from the past century that would support these types of methods in Iraq today. There is no doubt that coercive means are against the current rules of engagement, but the theory behind population control has some merit in parts of present-day Iraq.

ACHIEVING DEMOCRACY IN IRAQ

While waiting to see if the Iraq surge strategy of 2006 to 2008 would pay off, it "became commonplace for officials to assert that political compromise, not military force, would determine the outcome of the war."[63] Thus a litany of measures of both effectiveness and performance were presented by government officials and think-tank analysts. When the United States has become involved in counterinsurgencies in the recent past, a multitude of external forces have muddled the decision-making process, resulting in paths not taken and eventually a failure of sorts when prosecuting a fight against an insurgent-infested battlefield. In Iraq, the desired end state as defined early on in the fight was a regime change in favor of democracy.

Bremer gave the primary justification for the invasion as the development of democracy, for if Iraq achieved this, it would become that "shining city on a hill in the Arab world."[64] Others said, "If democracy could take root in a dirt-poor nation like Mali . . . then why couldn't it emerge just about anywhere?"[65]

The question many analysts asked early on in the war was "What should the government of Iraq after Saddam Hussein look like?"[66] Viewed on a regional level, the broader issue becomes who will and will not support a strong, stable, prosperous, democratic Iraq.[67] There is no doubt that the coalition has worked hard on this issue. The U.S. government has addressed the problem by creating working groups and planning cells, formulating options, and discussing ideas with U.S. allies, while pundits and analysts in the media, think tanks, and academia have further identified this issue as vital to ensuring that peace in Iraq and the region is secured.[68]

The concern is that the coalition tends to try to make Iraq mirror the United States in every area: military, government, and business. In *Imperial Life in the Emerald City*, Rajiv Chandrasekaran expounds on the response of John Agresto, a senior advisor to Bremer who undoubtedly had his focus right from the beginning, on the transfer of sovereignty to the Iraqi government:

> Thirty years of tyranny do terrible things to a people: It breeds a culture of dependency; it breaks the spirit of civic responsibility; it forces people to fall back upon tight-knit familial, ideological or sectarian groups for safety and support. . . . The transfer of sovereignty will bring about some form of "democracy." But a liberal democracy, with real notions of liberty and quality and open opportunity—without strongmen, or sectarian or sectional oppression—well, I think that's doubtful."[69]

Is the desire to replicate the U.S. model of democracy in Iraq today appropriate, much less doable?

Democracy nevertheless lies at the heart of all discussions when it comes to defining benchmarks for success. President George Bush has declared that "all Iraqis must have a voice in the new government, and all citizens must have their rights protected."[70] Yet skeptics argue that trying to build democracy in the Arab world would not only fail, but also further stoke anti-Americanism in the process. Overall, critics raise at least five related objections to creating a democratic Iraq that seem damning upon first review. First, they contend that acceptable alternatives to democracy exist for Iraq that, if hardly ideal, are more feasible and more likely to ensure the stability and cohesiveness of the country. Second, they argue that Iraq is not ready for democracy. Third, they state that Iraqi society is too fragmented for democracy to take hold. Even if Iraq held elections or had other outward institutions of democracy, in practice such a system would yield an illiberal result, such as a tyranny of the Shia majority. Fourth, they insist that the transition to democracy in Iraq would be too perilous and the resulting government too weak; thus the institutionalization of democracy, particularly a federal form of it, would fail. Critics often conjure a vision of an Iraq beset by civil strife, with rival communities seeking revenge on one another while neighboring armies trample the country. Finally, they assert that the United States is too fickle, and the Iraqis too hostile, to give democracy the time it would need to grow and bear fruit. Overall, primarily for these five reasons, the doubters do not so much question the desirability of democracy in Iraq as they do its feasibility.[71]

Iraq is hardly ideal soil for growing a democracy, but it is not as infertile as other places where democracy has taken root. Iraq's people are literate, and the country's potential wealth is considerable. A properly designed federal system stabilized by the military forces of the United States and other intervening powers could both satisfy Iraq's communities and ensure order and security. Creating democracy in Iraq would require a long-term U.S. commitment, but the United States has made similar commitments to far less strategic parts of the world. Creating a democracy in Iraq would not be quick, easy, or certain, but it should not be impossible either. The question we must ask ourselves is how the average Iraqi actually feels about what a democracy would bring to his or her society. Our guess is, and our experiences tell us, that a quest for democracy is unimportant to the Iraqis, even though the U.S.-led coalition makes it a focal point for success; having elections may be the saving grace and a backdoor way to establish a democratic state of Iraq. Some may argue that free elections are no guarantee for democracy, but isn't it true that if you have free elections, you have the beginnings of a democracy?

THE KEY CHALLENGES

According to Ali Allawi, "The nature and scope of the Iraq crisis can be encapsulated in the emergence of four vital issues that have challenged the entire project for remaking the Iraq state." As an Iraqi who suffered years of exile until the fall of Saddam, he believes that the following issues determine the outcome of the war if each is appropriately addressed.

First, Allawi believes that the invasion of Iraq tipped the scales in favor of the Shiites, who are now determined to emerge as the governing majority after decades, if not centuries, of perceived disempowerment and oppression. The consequences of this historic shift inside Iraq and elsewhere in the Middle East are incalculable. While we concur that his analysis is correct, we also believe that the U.S.-led coalition, mainly the CPA, has amplified the profound desire of the Shiites by marginalizing the Sunnis in the debaathification program.

Second, Allawi thinks that the invasion of Iraq legitimized the semi-independent region that Iraq's Kurds had forged over the past decade. The real issues here are how Kurdish control of the north plays out in the constitution; what the limit of advance of the Kurdish-Sunni fault line called the Green Line is; and where the oil-rich city of Kirkuk falls in the realm of control. The answers to these questions will have a keen role in, as Allawi puts it, "the integrity and self-definition of Turkey, Iran and Syria now or in the future."

Third, "the uneven, poorly prepared and messy introduction in Iraq of democratic norms for elections, constitution-writing and governance structures is a stark break with the authoritarian and dictatorial systems that have prevailed in the Middle East." We have already touched on the struggles surrounding the implementation of a democracy in this type of highly restrictive society with a full array of cultural norms that are foreign to Western ways of life. "While the Iraqi experiment has so far been marred by violence, irregularities and manipulation, it is quite likely to survive as the mechanism through which governments will be chosen in the future."

Finally, Allawi is very concerned about the influence of the Iranians. Clearly this challenge is a wild card, not only in how Iran influences the assembly of the government, but also in the Iranian government's reported support of the insurgents' capabilities to keep the Iraqi government unstable.[72]

CAN SUCCESS BE ACHIEVED?

Arguably, the War on Terrorism began with the Beirut bombings of the Marine barracks in October 1983. At that time, the United States established an unofficial policy: As casualties increased, the U.S. forces would retrograde. This unwritten but adhered-to policy was acknowledged by terrorist leaders as a win for their side. It essentially established that the United States didn't have the backbone for a large number of casualties. What ensued was a series of terrorist attacks with the goal of inflicting as many deaths as possible on American forces to cause us to withdraw. Unfortunately, the United States fell victim to this tactic. Time and time again, the world witnessed a tit-for-tat approach between Americans and terrorists, where the United States would suffer casualties, an outcry would ensue, and the policy makers would adjust the intent of the employed force—all in all, a win for the terrorists.

After 9/11, President George Bush was adamant that the terrorists would pay for the thousands of casualties caused that fateful day. Fortunately for the United States, there was no knee-jerk reaction to cause a premature withdrawal of forces as in Somalia in 1993. Instead, the massive attack against U.S. civilians that day galvanized our resolute approach to "defeating terrorism." The national decree to win the War on Terrorism had a shelf life, however, and the goal now was to determine, based on cause-and-effect actions, what that shelf life timeline was. Eventually the antiwar lobbyists and discontent congressional leaders would become a force to reckon with at the national level, and the resolve to find and destroy the terrorists who caused such devastation on U.S. soil would dissipate.

Most agree that our 2001 strikes on the Taliban in Afghanistan were indeed just. But was our decision to attack Saddam Hussein in Iraq a just decision based on the goals of defeating terrorism? This will obviously remain a question for the history books for years to come.

Now that we are years into the war, the issue of whether it is the right war to fight has become moot. Reflecting on the legitimacy of the war should be left to historical scholars. Assessing whether we are negotiating it correctly as it unfolds is the important question right now and should be the essence of all discussion at the military and political levels.

"'Stay the course' is not a strategy, it's a slogan," said House Democratic leader Nancy Pelosi nearly four years after September 2001, as she called for a new direction in a war she labeled "a grotesque mistake." Democrats denounced the GOP-orchestrated war with Iraq and the nonbinding resolution that says an "arbitrary date for the withdrawal or redeployment" of American forces is not in the national interest. Democrats viewed this as a politically motivated charade, and most, including California's Pelosi, state that supporting the resolution would have the effect of affirming Bush's "failed policy" in Iraq.[73]

In an August 2, 2006, CNN poll based on Sen. Joseph Lieberman's defeat in his party's primary in Connecticut showed that more than eighty percent of all Democrats opposed the war. It is not clear whether they opposed the general concept of the commencement of the war or any particular facet of it, but it was clear that they opposed the war—an outright disregard, publicly, for those prosecuting it up until that point.

An adage often used when defining a conflict is that one man's terrorist is another man's freedom fighter. Most insurgencies are fighting a war of ideas and attempt to mobilize a population toward a single line of thought or ideology with the goal of winning over the populace. The enemy in Iraq, originally termed anti-Iraqi forces (AIF), consists of a full array of elements whose main motivation seems to be ridding Iraq of the coalition, whereas the coalition forces are attempting to impart a Western way of defining freedom.[74] In defining which group is the real insurgency, the key is defining which is attempting to mobilize the population to their cause. One could argue, with great clarity, that the AIF is *not* attempting to mobilize the population. If they are, it's in an attempt to rid the nation of U.S. forces, an unorthodox approach to what many deem a classic insurgency. What the AIF does do, however, is mask it by using the populace to hide. They are a credible force in the eyes of many, so the populace allows this interaction to take place, whereas the coalition is not credible and therefore has a more difficult time "using" the populace.

Regardless, in a perfect world, most would prefer an ideological truce for the Kurds, Shiites, and Sunnis to live together in harmony so that democracy could flourish. We cannot help but think, however, that trying to force these diverse groups of people to live peacefully together is a fool's errand, and we are those fools. Many in Iraq want the land to be divided into three countries, and sooner or later it probably will. We can't force people to adopt a system of government they truly don't want. The Iraqis are just not willing, able, or ready to become democratized, for democracy is really not a natural process that will take place under certain conditions. It's a state of mind more than anything else.

An argument that will be less received by critics concerns our decision to turn our backs on the Kurds in 1991 following Operations Desert Shield and Desert Storm. One could argue that if we hadn't done so, the prosperity the Kurds have enjoyed in the north would not have evolved. If we hadn't turned our backs on the Kurds, they would be in the same position as the rest of the country today: in dire need of help and absolutely reliant on the coalition to "do it for them." Perhaps being weak everywhere may have been a better algorithm for a successful democracy.

One of the principles of a counterinsurgency in today's doctrine *(FM 3-24)* is that it leads to the legitimacy of a standing government, and Iraq now has an elected government of national unity that is made up of leaders with diametrically opposing goals. Even if the Iraqi government functioned perfectly, what would the government govern? Not Kurdistan. The Kurdistan regional government (KRG) insists on its constitutional authority to run its own region. Baghdad is not even allowed to open ministerial offices in that region. Not the Shiite south. Clearly it is run by a patchwork of municipal and governorate officials who front for the clerics, religious parties, and mili-

tias, which are the real power in the south. The region has been ruled
as an Islamic state where militias and religious police enforce religious law with varying degrees of strictness. Basra's rulers have
tapped into Iraq's oil wealth, siphoning off billions of dinars' worth of
oil. Not the Sunni Arab heartland. It remains a battleground where
the U.S.-led coalition, in concert with Shiite troops, is at war with
the insurgents and Al Qaeda terrorists. Not even Baghdad itself can
be governed, since it is simply a series of armed camps where the
wealthiest of Iraqis maintain personal security protection forces.[75]

What many forget is that President Bush cited early on that the
war would be a long one, and everyone appeared to accept that constraint. Unfortunately, political amnesia hit, and pundits like George
McGovern and William R. Polk now claim that the president is a
mere neoconservative in favor of the "long war." They go on to cite
the cataclysmic and apocalyptic nature of this war, talking about "the
terrible and useless waste," and casting the Americans as Orwellian
puppets "truly looking into the abyss toward hell on earth."[76]

Former marine, public servant, and author Bing West writes that
the troubles in Iraq are being compartmentalized and therefore over
simplified. He adds that former Chairman of the Joint Chiefs of Staff
and Secretary of State Colin Powell spoke of the "sectarian line" in
an interview on *Meet the Press,* asking, "Are we delaying the
inevitable conclusion of this civil war that ultimately will be fought
out between Sunnis and Shias, Shias and Shias, Sunnis and al-
Qaeda?" Bing answers this question by stating that "the Sectarian
Camp [of Iraqis] believes the current surge is too little, too late,
because the cancer of hate has already metastasized throughout Iraq's
body politic. They believe Iraq is being torn apart by religion, not
terrorism." The Anti-Terror Camp, on the other hand, sees the war as
winnable and fears that Al Qaeda in Iraq will become their ruler
when the Americans leave. According to West, the surge of 2007 pro-
ceeds on the hope that most militias can be reconciled to a civil
order. "The best hope is that those irretrievably bent on terrorism are
small in number and can be removed from the mainstream, setting

Iraq on a course to emerge as a pluralistic, democracy-based society, albeit plagued with intermittent violence, such as, say, Colombia." The Sectarian Camp believes that the surge will not work.[77]

As the saying goes, "When you're up to your ass in alligators, it's hard to remember that you came to drain the swamp."[78] Or in other words, it is easy to lose sight of your objectives if you are sidetracked by other factors. It is our belief that both camps are approaching this fight all too simplistically. The combination of sectarian strife and a desire for terrorist camps to thrive in this environment has left Iraq ripe for an insurgent success. What we believe is the anchor for success is simple and achievable. It is the most dynamic element of combat power: leadership.

CHAPTER 4

The Decisive Nature of Leadership

"One of my cardinal rules of battle leadership—or leadership in any field—is to be yourself, to strive to apply the basic principles of the art of war, and to seek to accomplish your assigned missions by your own methods and in your own way."

Gen. Matthew B. Ridgway
The Korean War, 1967

One man or woman in a leadership position can make a great deal of difference in the outcome of this war, as leaders influence others to achieve success. The leadership, both coalition and Iraqi, at each level of war—strategic, operational, and tactical—has had an impact on the current state of this fight.

"Leaders must have a strong sense of the great responsibility of their office; the resources they will expend in war are human lives."[1] While simple to understand, this is an incredibly important and fitting quote taken from U.S. military doctrine. In the end, the leaders of any fight are the custodians of the welfare of the soldiers whom they lead. This is a simple fact that is sometimes forgotten in the heat of battle. Although confusion and the tempo of operations often cause friction in the maintenance of leadership responsibilities, it is our opinion that for leaders of any rank on the battlefield, bureaucracy—and all that comes with it—is the main competitor for good order and discipline. Most leaders inherently know what to do, but as the well-known military adage goes, even the best of leaders with their best-laid plans can be easily overcome by the Clausewitzian fog and friction of war.[2]

The English military historian B. H. Liddell Hart, who greatly influenced the development of armored warfare and strategic theory in the twentieth century, writes in his classic book on military strategy that "in war the chief incalculable is the human will."[3] Hart spent a lifetime studying what willed a man or woman to fight.

Civil War general Stonewall Jackson was known to have said, "War means fighting. . . . The business of the Soldier is to fight." Jackson ultimately described what a military leader must do, or be prepared to do, and that is to fight. We view the ability to get ready to fight, skill in actual fighting, and the will (as Hart wrote) to prevail in combat against a foe as the critical dimensions of leadership.[4]

The majority of the combat force currently in Iraq consists of U.S. land forces. American land power is unique in its ability to decisively impose our nation's will on adversaries. It follows then, that land power, more than any other component, depends on human interaction and innovation while fundamentally seeking to change or control human will. The exact meaning of the term "human will" has been the subject of historical debates among philosophers and theologians. Most attempts at defining "human will" include the mind's power to choose. According to Carl von Clausewitz, "War is thus an act of force to compel our enemy to do our will." Will plays a significant role in current joint operations design in such things as identifying the adversary's center of gravity, which Clausewitz calls "the hub of all power and movement, on which everything depends."[5] For Iraq, we believe that the center of gravity is the will of the Iraqi people.[6]

To achieve our goals in this fight, we need to impose our will on our enemy and, most important in Iraq today, on the populace to turn them to support the Iraqi government. To ensure that there is a concerted effort to meet these needs, our leaders must maintain a keen eye on what motivates our soldiers to fight. Physically engaging through lethal means and employing combat power to "win the hearts and minds" of the populace both have challenges from a leader's standpoint. "Firm and decisive leadership during critical moments has the power to elevate the morale of troops, galvanize their energies, and increase the will to fight from within."[7] The inverse corollary for this rule is equally important: That is, the loss of trust and confidence in subordinates to do their job leads to building bureaucracies and a loss of focus on the goals of the fight. To accomplish the goal of defeating the insurgency by building the credibility of the Iraqi government and the Iraqi Security Forces, we need not only the right mission sets and rules of engagement, but also the appropriate leadership to motivate our soldiers, sailors, marines, and airmen to achieve victory.

Those in uniform, and even those who have a vested interest in our nation's ability to project power, know that when the bullets begin to fly, the thoughts of "red, white, and blue" and "God and country" become limited rallying cries for those in the fray. What matters most to a soldier in a fight is the soldier on his or her flank. Given this premise as the motivation to fight, there have been some leaders who managed to channel that energy in a positive manner. As leaders and key individuals in this war against an insurgency in Iraq, they knew what "right" looked like. Perhaps we can learn from them.

LEADERSHIP DEFINED

According to military doctrine, leadership is the most dynamic element of combat power. *JP 1-02* defines "combat power" as "The total means of destructive and/or disruptive force, which a military unit/force can apply against the opponent at a given time."[8] Therefore, if it is agreed that leadership is the most dynamic element—or perhaps more specifically, the most influential one—then it is the leaders who can bring to bear the "destructive" force against our enemies.

The U.S. Army field manual dedicated to the art of leadership, *FM 6-22: Leadership* says:

> The definitions of leadership and leaders address their sources of strength in deep-rooted values, the Warrior Ethos, and professional competence. National and Army values influence the leader's character and professional development, instilling a desire to acquire the essential knowledge to lead. Leaders apply this knowledge within a spectrum of established competencies to achieve successful mission accomplishment. The roles and functions of Army leaders apply to the three interconnected levels of leadership: direct, organizational, and strategic. Within these levels of leadership, cohesive teams can achieve collective excellence when leadership levels interact effectively.

Why is this important? You can understand the actions of military leaders if you clearly understand the doctrine from which they are trained.

The manual continues:

> An enduring expression for Army leadership has been BE-KNOW-DO. Army leadership begins with what the leader must BE—the values and attributes that shape character. It may be helpful to think of these as internal and defining qualities possessed all the time. An *Army leader* is anyone who by virtue of assumed role or assigned responsibility inspires and influences people to accomplish organizational goals. Army leaders motivate people both inside and outside the chain of command to pursue actions, focus thinking, and shape decisions for the greater good of the organization.

The doctrine makes it abundantly clear that military values and attributes are the same for all leaders, regardless of position.

The KNOW discussion of leadership defines what our professional soldiers know about tactics, technical systems, organizations, management of resources, and the tendencies and needs of people. *FM 6-22* goes on to convey that "while character and knowledge are necessary, by themselves they are not enough. Leaders cannot be effective until they apply what they know. What leaders DO, or leader actions, is directly related to the influence they have on others and what is done." It is clear from our doctrine that "all Army leaders must be warriors, regardless of service, branch, gender, status, or component. All serve for the common purpose of protecting the Nation and accomplishing their organization's mission to that end. They do this through influencing people and providing purpose, direction, and motivation." So in short, the doctrinal definition as derived from the manual is that "*Leadership* is the process of influencing people by providing purpose, direction, and motivation while operating to accomplish the mission and improving the organization."[9]

Rephrased, military leadership is the process of influencing others to accomplish the mission by providing purpose, direction, and motivation. *Field Manual (FM) 22-100: Command* defines military leadership as the authority a person in the military service lawfully exercises over subordinates by virtue of his or her rank and assignment or position. It goes on to convey that the responsibilities of a leader are accomplishment of the mission and the welfare of the soldiers.[10]

It is well known in the military that the most essential dynamic of combat power is competent and confident officers and noncommissioned officers and the leadership they display. It is from the capable and experienced officer and noncommissioned officer population across the force that the U.S. military derives its leadership power base.

Many have attempted to define leadership, as it means many things to many people and organizations, and it is instructive to explore how other sources convey what defines leadership. The *Collins English Dictionary* states that leadership is the ability to lead. Besides using a form of the word in its definition, the dictionary states that leadership focuses on the position, tenure, and ability of leaders. As such, it misses key points about the purpose and hallmarks of effective leadership.

The late management consultant and prolific author Peter Drucker gives the essence of leadership in the foreword to the Drucker Foundation's *The Leader of the Future:* "The only definition of a leader is someone who has followers. Some people are thinkers. Some are prophets. Both roles are important and badly needed. But without followers, there can be no leaders."[11]

This definition further adds that to gain followers requires influence, but it doesn't address the importance of integrity in achieving that goal. Indeed, it can be argued that several of the world's greatest leaders have lacked integrity and adopted values that would not be shared by many people today. This is a subtle point, but it's very necessary when judging leaders, especially those who are responsible for the lives of their subordinates like those in our military.

John C. Maxwell, an American pastor, author, and "leadership expert," sums up his definition of leadership in *The 21 Irrefutable Laws of Leadership* as follows: "Leadership is influence—nothing more, nothing less." Indirectly, it also implies character, as without maintaining integrity and trustworthiness, the capability to influence will disappear.[12] This moves beyond the dictionary in defining the leader by looking at his or her ability to influence others—both those who would consider themselves followers and those outside of that circle. Maxwell's definition closely relates to the military's doctrinal definition in that the military leader's influence on his or her soldiers is very important.

An American scholar, organizational consultant, and author who is widely regarded as a pioneer of the contemporary field of leadership is Warren Bennis. Bennis's definition of leadership, well known in many circles from the United Nations to the world of academics, focuses much more on the individual capability of the leader: "Leadership is a function of knowing yourself, having a vision that is well communicated, building trust among colleagues, and taking effective action to realize your own leadership potential."[13]

Attacks on Iraqi infrastructure such as electric plants, towers, oil pipelines, and refineries were to have been mitigated by the creation of the Strategic Infrastructure Battalions. The mission of the SIBs was to guard those facilities; they did not succeed. Corruption and tribal rivalries were two of the many obstacles preventing success. Seen here is an oil line fire in Bayji, north of Tikrit.

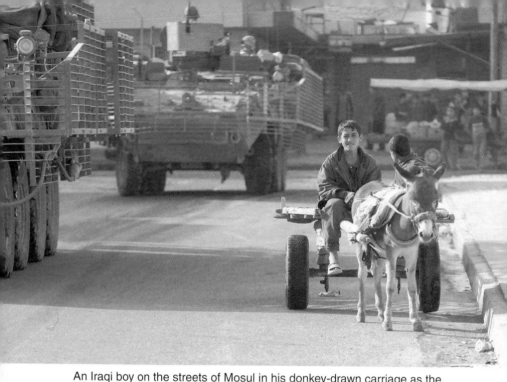

An Iraqi boy on the streets of Mosul in his donkey-drawn carriage as the mighty Strykers of the 172nd Stryker Brigade Combat Team drive by during a patrol of the second largest city in Iraq.

The effects of a SVBIED attack on a police checkpoint on the Jabouri Peninsula north of Baghdad.

Maj. Gen. Tom Turner, commander of Task Force Band of Brothers, meets with the commander of the 4th Iraqi Army Division and his key subordinates and staff officers. This would be the first of many meetings between the American and Iraqi generals.

A Rakkasan from 3rd Battalion, 187th Infantry Regiment (Iron Rakkasans), throws a grenade at an enemy position in the Quarghuli area of southern Baghdad.

Band of Brothers deputy commanding general for operations, Brig. Gen. Mike Oates, meets with members of the Kurdish political party PUK who had recently detected and intercepted a suicide bomber attacking their headquarters. The man responsible for killing the suicide bomber poses with Oates.

Lt. Col. Andrea Thompson on patrol in the city of Bayji, Salah ad Din Province, with the Rakkasans of 3rd Brigade Combat Team, 101st Airborne Division (Air Assault). Security of the Bayji oil refinery was one of the primary missions for Iraqi Security Forces in the area since the refinery served not only northern Iraq but also the city of Baghdad.

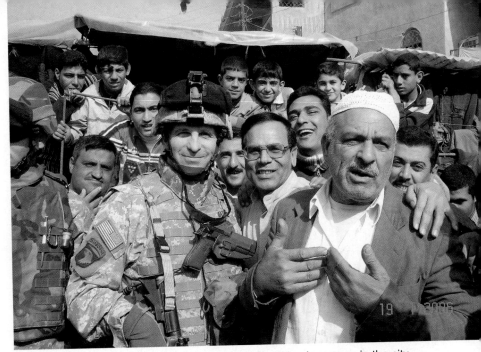

Brigadier General Oates is approached by local Iraqi businessmen in the city of Bayji. This bustling city was known for its oil refinery, but it also supported numerous small businesses. The men seen here ran multiple car sales stores.

A Rakkasan of the 3rd Brigade Combat Team overlooks a crowd of Iraqis.

The commander of the 101st Airborne Division, Maj. Gen. Jeffrey Schloesser, and Vince Camacho, division command sergeant major, visit the 3rd Brigade Combat Team outside the Rakkasans' headquarters at Camp Stryker, January 2008.

Col. Tom Vail, Currahee 6, talking with the Iraqi Security Forces in Adhamiyah in western Baghdad.

Coalition Forces are based across the country, collocated with Iraqis on smaller patrol bases (PBs) or larger bases like Forward Operating Base (FOB) Speicher, seen here outside the northern city of Tikrit.

Rakkasans of the 101st Airborne conduct a search near Quarghul village in southern Baghdad.

During Operation Swarmer, the 101st Airborne Division's largest air assault since the ground war, the Rakkasans of the 3rd Brigade Combat Team and their partnered Iraqi battalions found thousands of cached munitions and hundreds of IEDs. Andrea Thompson is seen here with a local Iraqi family elder during the operation, which was conducted outside Samarra in Salah ad Din province.

This Iraqi family was attacked by insurgents using a vehicle-borne improvised-explosive device (VBIED). Andrea Thompson is seen here with the wife and family of the Kirkuk chief of police, the target of the attack. Although their home was severely damaged, no one was injured in the attack.

A helicopter of the 101st Airborne on patrol.

Partnership and, more often than not, friendships were critical to the successful integration of Coalition and Iraqi forces. Here Dominic Caraccilo meets with the city of Kirkuk's chief of police, Maj. Gen. Tarhan Abdulrahman Yusif, who served in Caraccilo's partnered unit during OIF 1.

The women of this Iraqi family assemble in their family courtyard during Operation Swarmer while the men are searched for enemy equipment. The operations, conducted outside both Samarra and Tikrit in Salah ad Din province, resulted in the capture of thousands of munitions and hundreds of IED components.

A feast with Iraqi sheiks in a former Al Qaeda in Iraq holdout in Quarguli village.

The Iraqi Ground Forces commander inspects his troops from the 5th Iraqi Army Division in Diyala province. The 5th was the first Iraqi division to assume unilateral control for security operations in their area across Multi-National Division North.

The incoming and outgoing American commanding generals for Multi-National Division North—Maj. Gen. Tom Turner of the 101st Airborne Division (Task Force Band of Brothers) and Maj. Gen. Joe Talulto of the 42nd Infantry Division (Task Force Liberty)—meet with Lieutenant General Aziz, commander of the 4th Iraqi Army Division. By the middle of Band of Brothers' deployment, the 4th had taken control of security operations for the critical infrastructure security mission, guarding oil pipelines and electrical grids.

Command Sgt. Maj. Dennis DeFreese of 3-187 Infantry overlooking a Shia celebration in Yusifiyah.

Camp Hadar, Udaim, was the first Iraqi Army–controlled area in Iraq when in December 2005, the Iraqi Ground Forces commander directed a unit from the 5th Iraqi Army Division to control the road leading from Tuz in Kirkuk province to Baghdad through Diyala province. The Iraqi Army was attacked twice during its tenure here in a matter of two weeks, but they didn't break and run, and more importantly, Maj. Gen. Tom Turner did not direct a tactical intervention of U.S.-led Coalition forces. To this day, Camp Hadar is controlled strictly by the Iraqi Army with little assistance from the Coalition.

The transfer of authority (TOA) ceremony between the 42nd Infantry Division and the 101st Airborne Division (Air Assault) took place at FOB Danger, Tikrit, Iraq. Soon after the 101st's ceremony, it turned the base over to the Iraqi government.

Lt. Gen. Raymond Odierno, commander of Multi-National Corps-Iraq.

The Kirkuk city chief of police and his family were attacked by a VBIED seen here. Fortunately, none of his family members was killed, although the physical damage to his home and long-term emotional damage to his family were devastating. He continued to serve his country despite the attack.

Red Knight firing 105-millimeter artillery in south Baghdad.

Maj. Gen. Abdul Ameer (right) and Brig. Gen. Ali Jassim Mohammed Hassen Al-Frejee of the 6th Iraqi shake hands at an Iraqi Army Day celebration.

Urban development continues across portions of Iraq. Seen here is the new international airport in Sulimaniyah province in northeastern Iraq.

And finally, the Roman Catholic Archdiocese of Rochester, New York, defines leadership for the purposes of leader development as "the process of influencing the behavior of other people toward group goals in a way that fully respects their freedom." The emphasis on respecting their freedom is an important one, and one that must be the hallmark of successful leadership. Jesus influenced many diverse people during his ministry, but he compelled no one to follow him.[14]

There is obviously a wide array of beliefs and understandings associated with what it takes to be a good leader. Different parts of society relate leadership to their own experiences and backgrounds. When it comes to military operations, however, some types of leaders are better than others. Several characteristics are necessary to be a successful leader in the current war in Iraq, based on operational requirements and the existing environment.

STRONG AND WEAK LEADERSHIP IN IRAQ

We have gone through a multitude of sources from both public and private sectors looking at the characteristics and attributes of the wide variety of leaders who have been or are currently in Iraq, including ourselves, and have found clear examples of what qualities are attractive in a leader and what characteristics are appalling. It is truly amazing how much talent exists within our leaders conducting the war in Iraq. Few would argue that the military is undoubtedly the preeminent showground for what it is to be a leader. Flexible, agile, and adaptable are three characteristics that come to mind as requirements to succeed in the dynamic arena called Operation Iraqi Freedom.

After reviewing both doctrinal definitions and various input from societal leaders, we agree that the military leader must be influential. In Iraq today, leaders ranging from general officers housed in the Green Zone in Baghdad to the team leader patrolling the canal-filled backlands of southwest Baghdad have to influence not only their subordinates to do what is right, but also the Iraqis to abide by what the new government has defined in its constitution. Influencing

Iraqis—or "conducting an engagement," as it is now defined—is not a simple matter. In fact, the combat training centers require leaders to go through the "engagement university" established to train soldiers at the company command level and above to interact with Iraqi leaders, merchants, businessmen, security forces, and ordinary citizens as part of a unit's mission rehearsal exercise.

We agree that the dynamics of leadership are found in the competency and confidence of the military officers and noncommissioned officers in charge. We also believe that compassion is a key element of a good leader that has not been recognized thus far in our analysis of the leadership definition.

To be compassionate as a leader means to truly care for the soldiers (and their families) under one's watch. Often this requires leaders to make hard calls, such as whether to let a soldier leave the combat zone to take care of a personal matter. Conversely, compassion also may require a leader to make the hard call to deny a personal request to ensure that the mission is not compromised. Both forms of compassion are equally important.

The tangible part of leadership is having followers, people to lead, as the Drucker Foundation suggests. The need for a leader to initially be a good follower supports the premise that leadership is the most dynamic element of combat power. Further, integrity is absolutely necessary in the military. The personal capabilities of an individual are a telling sign of his or her ability to lead, as Bennis points out. Therefore, while we support the doctrinal definition of leadership, having a vision, conveying it to those you lead, and having the moral integrity to pursue it are equally as critical in Operation Iraqi Freedom as the need to kill terrorists.

Finally, we believe the definition from those in the religious world also has applicability when it refers to influencing others as a way to attain group goals. Ironically, though culturally much different, this Christian definition of leadership is applicable to the Muslim nation of Iraq. There is no doubt that attaining a group consensus while maintaining individual freedoms is an essential component to achieve what is obviously the ultimate goal: a unified nation of Iraq.

There are leadership and ethical imperatives that are prominent and, in some cases, unique to a counterinsurgency. The dynamic and ambiguous environment of modern counterinsurgency places a premium on leadership at every level, from sergeant to general. Combat in counterinsurgency is frequently a small-unit leader's fight; however, commanders' actions at brigade and division levels can be more significant. Senior leaders set the conditions and the tone for all actions by subordinates. As Clausewitz writes, "The more a general [the leader] is accustomed to place heavy demands on his Soldiers, the more he can depend on their response."[15]

Today's soldiers, marines, airmen, and sailors are required to be competent in a broad array of tasks. They must also rapidly adapt cognitively and emotionally to the perplexing challenges of counterinsurgency and master new competencies as well as new contexts. Those in leadership positions must provide the moral compass for their subordinates as they navigate this complex environment. Underscoring these imperatives is the common thread that exercising leadership in the midst of ambiguity requires intense, discriminating, professional judgment.

Military leaders are expected to act ethically and in accordance with shared national values and constitutional principles, which are reflected in the law and military oaths of service. These leaders have the unique professional responsibility of exercising military judgment on behalf of the American people for whom they serve. They continually reconcile mission effectiveness, ethical standards, and thoughtful stewardship of the nation's precious resources— human and material—in the pursuit of national aims.

Leaders across the U.S. armed forces work proactively to establish and maintain the proper ethical climate of their organizations. They serve as visible examples for every subordinate, demonstrating cherished values and military virtues in their decisions and actions. Leaders must ensure that the trying counterinsurgency environment does not undermine the values of their soldiers, marines, sailors, and airmen. Under all conditions, they must remain faithful to basic American standards of proper behavior and respect for the sanctity of life.

Leaders educate and train their subordinates. They create standard operating procedures and other internal systems to prevent violations of legal and ethical rules. They routinely check on what their subordinates are doing. Effective leaders respond quickly and aggressively to signs of illegal or unethical behavior. The nation's and the profession's values are not negotiable. Violations of these values are not just mistakes; they are failures to meet the fundamental standards of the profession of arms.[16]

We have learned over the past few years that in the war in Iraq, a single individual can make a difference, good or bad. The adage that no single person in an organization like the U.S. military is indispensable is correct only to a degree. Over the past few years, some individuals, whether they be in a command position, a key staff billet, or a central role affecting the war, have clearly made a great impact on the outcome of events in Iraq. Individuals' actions in a counterinsurgency count, perhaps now more than ever.

The idea that no one is so important that if that person is indisposed the unit or endeavor will fail is not universally true. This theory has been disproved in Operation Iraqi Freedom. A brigade combat team commander or legacy commander, a special staff officer or NCO, or an Iraqi leader can make the difference between success and failure. Everyone who has served a day in Iraq, as well as the American populace, can appreciate the fact that there are individuals working with the coalition and their Iraqi counterparts who are at the top of their game. Often these individuals have made a decisive impact, and their actions gave the coalition a marked advantage in achieving its task to provide security to Iraq and legitimize the Iraqi Security Forces and government.

Examples of such coalition leaders include Col. H. R. McMaster, who commanded the 3rd Armored Cavalry Regiment in Tal Afar, pacifying the key city in western Ninevah province; Col. Mike Kershaw, who commanded the 2nd Brigade, 10th Mountain Division, in southwest Baghdad and proved that local security forces could fill the gap where there was a lack of Iraqi Security Forces, thus providing a model other brigade combat teams could emulate; and Col. Sean

MacFarland, commander of the 1st Brigade, 1st Armored Division, who empowered the tribes into defeating the insurgencies in Ramadi. Another prominent leader is Maj. Gen. Mike Oates, commander of the 10th Mountain Division at Fort Drum, New York, who was the deputy commander for operations for Task Force Band of Brothers (101st Airborne Division) in Tikrit, Iraq, during 2005–2006. Oates was the epitome of a selfless leader whose presence on the battlefield was felt by subordinate commanders daily (a running joke was that he was shot at more times than any other soldier in the task force). One of the many examples of his positive leadership was the day he decided to travel throughout the Salahadin and Kirkuk provinces in his assigned UH-60 Blackhawk helicopter to pick up battalion commanders from various forward operating bases so they could link up together for an ad hoc lunch to discuss tactics, techniques, and procedures in their areas, an opportunity that perhaps could make the situation on the ground more clear for soldiers and their commanders. The move also showed battalion commanders that they could count on Mike Oates to take care of their commands, their soldiers, and their families.

Individual Iraqis who have made a difference in this war include Maj. Gen. Tarhan Abdulfahman Yusif, deputy chief of police for the province of Kirkuk, who accepted the number-two leadership position in the northern oil-rich city of Kirkuk. Kirkuk, which sits astride the Green Line, has long been an ethnic powder keg. Yusif stood out among all the Iraqi police leaders as an individual who was selflessly working to make his station in southwest Kirkuk better, and he therefore was hand-selected for the deputy position for the entire province of Kirkuk, by the commander of the 173rd Airborne Brigade, Col. Bill Mayville.

Some may argue that Prime Minister Ayad Allawi was "the right leader to steer Iraq out of its crisis."[17] The same excitement didn't exist for the Maliki administration in late 2007, however. Nouri al-Maliki was not our first choice to be Iraq's first permanent prime minister, and six months into his term, American officials had come close to losing confidence in him. When Maliki was chosen in April

2006, he was not a familiar figure to the Iraqi public, and he appeared stiff and nervous in his first press conference. But Maliki has clung tightly to power and to his agenda of putting an expanded Iraqi Army in charge of the country's security, and by the summer of 2007, he appeared to have retained and even deepened the support of the United States.

Maliki had served as a deputy leader in the Dawa party, a Shiite group that had long fought against the rule of Saddam Hussein, and was picked after months of wrangling in which Kurdish and Sunni officials combined to block the nomination of the interim prime minister, Ibrahim al-Jaafari, the Dawa leader. Jaafari had earned a reputation as being indecisive and had angered Kurdish and Sunni leaders by seeming to favor Shiite interests too much, in particular by allowing Shiite militias to infiltrate the new Iraqi Police Force. Maliki was viewed as more direct and forceful, and he stressed during his initial appearance a determination not to favor his sect above others.

The key votes in the caucus of Shiite parties that chose Maliki to be Jaafari's successor were cast by Muqtada al-Sadr, an anti-American cleric who was closely tied to the Mahdi Army, the militia believed to be the driving force in a wave of sectarian killings that had Baghdad in its grip. As time progressed, American commanders expressed frustration with Maliki, saying that he appeared to be protecting the Madhi Army and other militias. Maliki, for his part, pushed instead for an increase in the size of the Iraqi Army and insisted that Iraqi forces would be able to take control of the country far sooner than American generals were predicting.

Although the Bush administration gained Maliki's support for the early 2007 surge, friction clearly still existed. In mid-July, days after the administration released a report showing Maliki's government falling short on many political and security goals, Maliki gave a speech asserting that Iraqi forces were ready to assume control of the country any time the Americans decided to withdraw. It was unclear whether this meant abandoning democracy, for most would agree that the struggling nation of Iraq won't achieve democracy if the surge fails.[18]

Some people suggest that perhaps Iraq needs to disregard democracy for the time being and install a leader who is more apt to focus on bringing security to the country than trying to achieve a lofty goal based on a foreign framework for government. Regardless of the Iraqi chosen to do so, his ability to lead his country will determine the eventual success or failure of Iraq.

There is no doubt that the individual who has had the most impact on the recent outcomes in Iraq is Gen. David Petraeus, followed closely by Lt. Gen. Ray Odierno and now Lt. Gen. Lloyd Austin. Together, Petraeus and Odierno masterminded a path toward success in September 2007 in the form of a postsurge strategy. Before Petraeus gave his assessment to the administration, it was widely assumed that he would recommend that the U.S. stay the course in Iraq. In fact, most believed that Petraeus would recognize, as he had all along, that the chief of staff of the army, Gen. George Casey, had it about right when he was the MNF-I commander.

Withdrawing a sizable number of American troops as measures of success are met, meaning drawing down while ramping up the effort to train the Iraqi Security Forces, was the right strategy from the very beginning of Casey's tenure. What is unclear at this point in the war is that the tactical commanders, Odierno and Austin, clearly understand the process of transitioning battle space to the Iraqis and have given autonomy to subordinate commanders to complete that mission. Petraeus is also a leader who instills a level of trust in his subordinates, a characteristic too often absent among senior army officers. The jury is obviously out on the success of this plan. The events over the course of the next year will be telling, but the prognosis is good.

While the U.S. military has had an abundance of leaders who have had an impact on the progression of this war, insurgent leaders have also been attempting to direct its outcome in a different direction. Leadership has been critical in their efforts as well.

Saddam Hussein, the tyrannical dictator whose actions served as the catalyst for the initial invasion, had a decisive leadership role at all levels in this war, as did Abu Musab al Zarqawi, the Al Qaeda leader who met his demise in Diyala province in 2006, but not before establishing Al Qaeda in Iraq (AQIZ) in support of the insurgency, making it difficult for the coalition and Iraqi Security Forces to defeat Shia and Sunni extremists because of the AQIZ terrorist involvement.

Leaders from the various "constellations of insurgents" were responsible for enemy successes across Iraq.[19] These included organizations such as Jaysh Ahul-ul-Sunna (Army of the People of the Sunna), Jaysh al-Taifa al-Mansoura (Army of the Victorious Party), and Majlis Shoura al-Mujahideen (Mujahideen Advisory Council), among others, each of which had formed a terrorist arm of AQIZ in the years following the commencement of the war. There were also anti-Iraqi leaders who weren't as closely affiliated with the terrorist movements, such as the Jaysh al-Islami al-Iraqi (Islamic Army of Iraq), the Yaysh 'Umar (Army of Omar), Jaysh Muhammad (Army of Muhammad), and Kataib Thawrat al-'Ishrin (Battalions of the 1920 Uprising). Each of these groups, as well as dozens of others, had its own motivation and modus operandi for accomplishing its tasks—but in the end, they all tried to impede the progress of the Iraqi government and Iraqi Security Forces, with the ultimate goal of expelling the U.S.-led coalition from Iraq. No doubt these groups had individuals who inspired others to excel.

In many cases, leaders on either side excelled beyond the individual norm and set an example for others to emulate. Others displayed a bad attitude or unattractive leadership quality, and this negative example of leadership was equally powerful. In both cases, leadership made a difference in determining the outcomes of events.

THE IMPACT OF LEADERSHIP DECISIONS
A staff officer can have a huge impact on whether an operation succeeds or fails.

From 2007 to 2008, Task Force Rakkasan was stationed in the former "Triangle of Death" in South Baghdad. Decisions were made early on to allow for changes of command at the captain level and, perhaps more audaciously, to allow for the transitioning of primary staff officers (typically school-trained majors) during the fifteen-month deployment. Thus, all battalion-level operations officers—including the BCT's S2, S3, and executive officer—were transitioned without the force missing a step in its operational capabilities. This underscored the flexibility and adaptability of majors, captains, and lieutenants.

Nowhere was this more profound than in the case of the BCT's "senior" intelligence officer, a position that transitioned from a staff college–trained major to a talented captain, Rachel Sarles, and then to 1st Lt. Meg Fitzpatrick, who had barely two years in service when she was asked to fill this critical position for months while Sarles was on emergency leave. What was unique in this instance was the incredible leadership attributes and instinctive capabilities that Fitzpatrick displayed while conducting duties that most majors struggle to carry out proficiently. This example speaks volumes about the trust our leaders have in their subordinates and the incredible preparation provided by our commissioning sources.

In 2005 to 2006, Task Force Band of Brothers, stationed at Forward Operation Base Speicher in Tikrit, had established an Iraqi Security Forces cell responsible for manning and equipping the ISF. The development of credible and capable ISF was Maj. Gen. Tom Turner's main effort. However, ancillary tasks such as hunting high-value targets and countering IEDs often threatened to take the focus off the goal of developing an indigenous force capable of assuming the coalition role in securing Iraq. But Turner was not going to let his division be sidetracked by other tasks, even though they may have been both easier to accomplish and more attractive to execute for those with a military mindset.

For a year, Turner's division did all it could to focus on establishing a credible ISF in its area. This focus proved fruitful. By the time the 101st Airborne exchanged duties with Maj. Gen. Randy Mixon's Hawaii-based 25th Infantry Division, it had turned over forty battalion sectors to the Iraqis—nearly 90 percent of what it owned. Additionally, it transitioned two of the four Iraqi division headquarters to Iraqi control, a phenomenal task worth noting.

There were many challenges to completing the mission of manning, equipping, and training the ISF so it could conduct counterinsurgency operations unilaterally and autonomously. One of these challenges was the difficulty in finding talented and respected individuals who could work that task. The army does not have an identified billet that stipulates "ISF team chief" or "ISF cell leader," and few commanders wanted to pull their best officers from key positions to fill these slots, regardless of how important they were for success.

ISF training became part of the responsibilities of the partnership unit, where there clearly were enough talented brigade combat teams and subordinate commands to maintain the energy required. Coupled with the efforts at the highest echelons, training Iraqi police and army units seemed to be on a path for success. But the attainment of vehicles, arms, radios, and even uniforms for the many ISF elements springing up all over the Iraqi battlefield became much more difficult, as did paying the ISF soldiers and promoting deserving Iraqis. The Iraqi Joint Headquarters and Iraqi Ground Forces Command seemed to care little about managing the Iraqi soldiers' careers.

The Iraqi Ground Forces Command (IGFC) was established on May 15, 2005, as the operational fighting headquarters for the Iraqi Army. In a command directive dated August 4, 2005, the commanding general of the Iraqi Joint Forces (IJF) provided his implementing direction to the commander of Iraqi Ground Forces (IGF). The IGFC serves the dual functions of operational-level corps headquarters and the land component command of the IJF. The coalition's goal for the IGFC is that it eventually will not only direct the combat operations of assigned IGF units, but also take the following responsibilities:

- developing a robust training plan to enable units to maintain their operational capability and combat effectiveness
- identifying training requirements for units in anticipation of forthcoming operations and advising Joint Headquarters (JHQ) where support is required

- collecting and advising on lessons learned in accordance with direction from JHQ

These functions did not exist in this form or organizational level in the former Iraqi Army, and as such, the IGFC has met institutional resistance to its raison d'être. This is notwithstanding its key enduring roles as a buffer to politicization of the IGF and in delivering effective operational interpretation of strategic direction from JHQ, the Ministry of Defense, and the Iraqi government. As the Iraqi hierarchy developed, other key concepts came to include the following:

- gaining familiarity and proficiency with C4 (command, control, communications, and computers)
- revising the application of the Common Staff System (previously inherent, but employed differently to accommodate an autocratic and punitive system of directive control)
- adopting the U.S. schooled military decision-making process (MDMP) as a planning method

These factors and the effort to implement each had a great impact on the effective partnership of Multi-National Corps-Iraq (MNC-I) with the IGFC, a liaison that is fundamental not only to the success of the IGFC as a headquarters, but to the entire command-and-control construct adopted for the Iraqi Army, and thus ultimately key to the transition of the counterinsurgency fight.

While the IGFC military transition teams provide technical and individual training, the MNC-I partner provides additional mentorship, contextual understanding, and experiential advice to its IGFC counterparts.[20] It was obvious that the implementation of many of these concepts for command and control and, more importantly, the Iraqi higher headquarters' responsibilities for their subordinate units were foreign to the new generals in the Iraqi Army.

According to Australian Lt. Col. N. H. Floyd, coalition planner within MNC-I chartered to analyze the partnership requirements at the corps level in 2006, the concept of a higher headquarters dedicated to the Iraqi soldier was "entirely new to the senior Iraqi Army

Leadership."[21] To make the coordinations and processes work, it would take an engaged individual willing to go the extra mile to facilitate interaction with the Iraqi Army—a self-starter who could work through ongoing issues that were complex and often unsavory.

In exploring the need for appropriate manning and efficient partnership, Floyd determined that the following things were critical: dedicated senior action officer partners to engage Iraqi leaders, a whole cell support made up of a wide variety of functions to support that partnership, maintenance of a dual battle rhythm (coalition and Iraqi), accommodation of and accounting for cultural differences (interpreting, translation, time allocation, and work rates), meeting structures, situational awareness with the Iraqi Army, Iraqi input to policy and operational decision making, personal and institutional constraints and limitations, and personal support and credibility.[22]

Essential to this leadership partnering was a litany of items that required coordination and input between coalition and Iraqi partners. Most of these coordination efforts had to be done at the highest level to ensure appropriately nested mission sets along the parallel aligned headquarters. What was unclear was how the day-to-day actions would unfold so that the soldiers partnering with Iraqi counterparts at the lowest level could recognize progress.

Management of money and equipment to support the Iraqi Army had already become questionable over the years the coalition had been in Iraq. There may have been a master plan to manage funds and provide allocation of such, and the execution of the fiscal plan may have been meticulously done, but it was not readily apparent to the soldiers on the ground. It seemed that always, regardless of the province or unit level, the troops and junior leaders were left holding the bag with their Iraqi counterparts for radio deliveries that never came through, vehicle maintenance contracts that were never developed, compensation pay that was promised but never made, and infrastructure development for the ISF that was guaranteed but never up to par.

From the perspective of the junior level, it seemed that some of the senior leaders were unwilling to hear these issues. In fact, one very senior leader told a group of paratroopers in late 2003 that "the money is there to be spent for the Iraqi equipment; if the CERP [Commanders' Emergency Response Program] funds are being spent to fit the force then it's your own damn fault." This, of course, was an oversimplification of a remedy that was much more complex than what senior leaders believed or admitted at the time. In fact, in September 2003, the funding for the war through the delivery of CERP funding had all but dried up, leaving junior leaders throughout Iraq incapable of paying contractors for completed projects, an embarrassment we have personally suffered.

Nevertheless, tracking and managing of projects, funding, equipping, and manning were tedious and thankless jobs. What we have learned in Iraq, as well as other places that have somewhat ambiguous procedures and processes for getting the job done, is that it takes great initiative on the part of staff officers and commanders to define the process so that progress can be achieved.

For Task Force Band of Brothers in 2005 to 2006, Major General Turner gave the task of directing the team for developing a capable ISF to his deputy commander for support, Brig. Gen. Ricky Rife. Rife was indeed a meticulous planner and manager, and he also knew to surround himself with talented and hardworking people. Nearly every organization has a "go-to" person—a person everyone can count on for straight answers and for working beyond the required call to duty. For Task Force Band of Brothers, that individual was a young, energetic officer named Capt. Renee Vigilante, a quartermaster officer from the 101st Airborne Division. Captain Vigilante individually made a difference in this effort by nearly single-handedly establishing a method for tracking unit requirements and, more importantly, truly defining their shortages. At times she would go directly to the IGFC and JHQ (bypassing the MNC staff but always following up after progress was made), as well as to the Multi-National Security Transition Command-Iraq (MNSTC-I) logistical sections to coordinate supply deliveries and rectify issues. It was clear that the weakest trait of the newly formed ISF was the ability to maintain itself logistically. Vigilante helped develop logistics strategy for this fledgling security force and was Turner's go-to person for all things related to ISF at that stage in the war.

By mid-2006, many believed that the ISF in many parts of Iraq, especially in Turner's sector, was at the point where it could conduct small-unit collective tasks on its own, but it was unclear whether it could sustain itself in a fight without the help of the United States. Regardless of the hard work by a robust MNSTC-I headquarters, what was lacking was an established logistical network ensuring that the Iraqis could support themselves with all aspects of equipping and manning the force. It was clear in Task Force Band of Brothers, and in the task forces across Iraq in the years preceding the 2005-2006 rotation, that the weakest link in establishing a capable and credible ISF was its ability to sustain the fight without the coalition coming to its aid.

Although solving this challenge proved nearly impossible even as late as 2006, everyone in the task force knew they could go to Rife's ISF cell, and more specifically Captain Vigilante, for answers and action. She, like others in that particular staff, would go to great lengths to solve the problems even if there were no established solutions at that time. Vigilante clearly had a great impact in the war during the 101st Airborne Division's tenure.

There were other leaders in Iraq who *could* have made a difference but for some reason did not. As the leader for the post–Operation Iraqi Freedom effort, Lt. Gen. Jay Garner, the successful commander of Operation Provide Comfort in 1991 after Desert Storm, was one individual who likely could have had a decisive impact on our success in Iraq if given the chance.

Rajiv Chandrasekaran says in *Imperial Life in the Emerald City,* a critical view of the civilian leadership in the Green Zone, that Garner "arrived at the Pentagon . . . with no staff and no blueprint for the job ahead." According to Chandrasekaran's research, if there were a plan for postwar Iraq, Garner was never given it and was essentially set up for failure in his quest to rebuild the country. As Garner left Iraq after only a month on the ground, he warned the new envoy,

L. Paul Bremer, that the drawdown of the Iraqi Army and implementation of the debaathification executive order would have a negative impact on the prognosis for victory in Iraq, saying, "You're going to drive fifty thousand Baathists underground before nightfall . . . don't do this."[23] Bremer ignored that advice. He issued the executive order, and the impact is the situation we have today in Iraq: disenfranchised Sunnis fighting to ensure that their hopeless future is not set in stone with the establishment of a coalition-backed Shiite government.

It is unclear whether Bremer regrets debaathification and disbanding the Iraqi Army, but in his book *My Year in Iraq,* he does write that he thought the requirement to rid Iraq of the Baathists was so important that he wanted to be the one to convey it and not leave it up to Garner. What he did predict correctly, however, was that "assembling a New Iraqi Army (NIA) would not be easy."[24]

While the result of Bremer's decision—or in some respects, the inability of our leadership to trust Garner's instincts—was the increased effectiveness of the anti-Iraqi insurgency, a side effect that was just as damaging to the establishment of a democracy was the wholesale looting of the country's infrastructure. Disbanding the Iraqi Army amplified the disenfranchisement of the former power brokers in the Hussein government. Bremer writes that "a month after the liberation of Baghdad, General John Abizaid . . . reported in a videoconference that not a single Iraqi military unit remained intact."[25] The sanctions initiated by the end of Desert Storm had hollowed out the fundamental capacity of the Hussein government to provide services. Once the Iraqi military was disbanded, the government was unable to protect its country. With examples at almost every echelon, it is evident that those in leadership positions and the critical decisions made by them are the driving forces behind all successes and failures in Iraq.

INSPIRING LEADERS DEFINED

Leaders inspire soldiers with the will to win. They provide purpose, direction, and motivation in combat. Leaders determine how maneuver, firepower, and protection are used. They ensure that these

elements are effectively employed against the enemy. Thus no peacetime duty is more important for leaders than studying their profession, understanding the human dimension of leadership, becoming
tactically and technically proficient, and preparing for war. Studying
the profession of arms helps them understand the effects of battle on
soldiers, units, and leaders. Clearly, the regular study and teaching of
military doctrine, theory, history, and biographies of military leaders
are invaluable.

Commanders are selected for command because of their moral
character, willpower, and professional ability. They must imbue their
commands with their ideas, desires, energy, and methods. Professional
competence, personality, and the will of strong commanders represent
a significant part of any unit's combat power. The foundation of successful leaders must include strong character and ethical standards.
Good leaders are soldiers first, and to better achieve success at being
leaders, they must first know and understand their subordinates.

Leaders must act with courage and conviction in battle and build
trust and teamwork within their organizations. During combat
operations, they know where to be to make decisions or influence
the action by their presence. Clausewitz refers to a commander's
intuition as *coup d'oeil,* the recognition of the truth in battle based on
gut instinct.[26] Strong leaders and trained, dedicated soldiers are the
greatest combat multipliers.

When the enemy force represents a difficult challenge, as does an
insurgency, leaders provide the decisive edge. Once the force is
engaged, superior combat power is derived from the courage and
competence of soldiers, the excellence of their training, the capability
of their equipment, the soundness of their combined-arms doctrine—and above all, the quality of their leadership. Leadership continues to be the most dynamic element of combat power. As a result,
leadership and its development are studied both on and off the battlefield.

Field Manual (FM) 3-0: Operations defines the commander's leadership role in the following way:

Because it deals directly with Soldiers, leadership is the most dynamic element of combat power. Confident, audacious, and competent leadership focuses the other elements of combat power and serves as the catalyst that creates conditions for success. Leaders who embody the warrior ethos inspire Soldiers to succeed. They provide purpose, direction, and motivation in all operations. Leadership is key, and the actions of leaders often make the difference between success and failure, particularly in small units.

The duty of every leader is to be competent in the profession of arms. Competence requires proficiency in four sets of skills: interpersonal, conceptual, technical, and tactical. Army leaders hone these skill sets through continual training and self-study.

Leaders instill their units with Army values, energy, methods, and will. The professional competence, personality, and will of strong commanders at all levels represent a significant part of every unit's combat power. All Army leaders must demonstrate strong character and high ethical standards. Leaders are Soldiers first: they know and understand their subordinates and act with courage and conviction. During operations, they know where to be, when to make decisions, and how to influence the action.

Leaders build teamwork and trust. Trust is a key attribute in the human dimension of combat leadership. Soldiers must trust and have confidence in their leaders. Leaders must command the trust and confidence of their Soldiers. Once trust is violated, a leader becomes ineffective. Trust encourages subordinates to seize the initiative. In unclear situations, bold leaders who exercise disciplined initiative within the commander's intent accomplish the mission.[27]

Bold leaders in both the coalition and Iraqi ranks continue to make the hard decisions, leading their soldiers by example on a daily basis.

COMMANDERS WHO HAVE EXCELLED IN COMBAT

There are a number of brigade commanders who excelled since the war began some five years ago. These commanders knew what it meant to fight a counterinsurgency for their brigade, some of which transformed into combat teams while others remained legacy structured for the war. They used a multitude of resources and mission sets, both lethal and nonlethal, to counter the insurgents attempting to unseat the fragile security system in Iraq. The following are just some of these fine leaders, who are too abundant to list in this one volume. These examples clearly prove that one individual can certainly make a difference. Their actions are even more poignant when considered against the counterinsurgency culture, one that is so dependent on the commander's decision on how to fight.

Col. Joe Anderson, now a brigadier general and the chief of staff for MNC under Odierno, was the 2nd Brigade commander in the 101st Airborne Division in the northern city of Mosul, Iraq's second-largest city. He demonstrated early in the war an unmatched ability to integrate his forces to bolster the credibility of the local Iraqi military and governmental leaders.

Col. Bill Mayville, the commander of the 173rd Airborne Brigade, which parachuted into northern Iraq's Bashur drop zone on March 26, 2003, commanded the forces that eventually occupied the ethnically disputed oil-rich city and province of Kirkuk. His efforts were a graduate-level approach to multiple lines of operation, perhaps engaging in the LOO concept before it became the framework for success later in the war.

Col. H. R. McMaster, a well-known combat leader of Desert Storm fame and the battle of 73 Eastings, commanded the forces in the Nineveh province city of Tal Afar in 2005–06. McMaster led one of the first true counterinsurgent fights using the Galula principles in Iraq. Most notably, he showed that he knew how to divide the insurgency from the population through force and other means.

Col. Sean MacFarland was the commander of the 1st Brigade of the 1st Armor Division, a legacy unit sent from Tal Afar in a surge to restore stability in Ramadi. MacFarland's command was one of the first units in Iraq to determine that reconciling the local security forces could bring about security at the micro level.

Col. Mike Kershaw capitalized on the MacFarland model by bringing multiple counterinsurgent organizational leaders to the table. Kershaw's 2nd Brigade of the 10th Mountain Division immediately occupied his area, once heralded as the most dangerous in Iraq, by establishing seven patrol bases, two joint security locations, and two forward operating bases, all forward deployed and living among the population. This effort, as displayed by the Commando Brigade, employed the clear-hold-build concept even before General Petraeus began his tenure as the MNF-I commander and directed the use of this concept throughout Iraq. Additionally, this brigade was able to turn the "Triangle of Death" in southwest Baghdad into a reasonably secure area by co-opting the local populace in that area to join the ISF as neighborhood watch elements that were initially called concerned citizen groups. As of late summer 2007, Kershaw's command had established an environment where 7,000 concerned citizens, some of mixed sectarian representation, have augmented four Iraqi Army battalions and a handful of Iraqi Police, which drastically reduced the violence against the coalition, Iraqi Security Forces, and the Iraqi populace. In the fall of 2007, the 3rd Brigade of the 101st Airborne Division (Rakkasans) transitioned into this battle space under the command of Col. Dominic J. Caraccilo, coauthor of this work. As this work goes to press, there are more than 15,000 Iraqi volunteers serving at over 800 checkpoints throughout South Baghdad, and attacks have decreased by more than 90 percent from the previous year.

Col. Dave Gray, capitalizing on Mayville's success in Kirkuk, worked brilliantly with the Kirkuk Police, which arguably are a model for the rest of Iraq. Gray established a firm grasp of the confluence of the Kurdish, Arab, Turkoman, and Assyrian powder keg, capable of igniting at any time. After rotations of multiple brigades to Kirkuk, including a successful tour by Col. Lloyd Miles, now a brigadier general, from the 25th Infantry Division, Gray maintained a level of security in Kirkuk that most believed improbable at the beginning of the insurgency, knowing that the city would be a focal point for violence.

The Currahee Regiment (506th Infantry) commander Col. Tom Vail, now the 101st Airborne Division chief of staff in Afghanistan, commanded the forces in the Shiite stronghold of Sadr City in Operation Iraqi Freedom 05–07. Vail undoubtedly had a graduate-level challenge in this stronghold of Shia extremists. Nevertheless, he managed to quell the difficulties brought on by years of neglect by both the coalition and the Iraqi government in eastern Baghdad.

Col. Steve Salazar, now a brigadier general, identified the true nature of the fight in Baqubah (the "Baghdad of the north") and the rest of Diyala province, where the first Iraqi Army unit was given tactical control of a piece of terrain called Udaim. Salazar was probably the most diversified commander in Iraq at the time of his deployment, with his 3rd Brigade, 3rd Infantry Division, working for first the 42nd Infantry Division from New York and then Task Force Band of Brothers. Salazar's command brought to the table multiple economic initiatives in a way to better the lifestyles of the Iraqi populace. These initiatives were clearly an appropriate approach to a counterinsurgency determined to drive a wedge between the populace and the enemy.

Col. Mark McKnight, the most recent chief of staff for the 3rd Infantry Division in MND-C, was a brigade commander for 1st Brigade, 3rd Infantry Division, in MND-N during 2005–06. His command was one of the largest in the history of the war, at one time controlling seven and sometimes eight maneuver battalions.

Col. Mike Shields, commander of the Alaska-based 172nd Stryker Brigade in Mosul, established a model signal intelligence based operations environment in Iraq. Later in his rotation, Shields and his capable brigade were extended for ninety days to surge to Baghdad, the first unit to do so in the war.

These are just a few of the colonels who with their brigades have made a great difference in the fight against the insurgency in Iraq since 2003.

According to professional strategic planning consultant Roby Barrett, "For the commanders in Iraq, 'context' is a central aspect of most, if not all, important decisions."[28] The Iraq context is what Barrett calls "the 350-year-old applecart," meaning that in eight short weeks, we turned a system of rule that had existed for 350 years on its head. This invasion has resulted in the introduction of a level of fundamental regional political, economic, and social instability that is perhaps unrivaled since the decline of the Ottoman Empire, which in 1914 joined the Central Powers to form the Triple Alliance, ultimately resulting in redrawing the boundaries for the country of Iraq.[29] The descriptions of the commanders above are just snapshots of the quality leaders we have had in Iraq since 2003. These leaders understood that a creative, trustworthy, and educated approach to righting the apple cart overturned in 2003 is needed, and that it can be done. Looking at the specifics of how some of these leaders commanded will help in understanding their approach.

The Brave Rifles: 3rd Armored Cavalry in Tal Afar
In an interview by *Frontline* on February 2, 2007, Col. H. R. McMaster talked at length about his 3rd Armored Cavalry Regiment (ACR) in Nineveh province in western Iraq. The 3rd ACR initially worked for Multi-National Force-North (MNF-N), or Task Force Freedom, an ad hoc command led by the most recent commander of the 82nd Airborne Division, Maj. Gen. Rod Rodriguez. Task Force Freedom was disbanded in December 2005, and control of the entire MNF-N footprint passed to Tom Turner's Task Force Band of Brothers.

The 3rd ACR returned from Iraq in March 2004 and had only ten months to prepare to go back to Iraq in February 2005. They used that time to learn as much as they could from their experience in Iraq during their previous deployment, from 2003 to 2004.

McMaster applied those lessons to their training strategy and standard operating procedures on how they intended to conduct operations in Iraq, bring stability to communities, and develop indigenous security forces so that those gains would be sustainable over time.

McMaster identified early on that in order to deal with an insurgency, it is important to refer to it as such. Studying lessons learned from the British experience in Malaya, among other examples, helped in defining it as an insurgency. McMaster recognized at the beginning the importance of having complete unity of effort with indigenous forces and ensuring that their police and army components work well together. He also realized from studying historical military experiences in Algeria that population control, issuance of identity cards, understanding who the insurgents are, and isolating them from the population are critical to success.

As Galula defines in *Counterinsurgency Warfare,* the "destruction and expulsion of insurgents" is the first step in dealing with an insurgency.[30] Although offensive operations and hunting down the enemy are integral parts of any counterinsurgency approach, McMaster understood that destruction of the guerrilla force was not an end in and of itself. He identified that in Tal Afar there had to be an emphasis on initially establishing a degree of security. Once that was established, economic and political development and the development of indigenous forces could proceed.

When the 3rd ACR first arrived in Tal Afar, the situation was bleak. The enemy had essentially established control over the city. According to McMaster, it was sort of a franchise operation of Al Qaeda in Iraq. "The border was wide open at the time. Tal Afar was being used as a safe haven, support base, training area for insurgent operations across [Nineveh] province and all of Iraq. The enemy had really established a high degree of control over the city services, had . . . replaced the imams with laymen with third-or fourth-grade educations who were preaching hatred and violence, and recruiting adolescent and young males to the cause and enlisting them in the jihad."[31]

The enemy had caused the police force to collapse. The police force was essentially an exclusively Shiite organization that in many ways had become an adjunct retribution squad aimed against the Sunni tribes. So the cycle of sectarian violence had begun, creating a chaotic operational environment. Making matters worse, the enemy capitalized on the chaotic environment to establish control across the city, providing security to local residents where it did not exist.

What McMaster clearly understood, as did his West Point classmate Mike Kershaw in southwest Baghdad, was that brigade combat teams had to establish a clear-hold-build policy in order to "lift the pall of fear off of the population so that life can begin to flow back into these cities."[32] The clear-hold-build concept became popular once Petraeus took command of MNF-I, and it is clear that commanders like McMaster and Kershaw understood counterinsurgency and its principles and laws.

The 3rd ACR was able to develop credibility in Tal Afar. This credibility served as a catalyst for courageous Iraqi leaders—Tal Afar mayor Najim al-Jubouri, Gen. Khorshid Saleem of the 3rd Iraqi Army Division, Gen. Sabah Hamidi, the police chief—who began to broker reconciliation among the tribes that had been in direct military competition with one another. Everyone came to recognize over time that the source of their discontent, the source of the misery in that city, was Al Qaeda in Iraq, so they turned against these terrorists.

Although some would argue that the success in Tal Afar was an exception, McMaster remarked that one of the interesting characteristics about Tal Afar was that it generally replicated, in a microcosm, the complexity of Iraq. At the same time, he also recognized that the situation in Iraq differs greatly based on location and the unique ethnic-sectarian-tribal dynamics in a particular area.

The initial step of clear-hold-build, which is to clear an area or objective, has been conducted in military training operations for generations, and infantry soldiers know it "by the numbers." The "hold" part of the policy is not as routine, however. As 2/10 BCT and its successor, 3/101 BCT, have seen in southwest Baghdad, having multiple forward-based patrol bases causes a force to be fixed, meaning that it has no force available to conduct any other operation, since the force is fully engaged in holding terrain. This is a condition many believe the enemy wants us to attain.

Part of the solution to ensure that we don't get fixed in this methodology is to establish a strong logistical capability providing adequate facilities and the ability to communicate with and control forces. The capabilities are an essential framework that facilitates an expanded force to establish multiple locations and hold terrain forward.

It is imperative, in this concept, that forces are not withdrawn prematurely from an area. Time and time again, we see coalition leaders trapped by their initial success in an operation. Insurgents are defeated; populations flourish in that area; the markets are back open; and people are happy again. If the forces are withdrawn too soon and leaders give up terrain, what results is that the insurgency returns to influence and control what was once a pro-Iraqi populace.

So, according to McMaster, "what's important to understand is that the forces left behind have to be just not capable of sustaining the current situation, but they have to be capable of dealing with an intensified effort on the part of the enemy, which is certain to follow a successful operation."[33]

It is difficult to defend everywhere in a very dense urban area, so it is important not only to have security forces that the coalition may use to help hold terrain, but also to develop strong informant and source networks to provide access to good intelligence. It's also important that the forces develop good relationships in the community so that the locals are willing to come to them for assistance when suspicious people move into the neighborhood. This focus on local relations may seem obvious to many, but often cultural biases mask our efforts. Trust is essential among the leaders, the led, and the people they serve.

In the end, McMaster's success in Tal Afar was based on his understanding that withdrawal from a certain area should not be regarded as an end in and of itself. He knew it was important to focus on developing the conditions necessary to allow a transition to Iraqi control to occur. The 3rd ACR was very realistic in its assessments of the ISF's military capability, the strength of the police force, and effectiveness of the local government.

After the fight to rid the city of insurgents, McMaster used all the means in his control to ensure that the local government could provide for the basic needs of the people. This included pressuring the Iraqi government for millions of dollars so that the people in the region would go to the mayor and city council for assistance instead of to their sheikh and imam. McMaster believed that when the people go to their sheikh and imam for help, it reinforces their tribal and ethnic identities, which the enemy takes advantage of to continue the cycle of sectarian violence. Units in other parts of the country, however, such as Sean MacFarland's brigade in Ramadi, believe that tribal interaction, even if it marginalizes the elected government to an extent, is the answer. This confirms our belief that different areas of Iraq require their own specific solutions for success.

As in many other areas in the country, the 3rd ACR also determined that the rule of law had to be established so that there were consequences for criminal, insurgent, or terrorist activity. If Iraqis understand that if they are caught attacking their fellow Iraqis or coalition forces, an Iraqi judge is going to legitimately put them in jail for a full term, it would introduce a significant deterrent that would perhaps curb the violence.

McMaster concluded his description of how his unit conducted its counterinsurgency, which ended for him in February 2006: "Local governance, rule of law, economic development and improved security going hand in hand that set the right conditions for U.S. forces to withdraw. In many areas of Iraq still, coalition forces are the glue that holds this effort together, and so until Iraqis can develop the ability to fulfill their responsibilities to their people at the local level, I think coalition forces owe it to them to help hold the effort together."[34]

The Commandos of 2/10 BCT in Southwest Baghdad

Prior to the formalized clear–hold–build methodology for controlling battle space, a fundamental counterinsurgency concept described in M 3-24, Mike Kershaw's Commandos of the 2nd Brigade of the 10th Mountain Division (2/10 BCT) were executing this concept to standard in southwest Baghdad.

Historically, there were few to no police forces in this area, a canal-filled environment bordering on the Euphrates River in the south and Baghdad proper in the north. Multiple seams had existed, allowing insurgents and Al Qaeda to move freely from Fallujah in the west and other places in the south toward the capital through Kershaw's area of operations. It was also known to be a place where the Iranian influence was felt and the Shiite struggle grew its roots.

Therefore, Kershaw's Commandos turned the remnants of the 1920 Revolution Brigade, a Sunni militia group, into what initially was known as the Iraqi Provisional Volunteers (IPV) and has since morphed into what are commonly referred to as concerned citizen groups, Sons of Iraq, and now Iraqi Volunteers. These local initiatives to fight AQIZ and secure the neighborhoods are homegrown and generally follow tribal lines—again, much different from McMaster's action in the west.

Almost to a man, the Iraqi volunteers have indicated their desire to become part of the legitimate ISF and Iraqi government. Although some coalition elements do not agree with the initiative to legitimize the local security forces, which were once archenemies of the progress sought by the coalition and the ISF, in the end, the reconciliation effort perhaps is much more important than the effort to achieve success in a balance of power. The coalition continues to support this initiative with an eye toward moving the groups to Iraqi Police enrollment. The Commandos of 2/10 BCT led this effort by monitoring and controlling the various groups in southwest Baghdad, and the legacy of their efforts continues in the area today.

The First Team of 1/1 AR

The 1st Brigade, 1st Armored Division (1/1 AR), "Ready First Combat Team" (RFCT), commanded by Sean MacFarland spent fourteen months deployed to Southwest Asia in support of Operation Iraqi Freedom in 2006–07. The brigade initially served in the northwestern town of Tal Afar before being reassigned to the U.S. Marines' zone in Ramadi.

The Ready First's experience encompassed the full spectrum of counterintelligence operations, from fairly permissive ISF and Iraqi government support to heavy kinetic combat operations. In the process, the brigade learned a number of doctrinal, structural, and tactical lessons about fighting in a counterinsurgency and principles that gained some success in the unique environments of Tal Afar and Ramadi.

The RFCT is an "Army of Excellence" legacy armored brigade based in Friedberg and Giessen, Germany. What was unique about its success in Ramadi was that the brigade commander had to leave Lt. Col. John Tien's 2nd Battalion of the 37th Armor to secure Tal Afar when the brigade moved to Ramadi. Having been a legacy brigade, it was already short on personnel in comparison with the new modular forces.

The brigade's organization normally consists of two pure armor battalions, a mechanized infantry battalion, a headquarters company, and a brigade reconnaissance troop. About six months before deployment, the brigade received control of its direct support field artillery, engineer, and forward support battalions from the 1st Armored Division. The ad hoc brigade combat team (BCT) was augmented by a military intelligence company, a signal company, and a military police platoon provided out of 1st Armored Division assets. An additional mechanized infantry company from the 2nd Brigade Combat Team augmented this BCT for the deployment.

In the end, the brigade deployed with fifteen maneuver capable companies. This organization provided two tank companies, two dual-purpose companies, four motorized companies, four mechanized infantry companies, the brigade reconnaissance troop (BRT), and three combat engineer companies.[35]

Thus although MacFarland had a huge job to do, he had less force than most commanders with which to do it. But what he lacked in combat forces on the ground, he more than made up for with his brigade's leadership and operational successes.

An article by Jim Michaels titled "Behind Success in Ramadi: An Army Colonel's Gamble," in the May 1, 2007, issue of *USA Today,* gives a good picture of what MacFarland did in Ramadi in 2006. Michaels gives credit to MacFarland for surging to Ramadi when the U.S. strategy at that time called for pulling American forces back to large, heavily protected bases. In a bold move, he built small, more vulnerable combat outposts in Ramadi's most dangerous neighborhoods—places where Al Qaeda had taken root—in an attempt to hold the terrain and prevent the enemy from controlling it. In an interview, a humble MacFarland claims, in a tongue-and-cheek manner, that he "was going the wrong way down a one-way street" as he describes his negotiations soon after his occupation with a group of Sunni sheiks, some of whom have had mixed loyalties in the war.

For some time, MacFarland was indeed the lone wolf in Al Anbar province, as his superiors initially were wary of his plan. Despite the doubt at higher echelons, MacFarland forged ahead. His tactics have led to one of Iraq's rare success stories, with violence down today in Ramadi and the surrounding Anbar province west of Baghdad. Al Qaeda's presence has diminished, and Iraqis have begun to reclaim their neighborhoods. No one would have guessed that Al Anbar, the province that appeared red on all maps to indicate a high level of insurgent activity, would be the model for the rest of Iraq to follow.

According to the article, "Pentagon officials say the encouraging episode in Ramadi is a poignant reflection of shifting leadership

tactics within the U.S. military, which is trying to develop a generation of officers who can think creatively and are as comfortable dealing with tribal sheiks as they are with tank formations on a
conventional battlefield."

Whatever the case, it is clear that MacFarland "really understood
this is an argument between us and the insurgents." When most of his
1st Brigade was ordered from Tal Afar in northern Iraq to Ramadi in
late May 2006, MacFarland says he was given very broad guidance:
"Fix Ramadi, but don't destroy it. Don't do a Fallujah," referring to
the 2004 offensive in which U.S. Marines and soldiers fought block
by block to expel insurgents from that Sunni stronghold. The operation leveled large parts of the city and angered many Sunni Muslims
both locally and across Iraq.

The brigade immediately began building up to eighteen combat
outposts in Ramadi in areas where Al Qaeda was strongest. Rather
than following Galula's steps to defeating an insurgency linearly, Mac-
Farland's brigade didn't wait until a neighborhood was entirely secure
before launching construction projects, recruiting police, and trying
to establish a government.

The combat outposts helped drastically reduce violence by the
summer of 2006, but the brigade still wasn't close to winning over
the population, an essential part of defeating an insurgency. Ramadi
has a population of 300,000 people with strong ties to a multitude of
tribal affiliations. MacFarland says he soon realized the key was to
win over the tribal leaders, or sheiks.

While the combat outpost occupation was risky but necessary in
order to hold terrain, "the prize in the counterinsurgency fight is not
terrain," MacFarland rightly identifies. "It's the people. When you've
secured the people, you have won the war. The sheiks lead the people." Getting the sheiks to believe that supporting the coalition was
the right thing to do in order to protect their tribes and families was
MacFarland's plan.

The brigade made an offer: If the tribal leaders encouraged their
members to join the police, the army would build police stations in

the tribal areas and let the recruits protect their own tribes and families. They wouldn't have to leave their neighborhoods.

More than 3,000 new recruits had joined the police by the time MacFarland's brigade left in February 2007. More than 200 sheiks are now part of the alliance. They plan to form a political party in the near future.[36]

While Ramadi remains relatively calm today, it is important that the sacrifices made by MacFarland's brigade in their gutsy and successful endeavor are never forgotten. Over the course of its tour in Iraq, the brigade lost 95 soldiers, and 600 others were wounded. But because of Sean MacFarland's audacity as a combatant commander fighting a countersurgency, other BCTs emulated his actions in future deployments.

LEADERSHIP IS ESSENTIAL TO VICTORY

The majority of the decisions that got us where we are today in Iraq were the result of a set of conditions. These conditions created the need for additional decisions, and decisions made at each level caused a cascading effect up and down the chain of command. The war is framed by a continuous cycle of political and military decisions, and those responsible for making the critical decisions are our political and military leaders.

Through their actions, they lead, give guidance, and make decisions. All told, the profound impact of leadership has secondary and tertiary effects on the daily operations of the war. In the end, it is the leadership, with its influences both positive and negative, that will determine the outcome of this war and whether we achieve victory.

CHAPTER 5

The Good Enough
Solution

"Thus we may know that there are five essentials for victory:
(1) He will win who knows when to fight and when not to
fight. (2) He will win who knows how to handle both
superior and inferior forces. (3) He will win whose army is
animated by a same spirit throughout all the ranks. (4) He
will win who has prepared himself, waits, to take the enemy
unprepared. (5) He will win who has military capacity and
is not interfered with by his sovereign. Victory lies in the
knowledge of these five points. Hence the saying: If you
know the enemy and know yourself, you need not fear the
result of a hundred battles. If you know yourself but not the
enemy, for every victory gained you will also suffer a defeat.
If you know neither the enemy nor yourself, you will suc-
cumb in every battle."

Sun Tzu
The Art of War, c. 500 BC

A numinous chant of "No more Iraqs!" much like "No more
Vietnams!" can almost be heard in the distance as we head into
the national elections and continue to debate the status of this war.
Some, believing that the past repeats itself, identify the situation in
Iraq with that of Vietnam. In their view, the outcome of the

135

Indochinese conflict was a failure and the war in Iraq is headed toward the same. But failure is, in truth, never an option.[1] Even the harshest critics would agree that accepting failure is not the American way, and perhaps more importantly, it is not an acceptable outcome for global politics.

Achieving success in Iraq at this juncture is akin to snatching victory from the jaws of defeat. But this is what has to be done. We could take on a pessimistic tone, believing that the hearts and minds of an Islamic culture are impermeable. Other analysts, some of whom are noteworthy, believe that no amount of cultural sensitivity inculcated in the minds of U.S. troops will persuade fanatic believers to discard their religion, nor can any amount of American empathy change a foreign thug's ethnic identity.[2] Nonetheless, we believe that there is hope, and that victory can be achieved even this late in the effort to counter the insurgency.

In order to achieve victory, it is important to bring the fight, the approach, and the effort back down to the tactical level, where an impact can be felt. Pundits, talking heads, historians, and subject matter experts can explain what has to be done at the strategic and operational level. But if it cannot be done by boots on the ground, it cannot be done at all, and in the end, victory will never be achieved. The goal continues to be finding a realistic path for success.

Former Secretary of State Henry Kissinger once said, "If you do not know where you are going, every road will get you nowhere." So although benchmarks need to be defined, this cannot be done without first defining an end state that will be the catalyst for victory. The end state provides the framework, setting the conditions that will allow the Iraqi Security Forces to provide security for their nation. All the other lines of operation—communication, governance, economics, and transition—must support the one that will achieve victory for the U.S.-led coalition: the security line of operation. To attain security, we have to apply a full court press much like the Clinton administration's approach to campaigning in the 1990s, where the slogan "It's the economy, stupid," had a resounding effect on the election. In this case, the rallying cry might be "It's all about the ISF!"

But it is not merely about the ISF or the Iraqi government. It's also about establishing the *credibility* of the local power-based authorities. Those authorities, identified by coalition and Iraqi leaders, are chartered with bringing stability and services to their nation.

There is no doubt in our minds that there is a solution for achieving success in Iraq. We strongly believe that troops should not be withdrawn without first achieving a measure of effectiveness, or a benchmark for success. We believe an achievable benchmark has to be reached regardless of how long it takes or how difficult it is. Additionally, the solution is *not* merely to develop a timeline without a basis for achieving a benchmark for withdrawal. The solution requires an established phased operation that includes the incremental withdrawal of forces out of theater as desirable benchmarks are met.

As General Petraeus states in his September 7, 2007, letter to the troops: "My sense is that we have achieved tactical momentum and wrested the initiative from our enemies in a number of areas of Iraq. We are, in short, a long way from the goal line, but we do have the ball and we are driving down the field." He continues: "By living among the population with our Iraqi partners, you have been holding the areas you have cleared. By helping Iraqis reestablish basic services and local governance, you have helped exploit the security gains. And by partnering closely with Iraqi Security Forces, you have been strengthening Iraqi elements that will one day have sole responsibility for protecting their population."

Was the war in Iraq mismanaged early on? Perhaps, for a variety of reasons discussed in this book. Is the outcome of this war of importance to our nation? Yes, if for no other reason than to ensure that the hegemonic desires of the Iranians are kept in check.

Regardless of what pundits say, an insurgency left to run its course is potentially more dangerous than conventional war. As columnist Ralph Peters says, "Unless terrorists gain control of a full arsenal of weapons of mass destruction, they will not be able to do as much damage to states and societies as full-blown insurgencies."[3] Regardless of how we got to this point in the war, there is a full-blown insurgency in Iraq today, and it needs to be extinguished.

Those who say there was no plan for Iraq as we battle the insurgency need to review the sixty-three page report to Congress titled *Measuring Stability and Security in Iraq,* published in August 2006.[4] It is a definitive account of benchmarks and measurements laid out by the administration in the late summer of 2006, preceding the surge that occurred the following spring. This shows that thoughtful analysis has been ongoing in an effort to meet a level of measured success before pulling forces from Iraq.

But why is Iraq even important? The nation of Iraq and all its disputed territories are situated on sectarian fault lines where regional balance and world security are at stake. The clash of Persians, Turks, Kurds, Sunnis, Shiites, and other Arabs is amplified by the terrain centered on the "land of the two rivers." In a very simplistic view, harmony in this region is desired, if not required, for stability in the Middle East. We may have rocked the boat, but there is still time to ensure that it doesn't sink.

To achieve success in Iraq, we first have to establish how the U.S.-led coalition should approach the fight. Once this has been done, we then can define the action that needs to take place. Our conditions in this case are where we stand today—on the verge of a failed state, with U.S. forces taking the lead in a five-year-old counterinsurgency operation.

Before we can take these steps, we first must understand not only the chronological nature of what occurred starting in March 2003, but also the doctrine that directed the coalition and Iraqi actions, or in some cases inactions. As set forth in the report to Congress, politically, the goal was to help the Iraqis "forge a broadly supported compact for a democratic government." Economically, the goal was to assist the Iraqi government "in establishing the foundations for a sound market economy with the capacity to deliver essential services." And along the security line, the goal was to contribute to an environment where Iraqis are "capable of defeating terrorists and neutralizing insurgents and illegal armed groups."[5]

To achieve these goals, certain attitudes need to be ingrained in each soldier and senior leader. Key to the solution is the need to do it the Iraqi way, without attempting to mirror Western customs and systems, all the while focusing on the principles of a learned counterinsurgency doctrine. Helping the Iraqi government and the ISF gain credibility in all that they do along all the lines of operation is an overarching need for achieving victory. In the end, if the Iraqi populace believes in its government and security forces, then a level of victory can be achieved. At the same time, it's important not to marginalize the tribes, and employing local security forces has proved to be a good way to incorporate them. Sustainment of the seminal work being done to turn the security fight over to the Iraqis is a critical part of the solution.

Our recommendations are summarized in the form of "bottom lines" indicating the proposed solutions we offer for the various issues the coalition is facing as it strives to achieve success in Iraq.

GAINING AND MAINTAINING THE RIGHT ATTITUDE

Action speaks volumes in any endeavor, and having the correct attitude and focus clearly has an impact on one's actions. If the focus is skewed, the action and therefore the resultant outcome are undesirable. In the military, actions and attitudes are determined by the command climate and other factors, such as the experience of leaders, situational awareness, and willingness and ability to adapt to change. These all play an important part in gaining and maintaining the right attitude that will result in action leading to success. We believe that leaders' overall attitudes and subsequent actions in this war have at times been misguided, but the consequences are not irreconcilable.

Regardless of how we got into the fight in Iraq, we have been habitually negotiating it with a Western-centric attitude against a population whose experiences are mostly foreign to Western ways of thinking. Much has been said about the credibility of the Iraqi government and the ISF, as if the U.S.-led coalition expects them to meet the standards set by the United States. These standards happen to have been set by the sole superpower in the world, a nation that arguably has served as the model for democracy—which took more than 200 years to reach today's form.

While it has improved by an order of magnitude, from the onset of this war, the coalition has been training our "replacements," the Iraqi Security Forces, as if they were American soldiers on the verge of taking the lead. The coalition has been referring to its American checklists for even the most mundane tasks in an attempt to superimpose our attitudes on the Iraqi people.

When the Iraqis lived in neighborhoods surrounded by garbage and sewage, we thought it not only appropriate, but necessary to make these neighborhoods look more like downtown Mayberry, U.S.A. When the Iraqis wanted a soccer field built instead of developing a business center, we took it upon ourselves to "tutor" them into the "right" decision, as the business center clearly is the more appropriate and more important project to pursue because that is the way Americans would do it. When our soldiers hired Iraqi workers to clean their streets, because we believe the cleanliness of the streets is paramount to success, those same workers would discard their MRE (meals ready to eat) trash on the freshly swept streets before departing the area.

Because our expectations of the Iraqis are faulty, our actions often result in less than favorable results, playing a large part in extending the time the coalition needed to be engaged in a particular area. This also has contributed to the time-consuming task of finding answers to some problems that the Iraqis themselves could solve. In one case, a command bought ten garbage trucks to assist in the sanitation effort for a large city in Iraq. The city now "owned" the vehicles, but there was no national or even municipal program to maintain the equipment, and the Iraqis eventually cannibalized the trucks, which ended up on cinder blocks some weeks later.

There is no doubt that we need to understand the culture. This need has been reinforced numerous times during deployments and in training exercises in preparation for deployment. Today the American-led coalition, for the first time, universally understands this paradigm. Some of the scars left by our ignorance have had lasting effects on the fledgling nation of Iraq, however.

"Better the Arabs do it tolerably than you do it perfectly." This isn't a quote by a transition team, nor is it well-thought-out advice from a think tank in the basement of the Al Fatah Palace on Camp Victory, home of the MNC-I command. Instead, it is drawn from one of the most popular books among American military officers serving in Iraq: *Seven Pillars of Wisdom,* the accounts of T. E. Lawrence, the British colonel who rallied Arab tribal leaders during World War I.[6] Some ninety years ago, T. E. Lawrence, called "Lawrence of Arabia," already had this figured out. Unfortunately, it has taken the coalition several years to relearn this fact.

As Chandrasekaran writes in *Imperial Life in the Emerald City,* the coalition had an intense desire for success early on in this conflict, but unfortunately that desire was not harnessed. As a result, we had staffers doing things like studying the feasibility of giving each Iraqi family a debit card when there were no ATMs in the entire country. Coalition Provisional Authority (CPA) advisor Jim Otwell, a firefighter from Buffalo who was trying to build Iraq's firefighter directorates but was snubbed by Bernie Kerik, tried to tell Bremer that establishing a debt-based society without the proper systems or even the appropriate attitudes in place was a bad idea. But Bremer apparently would have none of it, for he was insistent on monetization.[7] This American imperialism has had a lasting effect on the Iraqi-U.S. relationship.

In the first few years of the war, it was obvious that many in the CPA believed that if we wanted to change something in Iraq, we simply needed to change the law. It is well known that Bremer signed hundreds of orders before he left, including directions defining the traffic code, rules for elections, and obscure topics such as laws governing patents, industrial design, and copyright regulations. It has been learned and relearned at every level of government over these past few years that a proclamation or decree doesn't replace the requirement for "laborious, on the ground work."[8] Just because the coalition says so doesn't make it so. But the Iraqis were looking at us, the sole superpower, as capable of doing anything—a false expectation that the coalition allowed to take root.

Another example is the CPA's approach to the health-care system in the new Iraq. James K. Haveman, a social worker with no medical degree who was virtually unknown in the international health community, got the nod as the lead for establishing a new Iraqi health-care system. As did all agency heads at that time, Haveman approached problems as a health-care administrator would do in the United States. He reportedly was set on devising efforts to develop an antismoking campaign in Iraq, a country where smoking is a national pastime. Another noble but untimely program was one dubbed Operation Smile, an American charity that sent physicians overseas to provide reconstructive surgery to children with facial deformities.

There is no doubt that programs like this were created with absolutely good intentions. The initial focus, however, should have been on more critical health issues, such as preventing epidemic diseases, childhood diarrhea, and other fatal maladies. Most would agree that the first step for any health-care effort in a third-world environment should be to work hard to provide decent drinking water in areas where disease from filth runs rampant. But above all, the primary issue concerning the health team efforts was the complaint by most Iraqis in the wake of the U.S.-led invasion: "Health care was free under Saddam—so why now charge?"[9]

The legal system was another place where the United States attempted to replicate itself in the development of solutions for an Iraqi problem. The concern for the rule of law following the fall of Saddam was very real. Nefarious individuals were being captured daily, and they deserved confinement. But there existed—and continues to exist—a great void in the capabilities of the Iraqis to bring justice to those criminals and terrorists responsible for so many violations of the law and attacks on progress in the country. Nonetheless, the way the coalition has tried to superimpose the Western justice system onto Iraq's court system is another misdirected approach to bringing democracy to a place that is just not ready for such government based on the principle of majority decision making. Court systems, jurisdictions, evidential requirements, and other legal parameters are expected under the U.S. way of bringing justice to its people. Perhaps we should allow the Iraqis to do it their way—which differs depending on the region, such as in Al Sulimaniyah with the Kurds in the north or in southwest Baghdad with the Quarghuli tribe.[10]

Bottom line: We need to explore the ways justice can be served without violating the Geneva Conventions and Laws of Land Warfare, and understand that when the coalition finally departs Iraq, the Iraqis will most likely return to what they know best. We should assist in refining whatever system is in place in each specific area of operation, rather than trying to make them all mirror the U.S. way. As time has progressed, we have learned that it is now time to have detainees incarcerated and sent to trial in the Iraqi system, not the coalition's. This may be perceived as an obvious solution, and it is being applied in most areas but is not universal to all.

When it comes to defining how the government of Iraq and the ISF are formed, we have to embrace the nation's cultures and assist the Iraqis in developing their government so that it can operate on its own when we leave. For example, Iraqis discipline their *jundis* (soldiers) for infractions much differently than Americans discipline their soldiers. Through Western eyes, their treatment of subordinates, which usually includes physical punishment, seems overly harsh. When we leave, however, the Iraqis will not fully adopt our methods, but revert to what works for them.

We also need to accept that the ISF will not be able to match the U.S. military in its tactical and technical abilities. It has taken the U.S. Army, in a focused leader-development effort, since the mid-1980s to build what it currently has today—an unmatched arsenal and leaders without peer. Still, the coalition continues to judge and subsequently measure the ISF against the U.S. standard. The coalition will never leave if we continue to do this, as our expectations for the ISF will never be met. We need to measure the effectiveness of the ISF by asking whether the Iraqi forces have learned not to flee when attacked, can generate their own mission sets, and can logistically sustain themselves through their own cumbersome systems.

The same attitude goes for the coalition interaction with the government of Iraq, whether it be at the national or provincial level. "If the government doesn't . . . respond to the demands of the people, they [the Iraqis] will replace the government," President Bush said at a news conference in Quebec, Canada. "That's up to the Iraqis to make that decision, not American politicians."[11]

Bottom line: The coalition has to stop trying to get Iraq to mirror the West. We need to do things, or enable them to be done, the Iraqi way. The coalition needs to recognize how the Iraqis will perform after we leave and work to assist in optimizing the appropriate support for that activity. There should be no more "ivory-tower schemes invented in the Emerald City" or elsewhere in our leadership hierarchy. We need to define how the Iraqis want to accomplish their mission, whatever it may be, and then decide on how best to engage with coalition resources to allow the Iraqis to accomplish the task.[12]

ENGAGING THE TRIBES AND CITIZENRY

Undoubtedly, we should support the government of Iraq, doing all we can to provide credibility to this fledgling government. Based on his success in Ramadi, Col. Sean MacFarland says that although it's important not to marginalize the government, we also have to get the tribes involved.[13]

As Ralph Peters says in the last line of his recent book, "From Liege to Lagos, the tribes are back."[14] He also writes that "the bleeding over political systems is largely finished; we have returned to the historical norm of wars of blood and belief, of conflicts driven by faith and tribe."[15] There has been a shift from an age of ideology consumed by the individual desires of those who "convinced themselves that [they] could reason out a better architecture for human societies than human collectives could arrive at it organically."[16] This change in the last two decades has had an enormous effect on "our statecraft and our approach to warfare, since the techniques that work against opponents inspired by ideology fall woefully short when applied to enemies aflame with divine visions or the lust to avenge old or imagined wrongs done to their kind."[17]

Engaging the tribes is counter to Western ways of interacting with established governments during conflict. The attempt to do so, though tacitly approved above the MNC level, is equally foreign to those at the diplomatic level, because the concept "overturns the entire system of diplomacy upon which we rely."[18] The southwest Baghdad model described in chapter 4, developed in early 2007, has proven to be the necessary framework to follow in Iraq.

Bottom line: Supporting the Iraqi government should be the first order of business, including getting a provincial electorate in place as soon as possible. But while we enable, empower, support, and ensure the credibility of the government of Iraq, it's critical that we don't marginalize the true power base of the Islamic nation of Iraq—the tribal network—and that we engage their support at the local level.

In southwest Baghdad, the former "Triangle of Death," local security forces have made a big difference. As of spring 2008, more than 15,000 concerned Iraqi citizens in that region had been entered into the U.S. Army's computerized tracking system, a censuslike database that most counterinsurgency experts say is an imperative part of controlling a population. Formalized contracts have been drawn up chartering these Iraqi volunteers in support of the coalition as local security forces that protect their neighborhoods. Compensation in the form of rewards is controlled initially by the coalition and soon will be transitioned to the Iraqi government.

Since the beginning of this program, attacks in this area, especially IEDs, have been reduced by more than 90 percent. In fact, these concerned citizens are leading ISF and coalition forces to an average of two to three ammunition caches per day. Here the coalition has turned the population against Al Qaeda in Iraq, among other insurgent groups, in a very visible manner. Though not uniformed, these Iraqis sport reflective belts, carry AK-47s, and support pro-Iraqi efforts. This is a win for the counterinsurgency and clearly a loss for the insurgents. The Iraqis in this area have clearly chosen peace over violence.

The next step to empowering the tribes while maintaining a credible government is to formalize these concerned citizen groups as an extension of the government and maintain local security forces as an extension of the ISF.

Indeed, Gen. David Petraeus referred to the importance of both the development of the ISF and the reconciliation of the tribes in his opening testimony to Congress on September 10, 2007:

> Iraqi Security Forces have also continued to grow and to shoulder more of the load, albeit slowly and amid continuing concerns about the sectarian tendencies of some elements in their ranks. In general, however, Iraqi elements have been standing and fighting and sustaining tough losses, and they have taken the lead in operations in many areas.
>
> Additionally, in what may be the most significant development of the past 8 months, the tribal rejection of Al Qaeda that started in Anbar Province and helped produce such significant change there has now spread to a number of other locations as well.[19]

An online report titled "Signs and Progress at the Local Level" includes a series of comments, both U.S. and Iraqi, from the spring and summer of 2007 on the successes both MND-B and MND-C have had in the southwest Baghdad region in getting locals to defend their own neighborhoods. Some of those comments are as follows:

Michael O'Hanlon and Kenneth Pollack of the Brookings Institution note that "reliable police officers man the checkpoints in the cities, while Iraqi Army troops cover the countryside. . . . Outside Baghdad, one of the biggest factors in the progress so far has been the efforts to decentralize power to the provinces and the local governments. . . . In response, many towns and neighborhoods are standing up local police forces, which generally prove more effective, less corrupt and less sectarian." Pollack goes on to say that a lot of the current progress is attributable to this change in strategy, with the emphasis on counterinsurgency, securing the Iraqi people, and helping them rebuild their lives. Power, water, and sanitation—all the things that people have been talking about for years—are now the principal mission of the U.S. military and civilian personnel in Iraq, and it does seem to be paying off, at least at the local level in certain important areas of the country.

The CENTCOM Public Affairs Office added its own comment: "For some provinces of the country, that [security] independence has been achieved. Setting a milestone on July 13, 2006, Muthanna became the first province to transition its security to Provincial Iraqi Control (PIC). The second province to transfer authority was Dhi Qar on September 21 and [the third was] An Najaf on December 20. Most recently, Maysan transferred authority on April 18."

Brig. Gen. Edward Cardon of the U.S. Army, deputy commander of Task Force Marne, observes that "what's starting to fill the gap with the Iraqi security units are these concerned citizens that are . . . tired of al Qaeda, of the extremist groups, and have [decided to] protect their own neighborhood."

Even the local citizens are enamored with this somewhat counterintuitive approach to achieving security. Badriyya Abdullah, an Iraqi citizen in Quarghuli village, reports that "since the Soldiers got rid of the terrorists, we've been able to start negotiations for power and water improvements."

Maj. Gen. Martin Robeson, of the U.S. Marines, the deputy chief of staff for strategy and plans, MNF-I, perhaps says it best: "I think it is the most significant thing that's happened in the past couple years. . . . [citizens] actually have come to us saying, 'We want to join you, we want to fight al-Qaeda.'" And the commander of Multi National Force—Iraq, Gen. David Petraeus, concluded in an

article in *USA Today* on August 15, 2007 that "what we're starting to
realize more and more is that reconciliation at the bottom may be
the more important element in the short term."[20]

During his September 2007 congressional testimony, Petraeus
also pointed out:

> The most significant development in the past six months
> likely has been the increasing emergence of tribes and local
> citizens rejecting Al Qaeda and other extremists. This has, of
> course, been most visible in Anbar Province. A year ago the
> province was assessed as "lost" politically. Today, it is a model
> of what happens when local leaders and citizens decide to
> oppose Al Qaeda and reject its Taliban-like ideology. While
> Anbar is unique and the model it provides cannot be repli-
> cated everywhere in Iraq, it does demonstrate the dramatic
> change in security that is possible with the support and
> participation of local citizens.

Perhaps more important is to integrate the local security forces
into the ISF structure. "We have, in conjunction with the Iraqi
government's National Reconciliation Committee, been engaging
these tribes and groups of local citizens who want to oppose extremists and to contribute to local security," Petraeus continued. "Some
20,000 such individuals are already being hired for the Iraqi Police,
thousands of others are being assimilated into the Iraqi Army, and
thousands more are vying for a spot in Iraq's Security Forces."[21] Iraqi
Army commanders like Brigadier General Ali of the 25th Iraqi Army
Brigade have shown their nationalistic attitude in the Mamudiya Qada
by taking the lead in assisting with the transition of the thousands of
Iraqi volunteers who thicken their lines in southwest Baghdad.

The surge of forces in early 2007 led some U.S. officials to predict that American combat deaths in Iraq would increase as well. But
in fact, by the fall of that year, fatalities had dropped by 50 percent in
three months since the buildup of 28,000 additional U.S. troops

reached full strength, even though U.S. forces launched major offensives involving thousands of troops north and south of Baghdad.

This has surprised analysts, who are divided in explaining why. Most agree that one secondary reason for the decline in casualties is the dramatic change of conditions in Anbar province, where former Sunni insurgents have teamed up with American troops to rid the province of Al Qaeda in Iraq. About one-third of all U.S. casualties in Iraq had been in this province, but that has shifted since the troop increase began. In August 2007, about 10 percent of U.S. casualties occurred there, compared with 30 percent in January, when the buildup began.

Another factor contributing to the successes of local security forces in the Baghdad region is that the Shiites are fighting one another for control of the southern provinces. Some military officers believe that rebel cleric Muqtada al Sadr's (MAS) Mahdi Army left Baghdad before the buildup of forces began. Throughout the troop surge, Sadr has issued statements discouraging his followers from attacking U.S. forces and Baghdad's fortified Green Zone. The official freeze that MAS put in place in late summer 2007 remains a critical factor in the decrease in Shia extremist activity in many parts of the country.

SHOULD DEMOCRACY IN IRAQ REMAIN A GOAL?

In a democracy, the rule of law protects the rights of citizens, maintains order, and limits the power of government. A democratic state, as represented by Western culture, is one that has three branches to support the governance: legislative, judicial, and executive. The legislative branch develops laws based on a true representation of power. The legislative process is lacking in Iraq, however, and this absence defeats the purpose of the Council of Representatives (COR). The judicial branch ensures that laws are followed and justice is met. In Iraq, the judicial branch is also inept, partly due to the flawed rule of law, as outlined by the constitution, that was established with a primarily Western and not Iraqi influence. The executive branch provides the leadership in a democracy. The executive branch in Iraq has credibility issues with its perceived lack of support for its own people. All three branches must have some semblance of operational functionality in order for a democracy to flourish. All three branches in Iraq today, however, are ineffective at best.

Is a democracy really what Iraq needs at this point? Can harmony be achieved without a democratic framework superimposed on this Muslim state? Perhaps it is time to table the quest for democracy and settle instead for a government that is run by a credible leader, trusted by the populace and determined to set a path for success in economic pluralism and the overall security of the nation. But "if the price of a unified Iraq is another dictatorship," as former Croatian ambassador Peter Galbraith writes in *The End of Iraq,* "it is too high a price to pay."[22]

Fareed Zakaria has it right in his book *The Future of Freedom: Illiberal Democracy at Home and Abroad,* when he ties democracy to liberty. Zakaria writes, "In 1900 not a single country had what we today would consider a democracy: a government created by elections in which every adult citizen could vote. Today 119 do, comprising 62 percent of all countries in the world." There is no doubt that democracy is the model for success in any government, but it's more than a model for governance. Zakaria admits that "democracy has gone from being a form of government to a way of life."[23] Though we must ask ourselves, is that "way of life" timely, or even required, for Iraq today?

"Democracy" is defined, first and foremost, as "the rule of the people," the meaning of the word's Greek root. Such a nation is defined by those democratically involved with governance in Western societies, who in reality are living within a "liberal democracy," which Zakaria defines as "a political system marked not only by free and fair elections, but also by the rule of law, a separation of powers, and the protection of basic liberties of speech, assembly, religion, and property." If a nation is set on establishing a democracy, then it needs to have liberalism. "With time," says Zakaria, "constitutional liberalism led to democracy, which led to further liberty," and so on.[24] This cycle of freedoms is a perpetual process in a democracy. Is Iraq even close to recognizing those freedoms?

The coalition, and therefore the Iraqi government, has defined as a goal the creation of a lasting and genuine democracy in Iraq. One of the primary missions of the coalition is to support that goal. The skill of our military is to win battles, however, and the tasks associated with building a democracy and reshaping a political culture like the Islamic state in Iraq may be beyond its means and abilities.

As Ambassador Ryan Crocker noted in his September 2007 address to Congress:

> [The Iraqis are not] simply grappling with the issue of who rules Iraq, but they're asking what kind of country Iraq will be, how it will be governed, and how Iraqis will share power and resources among each other. . . . Some of the more promising political developments at the national level are neither measured in benchmarks, nor visible to those far from Baghdad. For instance, there is a budding debate about federalism among Iraq's leaders and importantly within the Sunni community. Those living in places like Anbar and Salahuddin are beginning to realize how localities' having more of a say in daily decision-making will empower their communities. No longer is an all-powerful Baghdad seen as the panacea to Iraq's problems. This thinking is nascent, but it is ultimately critical to the evolution of a common vision among Iraq's leaders.[25]

Can we establish a democracy in Iraq when the country itself cannot determine how it wants to be governed? Or is this perhaps the most fertile time to make such a decision?

Merely holding elections doesn't equate to developing a democratic state. Nevertheless, one of the most important objectives we can seek to accomplish is to hold provincial elections whose results will ensure that the Council of Representatives clearly represents Iraq's eighteen provinces, not just the multiple religious-based party affiliations. For this to occur, immediate assignment of the COR members to geographic locations is needed. At present, there is no affiliation between the geographic location of citizens and their elected representatives. If an Iraqi demanded to see his or her congressman over a point of contention or concern, that representative doesn't exist.

The three-branch system offered as the model for Iraq is dependent on the legislative representation. If this were developed to support the new government, it could be a powerful driving factor toward the security and stability of Iraq. As Zakaria states, constitutional liberalism in a democracy hinges partly on the power of representation in government.[26] Without it, the potential for a liberal democracy decreases.

Not only must the constitution give power back to the people, but the legislative branch must also allow them to have a voice, a veto, and a vote as laws are enacted. Currently, members of the Council of Representatives are appointed by their particular parties, through the general election, to form the legislative branch of the Iraqi government. Again, there is no connection between the people and their representation. The delay in holding district or provincial elections has created a void that clearly denies the people's ability to speak through their COR.[27] Establishing provincial elections is only a small step toward achieving victory in Iraq, but it will give the Iraqi people a voice in their government along provincial lines rather than tribal or party lines and will set the country on a path toward a true democracy.

If a democracy is a definitive requirement for Iraq, then major changes would have to occur, including making, as Larry Diamond says in *Squandered Victory,* "a political accommodation with the bulk of the Sunni population that feels marginalized from the emerging political order."[28] This can be achieved only by the establishment of provincial elections.

Bottom line: Provincial elections should be held as soon as possible. We need to publicly recognize the COR as a means for the people to have their voices heard. As Ambassador Crocker stated during his congressional testimony in September 2007, "With provincial powers, Iraqis are grappling with very serious questions about what the right balance between the center and the periphery is for Iraq. Some see the devolution of power to regions and provinces as being the best insurance against the rise of a future tyrannical figure in Baghdad. Others see Iraq with its complex demographics as in need of a strong central authority."[29] Provincial elections will give the Iraqis an opportunity to stake their claims.

When asked in February 2004 what type of government they wanted, Larry Diamond reports, "86 percent of Iraqis polled approved of democracy, but 81 percent also endorsed having a single strong leader, and 53 percent support government made up mainly of religious leaders. When asked to choose between democracy, a strong leader 'for life,' and an Islamic state, half chose democracy and half one of the two authoritarian options."[30]

Before Iraq can become a democratic state, however, it must first become a state, which establishes a monopoly over the means of violence.[31] To do this requires strong Iraqi Security Forces answering to the state.

Bottom line: In order for Iraq to eventually become a legitimate democracy, much change must occur. Essential to this development is a change in Iraqi leadership. A legitimate democracy will not occur without a strong leader, but it is most important that he not be a Saddam in sheep's clothing.[32] The greater challenge now becomes who should lead this country, for the necessity of Iraqi autonomy becomes greater and greater as time unfolds.

Ambassador Crocker also briefly addressed Iraq's leadership challenges:

Saddam Hussein ruled without mercy, not hesitating to use lethal force and torture against even those in his inner circle. His genocidal campaign against the Kurds and savagery toward southern Shia are well known. But he also used

violence and intimidation as tools in the complete decon-
struction of Iraqi society. No organization or institution survived that was not linked in some way to regime protection.
He created a pervasive climate of fear in which even family
members were afraid to talk to one another. This is the legacy
that Iraqis had as their history when Saddam's statue came
down on April 9, 2003. No Nelson Mandela existed to
emerge on the national political scene. Anyone with his leadership talents would not have survived.[33]

Assisting Iraq in finding the right leader for all parties has been
fraught with challenges over the past five years. The Bush administration's preferred candidate in the early days was the nominee of the
Supreme Council for the Islamic Revolution in Iraq (SCIRI), Adel
Abdul Mehdi, who was well liked by the Kurds and generally
accepted by the Sunni Arabs in the COR.[34] As we've seen in our
own political leadership, operating in a democracy is difficult at best
without partisan buy-in from all involved. The Sunni-Shiite power
brokering has been defined as the single greatest challenge in this
political struggle. Why then would we not back a Shiite who has
Sunni support?

In a fledgling democracy, it takes time for a leader to rise to the
occasion. Democracy itself takes time, labor, commitment, and sometimes the willingness to fight against the forces of the past.[35] As Ryan
Crocker said in his opening remarks to Congress:

There will be no single moment at which we can claim
victory. Any turning point will likely only be recognized in
retrospect. This is a sober assessment, but it should not be a
disheartening one. I have found it helpful during my time in
Iraq to reflect on our own history. At many points in our early
years, our survival as a nation was questionable. Our efforts to
build the institutions of government were not always successful in the first instance, and tough issues such as slavery,

universal suffrage, civil rights and states' rights were resolved only after acrimonious debate and sometimes violence.[36]

Ousting Saddam Hussein was relatively straightforward; finding a leader who can unite Iraqis and move the country ahead is much more complex.

DEVELOPING THE IRAQI SECURITY FORCES

Jay Garner had a plan to bring the Iraqi Army back. "I'd brief the President on it. . . . Abizaid was all for it. Tommy Franks, McKiernan . . . beat me up every day, saying, 'When are you going to get the army back?' Even the Saudi Arabian ambassador to the U.S., Prince Bandar bin Sultan, strongly suggested to the U.S. that it find a way to keep together some remnant of the Iraqi military."[37] Garner wanted to use the likes of U.S. contractors to train the Iraqi Army, but with the dissolution order given by Bremer just weeks later, that plan went to the winds. Now that the Iraqi Security Forces are reestablished and training plans are developed, partnership will be the key to success. Coalition forces have to work hand in hand with the ISF in order for the plan to turn over the nation's security to them to work. This means that the United States has to stay forward-deployed and away from the large forward operating bases (FOBs) that it's used in the past.

Between 2003 and 2007, three major directives have caused the surge of coalition forces to and from large contingency bases. "Get out of the cities, the palaces, and towns and out of sight" was the guidance in 2004. "Close the FOBs following an established 100 day model" was the edict in 2006. "Live amongst the people and the ISF" was determined as the course of action in 2007. Today the coalition is following counterinsurgency doctrine as outlined by both history and the school of thought captured by General Petraeus in *FM 3-24*.

Bottom line: Immersion in the populace is the solution, for it has proven to be successful in the short term.[38]

There is no doubt that the ticket out of Iraq for the U.S.-led coalition is to help the Iraqi Security Forces reach the point where they can assume with some credibility the responsibility of securing Iraq. Most would argue that this solution is already known, but many, if not most, of those involved don't follow this premise. Time and time again, the coalition has come to the rescue if there were indications that an Iraqi Security Forces mission, for instance, may be going awry.

Bottom line: Our military needs to have the restraint and discipline not to interfere. We must realize that if the Iraqis stand their post, then they are achieving some level of success. The coalition has to stop tactically intervening and allow the Iraqi forces to learn through experience.

Although "the natural tendency is to build forces in our own image, with the aim of eventually handing them our role," this will not allow the ISF to develop into an entity capable of securing Iraq on its own. "Instead, it must be made clear that the local indigenous forces need to mirror the enemy's capabilities, and seek to supplant the insurgent's role." The MNF-I strategist, retired Australian lieutenant colonel David Kilcullen, includes this as one of the twenty-eight fundamentals of company-level counterinsurgency for all junior leaders to read before planning to deploy to the Iraq theater.[39]

Bottom line: The main effort guiding all lines of operation across Iraq has to be spending the time and effort in developing and training the ISF. The readiness of the ISF must be the common theme throughout all discussions for achieving victory in Iraq, and it must be instilled in all military leaders in the theater, as well as our politicians. This has been mentioned by squad leaders on the ground, in congressional testimonies, and in the recent 152-page independent report from the commission headed by the retired U.S. Marine Corps general James Jones. In the report, Jones tells the Senate Armed Services Committee that the United States should lighten its military footprint in Iraq to counter its image of an occupying force. He also recommends "giving the Iraqi Army—which is showing signs of real progress despite its limited operational effectiveness—a greater profile in security patrols, but with U.S. troops still playing a substantial support role."[40]

STAYING THE COURSE

Let's get over it: *There is no quick fix* for Iraq, or any insurgency for that matter. It takes time for a counterinsurgency to work. One of the challenges we face is that this particular counterinsurgency started well after the actual ground war began. The insurgency gained ground in late 2003, and the coalition has been working on developing potential solutions to counter it ever since. The war has become a series of twelve- to fifteen-month engagements for those in the army, leaving many wondering why the rotation of fresh forces to and from theater annually is not providing a decisive edge.

The executive officer for the 3rd Brigade, 101st Airborne Division (Rakkasans), in southwest Baghdad, Lt. Col. J. B. Becker, got to the root of the problem when he asked, "When was the last time in history that a victory was won by the side that rotated forces to and from the battlefield?" Perhaps we should just put a competent force on the ground that stays until benchmarks are met. Nations traditionally haven't done well in wars where rotating forces has been the method to generate combat power in a fight. In fact, we would be hard-pressed to identify a single conflict that was won by rotating combat power to and from the fray on a periodic basis with hopes of winning the war.

We also need to develop some perspective. Whereas the Sunnis and Shiites have been at odds for thirteen centuries, our nation is accustomed to wars that have resolved in a relatively brief time, which have "clouded our understanding of the longer, great tides of history."[41] Additionally, in an age of fast food and video games, it is difficult for our society to have the patience to allow processes to take their course.

Dr. Roby Barrett's 350-year-old applecart analogy speaks of our society's belief that centuries of ingrained attitudes could be changed overnight by wielding a new-age weapon system. But once we removed the only obstacle to Iranian dominance in the region, a secular Baathist government in Iraq, we set up a power struggle that is difficult to get our arms around at this point.[42]

Bottom line: We need to put a capable force in Iraq, commit all resources available to that force, and leave it there until the job is done. Stop piecemealing combat units to and from the theater and mission rehearsal exercises, and stop "salami slicing" the resources. Commit all that we have now to the fight. It may not be a popular decision in some political circles, but in the end, it's the most efficient and effective solution for our soldiers in the fight, the people of Iraq, and perhaps most important, the global issue of stability in the Middle East.

DETERMINING WHEN TO TRANSITION BATTLESPACE

Once it has been decided that a headquartered force would remain in place until success has been achieved, the question becomes how soon can we transition parts of Iraq to the control of the Iraqi Security Forces? In order to achieve this—which we believe will lead to victory—certain factors must be obtained. First, elections must take place so that the government, from the national to the local level, can provide for its people. Second, the government of Iraq needs to take responsibility for the thousands of volunteers standing watch over their tribal neighborhoods. Finally, a controlled transition plan for transferring operating bases to a "capable" Iraqi Army (working outside the urban areas) and a "functional" police force that can control the cities must be methodically structured and mutually supported by both the Iraqis and the coalition.

This effort is not unprecedented. In 2005–06, Maj. Gen. Tom Turner's MND-N transitioned dozens of patrol bases, decreasing its footprint from thirty-five to ten in less than one year. Arguably, this transition effort was premature, for the rest of the MNC-I had not followed suit. Regardless, the process and concept existed. Blueprints are in place for how coalition headquarters would maintain a superimposing footprint while moving coalition troop formations out and Iraqi units in; this can be executed once the conditions are set. Notable here is the need for BCT and battalion headquarters to provide oversight as the Iraqis take the lead.

We must keep in mind, however, that once U.S. forces are pulled from Iraq, there would be enormous domestic opposition within our country against going back in for any reason, such as a threat of weapons of mass destruction or a terrorist cell safe haven.[44] Therefore, we should be as certain as possible that the withdrawal not only is prudent, but also will be permanent.

Bottom line: The security is such that in some areas of Iraq, large formations of coalition forces can begin the piecemeal plan that recognizes that certain elements (headquarters, command structures, logistical capacity, and air assets) should remain in place to support the ISF as it forges on to its next level of mission capability. The true bottom line is that the coalition can now work hard to transition from "leading from the front" to "leading from behind."

ESTABLISHING A KURDISH GATEWAY

Although the search for a solution is difficult at best, a process of elimination can be done. A timeline without benchmarks is not a preferred course of action, nor is withdrawing hastily, as if the proverbial plug were pulled. Staying the course without an added emphasis on specified measures of success also is not a reasonable solution.

Democratic Sen. Joseph Biden of Delaware, among so many others, has said, perhaps wishing to end all discussion on the topic, "Failure is not an option."[45] But unfortunately, some leading congressmen honestly believe that "if American troops begin to leave and the remaining forces assume a more limited role . . . it will galvanize the Iraqi government to assume more responsibility for securing and rebuilding Iraq."[46] Kenneth M. Pollack, an expert at the Brookings Institution who served on the staff of the National Security Council during the Clinton administration, argues the counterpoint, stating that a push for troop reductions would backfire by contributing to the disorder in Iraq: "If we start pulling out troops and the violence gets worse and the control of the militias increase and people become confirmed in their suspicion that the United States is not going to be there to prevent civil war, they are going to start making decisions today to prepare for the eventuality of civil war tomorrow. That is how civil wars start."[47]

On July 23, 2007, the Democratic presidential candidates faced questions directly from voters in the first CNN/YouTube debate. A politically charged question for all candidates was "How do we pull out of Iraq now?" Sen. Barack Obama of Illinois answered: "Look, I opposed this war from the start. Because I anticipated that we would be creating the kind of sectarian violence that we've seen and that it would distract us from the War on Terror." He finished his statement by saying, "I think we can be as careful getting out as we were careless getting in. But we have to send a clear message to the Iraqi government as well as to the surrounding neighbors that there is no military solution to the problems that we face in Iraq." Obama, now the Democratic nominee, also believes that if we didn't have a plan to get out before we planned to "get in," then we shouldn't have gone in the first place. This is what war termination strategists have struggled with for centuries, ever since Clausewitz put pen to paper. But we should ask ourselves whether that strategy is ever supportable.

Biden had a different answer to the same question: "You know we can't just pull out now. . . . The truth of the matter is: If we started today, it would take one year, one year to get 160,000 troops physically out of Iraq; logistically . . . you cannot pull out of Iraq without the follow-on that's been projected here, unless you have a political solution." He then went on to explain that partitioning the state of Iraq may be the only solution: "Separate the parties; give them jurisdiction in their own areas; have a decentralized government, a federal system. No central government will work."[48]

There is some merit to Biden's comments about partitioning the state of Iraq. But instead of dividing the country into thirds as many have suggested—Kurdish north, Sunni central, and Shia south—why not reinforce successes like those found in the Kurdish regions with their *peshmerga* forces? By tacitly promoting Kurdistan to investors as the safe part of Iraq, it could become the gateway for the rest of the country for the delivery of services such as education, policing, and health care.[49] Although this effort would be controversial in some camps, the administration could execute the plan with the caveat that it would not enter into discussions about Kurdish independence—a sensitive topic not only for the current Iraqi government, but also for Turkey and Syria, which oppose an independent Kurdistan.

Bottom line: Partitioning the nation-state of Iraq has its merits. If we want the country of Iraq to flourish economically, however, then we need to allow the Kurdish north to become a gateway for military strength and basic services. Will it cause a political divide? Yes, but most would argue that the divisiveness already exists, and "a two-way split into Arab Iraq and Kurdistan is much more likely in the near future than a three-way split into Kurdistan, a Sunni state, and a Shiite south."[50]

ASSESSING THE BENCHMARKS

There has been much discussion on timelines with benchmarks, timelines with measures of effectiveness and performance, and timelines without either. What has not been described in any detail thus far are those benchmarks being addressed today as essential for achieving victory.

In July 2007, an assessment of the Iraqi situation left us with an understanding that there were clearly two camps: one willing to define the measures of success to achieve victory, and the other willing to develop benchmarks to determine when we should withdraw from Iraq. The *Initial Benchmark Assessment Report* offered a preliminary review of security, political, and economic progress in Iraq. When the benchmarks were defined in July 2007, the report showed that Iraqis were making good progress toward meeting eight of eighteen benchmarks set by Congress.[51]

In September 2007, a written report outlining both Petraeus's and Crocker's assessments of these benchmarks was released. This report was far more telling, because it reflected the impact of the 30,000-troop surge in Iraq. It marked a critical fork in the road, as its contents would quite possibly provide the path to be taken by the

United States as it defined its role for the coalition in Iraq for the coming years. The report included the following benchmarks and their subsequent evaluations, satisfactory, unsatisfactory, or mixed:

1. Forming a Constitutional Review Committee and then completing the constitutional review. Satisfactory.

2. Enacting and implementing legislation on debaathification. Unsatisfactory.

3. Enacting and implementing legislation to ensure the equitable distribution of hydrocarbon resources to the people of Iraq without regard to the sect or ethnicity of recipients, and enacting and implementing legislation to ensure that the energy resources of Iraq benefit Sunni Arabs, Shia Arabs, Kurds, and other Iraqi citizens in an equitable manner. Unsatisfactory.

4. Enacting and implementing legislation on procedures to form semiautonomous regions. Satisfactory.

5. Enacting and implementing legislation establishing an Independent High Electoral Commission, provincial elections law, provincial council authorities, and a date for provincial elections. Mixed.

6. Enacting and implementing legislation addressing amnesty. Mixed.

7. Enacting and implementing legislation establishing a strong militia disarmament program to ensure that such security forces are accountable only to the central government and loyal to the constitution of Iraq. Unsatisfactory.

8. Establishing supporting political, media, economic, and services committees in support of the Baghdad Security Plan. Satisfactory.

9. Providing three trained and ready Iraqi brigades to support Baghdad operations. Satisfactory.

10. Providing Iraqi commanders with all authorities to execute this plan and to make tactical and operational decisions, in consultation with U.S commanders, without political inter-

vention, to include the authority to pursue all extremists, including Sunni insurgents and Shiite militias. Unsatisfactory.

11. Ensuring that the Iraqi Security Forces are providing even-handed enforcement of the law. Unsatisfactory.

12. Ensuring that, as Prime Minister Maliki said, "The Baghdad security plan will not provide a safe haven for any outlaws, regardless of [their] sectarian or political affiliation." Satisfactory.

13. Reducing the level of sectarian violence in Iraq and eliminating militia control of local security. Unsatisfactory.

14. Establishing all of the planned joint security stations in neighborhoods across Baghdad. Satisfactory.

15. Increasing the number of Iraqi Security Forces units capable of operating independently. Unsatisfactory.

16. Ensuring that the rights of minority political parties in the Iraqi legislature are protected. Satisfactory.

17. Allocating and spending $10 billion in Iraqi revenues for reconstruction projects, including delivery of essential services, on an equitable basis. Satisfactory.

18. Ensuring that Iraq's political authorities are not undermining or making false accusations against members of the Iraqi Security Forces. Unsatisfactory.[52]

Weeks before the September 2007 report, congressional leaders released their own report trumping the expectation of success for Petraeus. The congressional assessment of the surge made a huge splash in Washington when the Government Accounting Office (GAO) said Iraq had met only three out of eighteen established benchmarks for success.[53]

The White House, in turn, said that the GAO report "was 'unhelpful' because it set the bar for success so high that it was almost guaranteed to find failure," while the Pentagon said it portrayed the situation in "only in 'blacks and whites' instead of considering some of the 'gray' areas of progress." Striking a harsher tone, the Associated Press said the report "drew fierce objections from the White House and provided fresh ammunition for Democrats who want to bring troops home."[54] No surprises, really, as benchmarks are set with a clear understanding that assessments will drive the decision on how to draw down our forces. Also of no surprise was the political wrangling, which will continue as the 2008 elections near.

It's important to note that the assessments of the benchmarks aren't necessarily binary in their "score." White House spokesman Tony Snow put it well: "The standard that is set by the legislation is to assess whether a benchmark has been met. . . . It's no secret that many of the benchmarks have not been met. What is significant is that there is progress towards a great number of them."[55]

An example of progress, but not full achievement, is in limiting the levels of violence across Iraq. Expecting no violence is not only unreasonable, but also unnecessary. A certain level of Darwinism is acceptable whenever a power brokerage is newly formed. To expect violence to end in Iraq is not realistic.

Bottom line: Leaders need to establish achievable and sensible benchmarks in their areas, nested with those defined by the president, Congress, and senior military leaders. For example, the measure of success in achieving victory is not how many enemy forces we can kill, but how many pro-Iraqi security forces stand their posts.

FOLLOWING THE MULTI-NATIONAL FORCE-IRAQ COMMANDER'S GUIDANCE

All reasonable suggestions for potential military courses of action need to be considered within the framework of the Multi-National Force-Iraq (MNF-I) commander David Petraeus's guidance.

Both Petraeus and the MNC-I commander, Lt. Gen. Ray Odierno and Odierno's successor, Lt. Gen. Lloyd Austin, realized in the late spring of 2007 that the war in Iraq had reached a critical stage. As he assumed command in April 2007, General Petraeus directed that "coalition and Iraqi forces work together to create security improvements and, in doing so, provide Iraqi leaders with the time and space to tackle the tough political issues that must be resolved in order to achieve national reconciliation and build a secure and stable Iraq."[56]

Petraeus was very clear in his approach. Upon taking command, he changed the focus of military policy to securing the Iraqi people—clearly an indication that the author of modern counterinsurgency doctrine was going to follow the age-old counterinsurgency principle that the population was, in fact, the prize.

The MNF-I initial main effort, as it had been at the tail end of the Casey command, was to secure the capital city of Baghdad, with a follow-on mission to later expand to other areas in Iraq. Effectively securing the Iraqi people, in Baghdad and throughout the rest of the country, would require close coordination with Iraqi leaders; this was paramount to the Petraeus plan. The MNF-I commander saw this focus as being so important that he provided a list of ten points that would serve as a framework for key requirements in the initial months of the Petraeus-Odierno command. Ambassador Ryan Crocker was also included in the decision-making process in the early summer of 2007, an emphasis ignored to a degree during the initial Sanchez-Bremer era.

When issuing these directives, Petraeus asked subordinate commanders to internalize each, think through how it would be implemented, and operationalize it so that the coalition could visibly improve security. He concluded by stating that "business as usual" would not be good enough and complacency was a killer in this fight. "A sense of urgency and good situational awareness will also be critical. Troopers on the spot, and their immediate instinctive reactions, will win or lose the perception battle at the local level. Everything we do supports and enables this battle of perceptions, locally here in Iraq and also in the global audience."[57]

Following are the directives that served as the MNF-I commander's intent for the forces in Iraq starting in the spring of 2007:

1. Secure the people where they sleep. Population security is our primary mission. And achieving population security promises to be an extremely long-term endeavor—

a marathon, not a sprint—so focusing on this mission now is essential. Most extra-judicial killings occur at night and in people's homes, while most spectacular terrorist attacks occur during the day, where people shop, work and play—anywhere they gather publicly. These key areas must be secured. Once secured, an area cannot be abandoned; it must be permanently controlled and protected, 24 hours a day, or else the enemy will re-infiltrate and kill or intimidate those who have supported us. This protection must be kept up until the area can be effectively garrisoned and controlled by Iraqi police (ideally from the area being secured) and other security services. We can't be everywhere—therefore you must assess your AOR [area of responsibility], identify priority areas, work to secure them first, and then expand into other areas.

2. Give the people justice and honor. We think in terms of democracy and human rights. Iraqis think in terms of justice and honor. Whenever possible, help Iraqis to retain or regain their honor. Treat Iraqis with genuine, not patronizing, dignity and respect; that will win friends and discredit enemies. You must act quickly and publicly to deal with complaints and abuses. Never allow an injustice to stand unaddressed; never walk away from a local Iraqi who believes he or she has been unjustly treated. Second only to security, bringing justice to the people and restoring their honor is the key task.

3. Integrate civilian/military efforts—this is an inter-agency, combined arms fight. Embedded Provincial Reconstruction Teams [PRTs] now operate directly alongside military units, adding new capabilities, skills, and funds to our counterinsurgency effort. PRTs bring political and economic expertise to the brigade and regimental combat teams with whom they serve, operate under

force protection rules that allow them to accompany our military forces on operations, and conduct extended engagement with local communities. In order to exploit military and civilian capabilities to their fullest potential, we must fully integrate our civilian partners into all aspects of our operations—from inception through execution. Close working relationships, mutual respect, and personal interaction between BCT/RCT commanders and PRT Team Leaders are critical to achieving "interagency combined arms."

4. Get out and walk—move mounted, work dismounted. Vehicles like the up-armored HMMWV insulate us from the Iraqi people we are securing, limit our situational awareness, and drastically reduce the number of Soldiers able to dismount. Furthermore, they make us predictable as they often force us to move slowly on set routes. Meanwhile, an underbelly attack by an IED or an EFP [explosively formed penetrator] may still damage the vehicle heavily—so we gain little in safety, but sacrifice much in effectiveness. HMMWVs are necessary for traveling to a patrol area or for overwatch, heavy equipment transportation, and communications. But they are not squad cars. Stop by, don't drive by. Patrol on foot to gain and maintain contact with the population and the enemy.

5. We are in a fight for intelligence—all the time. Intelligence is not a "product" given to commanders by higher headquarters, but rather something we gather ourselves, through our own operations. Tactical reporting, from civilian and military agencies, is essential: there are thousands of eyes out in your area—all must act as scouts, know what to look for, and be trained and ready to report it. Also, units should deploy analytical capacity as far forward as possible, so that the analyst is close—in

time and space—to the commander he supports. Our presence, living alongside the people, will turn on a "fire-hose" of unsolicited tips about the enemy. Units must be prepared to receive this flood of information. Intelligence staffs and commanders must learn how to sort through reports, separating the plausible from the fictitious, integrating the reports with other forms of intelligence, and finally recognizing and exploiting a "break" into the enemy network. Once you make a break, stay on it until it pays off. Most actionable intelligence will come from locally produced HUMINT, tactical reporting, follow-up of IED and sniper attacks, detainee interrogations, and SIGINT. Work with what you have.

6. Every unit must advise their ISF partners. Joint Security Stations and Combat Outposts have put coalition and Iraqi forces shoulder-to-shoulder throughout the battle-space. Regular MiTTs [military transition team] can't be everywhere, so units must help the MiTTs enforce ISF standards, enable performance, and monitor for abuses and inefficiencies. Any coalition unit working with ISF will be studied, emulated and copied—for better or worse. Therefore we must always set the example. Regardless of mission, any coalition unit operating alongside ISF is performing a mentoring, training, and example-setting role.

7. Include ISF in your operations at the lowest possible level. As foreigners, coalition forces lack language capacity, situational and cultural awareness, and a "feel" for what is normal in the environment. ISF possess all these abilities, but lack the combat power of coalition forces. Working together, with the ISF and the local populace, we are an extremely powerful combination; working unilaterally, we can be defeated piecemeal. Therefore,

units should operate with an ISF presence at the lowest feasible tactical level—ideally, at squad or platoon level. And when operating together, you must plan, sequence, and conduct operations together with local Iraqi commanders right from the outset. Units should build a genuine, field-based partnership with local ISF units: move, live, work, and fight together.

8. Look beyond the IED—get the network that placed it. Every IED provides a window into the network that placed it. If properly exploited, this window can be used to damage and roll back that network, thus ultimately defeating the threat. Of all key locations, the actual IED site is least important. Instead, units should look for early warning observation posts, firing and assembly points, and infiltration/exfiltration routes. Commanders should map IED patterns and use friendly convoy movement to trigger enemy action, having first pre-positioned SIG-INT and reconnaissance assets to identify IED teams moving into position, and to listen for communications between OPs [observation posts] and firing teams. Lastly, use UAVs [unmanned aerial vehicles] to trace enemy firing teams back to caches and assembly areas. Over time, units that adopt a pro-active approach to IEDs will degrade enemy networks and push back the IED threat in their area. This will ultimately save more lives than a purely reactive approach.

9. Be first with the truth. Public Affairs Officers [PAOs] and Information Operations organizations can help manage the message and set general themes. But what Soldiers say and do speaks louder than what PAOs say; the trooper on the spot has a thousand daily interactions with Iraqis and with the global audience via the news media. While encouraging spontaneity, commanders should also communicate key messages down to the

individual level, so that soldiers know what message to convey in interactions with the population and the media. When communicating, speed is critical—minutes and hours matter—and we should remember to communicate to the local (Arabic/Iraqi) audience first—the U.S./global audience can follow. Tell the truth, stay in your lane, and get the message out fast. Be forthright and never allow an enemy lie to stand unchallenged. Require accuracy, adequate context, and proper characterization from the media.

10. Make the people choose. Some in the Iraqi civilian population want to "sit on the fence" and avoid having to choose between the insurgents and the government. They attempt to protect themselves by supporting the strongest local power; however, this makes them vulnerable to enemy intimidation. We must get the Iraqi populace off the fence—and on the side of the Iraqi government. To do this, we must first persuade the population to choose to support the government. Having done this, we must make this choice irrevocable by having the citizens publicly support government programs or otherwise declare their allegiance. Once the population has chosen to support the government, they will become vulnerable to the insurgents were we to leave. So, together with the ISF, we must protect the population, where they live. People in Iraq exercise choice collectively, not just individually; win over local leaders to encourage the community to shift to the side of the new Iraq.[58]

As we finish this manuscript, the long-awaited written assessment of the situation in Iraq by Petraeus and Crocker was unveiled. We believe that the president will choose to stay the course but allow the surge forces from the spring of 2007 to go unfilled in 2008. The key political event in the near term is obviously the 2008 national elections, which will set the tone for the years to come.

Regardless, in the aftermath of the MNF-I report, we get a sense that much analysis has in fact been accomplished, and that the inclusion of the senior civilian diplomat in theater, Ambassador Ryan Crocker, in the decision-making process is indeed a welcome sign.

"If there is one word I would use to sum up the atmosphere in Iraq—on the streets, in the countryside, in the neighborhoods and at the national level—that word would be fear," Crocker said. "For Iraq to move forward at any level, that fear is going to have to be replaced with some level of trust and confidence and that is what the effort at the national level is about." Crocker then downplayed the importance of meeting major reforms right away and said that less ambitious goals, such as restoring electricity to a neighborhood, could be just as beneficial. He also pointed toward political headway being made at the local level and said that agreements there might inspire further cooperation among sects. The much-cited benchmarks "do not serve as reliable measures of everything that is important—Iraqi attitudes toward each other and their willingness to work toward political reconciliation." Crocker also warned against a withdrawal of U.S. troops, contending that such a move could increase sectarian attacks and create a "comfortable operating environment" for Al Qaeda.[59]

On the military front, Petraeus told members of Congress in a private meeting that he had seen some "tactical momentum" since infusing Baghdad with additional U.S. soldiers. That infusion appears, at this point, to be the effort by Maj. Gen. Rick Lynch's Task Force Marne to reconcile the locals into supporting a plan to augment local security forces. Petraeus's deputy in Iraq, Lt. Gen. Raymond Odierno, later told reporters he would need beyond September to tell whether improvements represented long-term trends. "In order to do a good assessment I need at least until November," he said.[60] In the end, the assessments presented in both the fall of 2007 and spring of 2008 confirmed the stance we have taken thus far in this book: reduce the enemy's capability to fight while winning over the populace and improving the capabilities of the ISF.

FACILITATING RECONCILIATION

Reconciliation and all that is associated with it may be the most talked-about success story in recent headlines. Above all other actions, the effort toward reconciliation—of not only the disenfranchised Sunnis, but also the local populace regardless of religion—appears to be the most effective method in achieving security in Iraq and is bringing a marked advantage to the coalition.

In a June 24, 2007, unclassified document to the armed forces of MNC-I, Odierno formally cites the process that commanders such as MacFarland and Kershaw have used with success since the spring of 2006. As defined by Odierno, reconciliation "means getting Iraqis to set aside their sectarian differences and focus on the future of free Iraq. The success of Iraq's young democracy depends upon this process." He goes on to state that "reconciliation is an Iraqi process. There is a day in the future when Coalition forces will step back. When that day arrives, we must have adequately prepared this Nation to function as a civil society free from the terror of extremists." The goal, he writes, "is an improved level of stability" in the longer term, a "self-reliant Iraq which is free from terror and an engine for regional economic growth."

Odierno clearly believes that "reconciliation is the key catalyst" for this end state and could be achieved by successfully accomplishing four key tasks that he directed his subordinate division commanders to complete:

1. Influence key leaders and communicators to leverage their positions in order to stop attacks against coalition forces and Iraqi Security Forces.
2. Facilitate peace arbitration between key leaders and communicators of groups that are attacking one another.
3. Influence key leaders and communicators to actively resist Al Qaeda in Iraq.
4. Engage all key leaders and communicators willing to dialogue with CF, ISF, and the government of Iraq.[61]

In a follow-on document, Odierno concluded that reconciliation is local and there is no one-size-fits-all solution set.[62]

Ambassador Crocker also commented on reconciliation during the September 2007 address to Congress: "The government, without much public fanfare, has contacted thousands of members of the former Iraqi army offering them retirement, return to the military, or public sector employment. So without the proclamation of a general amnesty, we see provisional immunity being granted, and we see de-Baathification reform in advance of national legislation. In both instances, the seeds of reconciliation are being planted."[63]

With the army's senior leadership heading the effort for reconciliation in Iraq, there is great hope for capitalizing on the success achieved thus far.

Bottom line: Reconciliation supports the goal of bringing a sense of harmony to Iraq. This fight is one of persuasion. The insurgent attempts to persuade the populace that the new government and what it represents are not in their best interests, and that the occupying forces are the root of the problem. Conversely, we are trying to persuade the populace that the insurgents are there for their own ideological interests and not the interests of the Iraqis, and that the populace has the ultimate impact on the success of operations and securing their freedoms. To win this fight, we must maintain contact with the populace, encouraging the influential Iraqi leaders. This is not primarily a kinetic battle, but a battle of influence. Therefore, commanders on the ground must use all the tools available to facilitate reconciliation with all disenfranchised Iraqis and encourage them to become integrated into legitimate governmental institutions.

HAVING THE RIGHT LEADERS IN PLACE
Thus far, we have been generally critical, at least indirectly, toward the architects of this fight. It is clear, however, that the right leaders are in place now, at the defining moment. The point of culmination, both

nationally and internationally, seems to have arrived in the spring of 2007. Political discussions were heated, and doubts were rising about the Iraqi government's contributions, or lack thereof. The arrival of General Petraeus, however, offered an opportunity to take a fresh look at the fight in Iraq.

Fortunately for the coalition and our nation, along with a strong leader at the strategic and operational levels, we also had a confident and competent senior commander at the tactical level. Starting in 2008, Lt. Gen. Lloyd Austin's XVIII Airborne Corps took the lead as the command element for MNC-I. Lt. Gen. Ray Odierno was the lead for MNC-I from 2007 to 2008, and before him was the incoming Vice Chief of Staff of the Army, Lt. Gen. Peter Chiarelli, preceded by the equally intelligent and charismatic Lt. Gen. J. R. Vines, who brilliantly commanded MNC-I from 2005 to 2006. Much like General Petraeus and Gen. George Casey, the MNC-I commanders had trust and confidence in their subordinate commanders.

Although many senior leaders in Iraq did not have relevant counterinsurgency experience, this was not the case when it came to the number one and two men in Iraq in 2007 and 2008. Both were division commanders in Operation Iraqi Freedom 1, the ground war to topple Saddam Hussein, and both are soldiers' soldiers who lead from the front. Their earlier experiences in Iraq, as well as the relationships established in their previous tours, proved to be combat multipliers under their leadership.

Most of the leaders and the majority of the soldiers under their command are on their third or fourth deployment since 9/11. Almost 50 percent of the soldiers of the 3rd Brigade, 101st Airborne Division (Air Assault), which controls the southwest portion of Baghdad, are on their fourth tour since the war began. Gen. David Petraeus has been deployed four out of five years since the beginning of the war. The number-two man from MND-C for 2007 to 2008, Brig. Gen. Jim Huggins, is arguably the single most deployed officer in our army, having served in multiple rotations in Afghanistan and Iraq as well as in numerous combat deployments before the War on Terrorism began. Most of the current one-star generals were brigade commanders in combat, and many of the subordinate commanders and command sergeants major (CSMs) were junior commanders and CSMs in the early stages of this war.

Bottom line: Our leaders and soldiers have gained an immeasurable amount of combat experience in this war. The rash of articles criticizing our senior officer corps misses the mark. Many of our senior officers have counterinsurgency experience, perhaps more than ever before in our all-volunteer army. We must continue to have trust and confidence in our leaders both up and down the chain of command as they remain confident in and trustworthy to their men and women in their command. They have proven in combat that they know what to do and can accomplish the mission.

EVALUATING THE COUNTERINSURGENCY FRAMEWORK

As we progress through our proposed solutions to this counterinsurgency effort, let's take a hard look at the framework itself and focus on some areas that in the past have been successful and unsuccessful in supporting it.

Areas that have been successful:

- Emphasizing intelligence sharing across the coalition and ISF and using intelligence to drive operations
- Focusing on the population, their needs, and security
- Establishing, then expanding, secure areas
- Isolating insurgents from the population (population control)
- Having a single authority who is a charismatic and dynamic leader at each level of command
- Using effective, pervasive psychological operations (PSYOP) campaigns
- Establishing amnesty and rehabilitation programs for insurgents
- Having the police in the lead and the military in a supporting role

- Expanding and diversifying the police force
- Reorienting conventional military forces for a counterinsurgency
- Embedding special forces and advisors with indigenous forces
- Denying insurgents sanctuaries

Areas that have been unsuccessful:
- Having a lack of combat multipliers in the form of State Department PRI experts and others (NGOs, civilian agencies) to augment the ability to train for other LOOs besides security
- Putting the priority on killing and capturing the enemy, not on engaging the population
- Having battalion-size operations as the norm
- Concentrating military units on large bases for force protection
- Having special forces focused primarily on conducting raids
- Making advisor effort a low priority in personnel assignment
- Attempting to build and train the indigenous army in the image of the U.S. Army
- Using peacetime government processes
- Having open borders, airspace, and coastlines[64]

The current counterinsurgency doctrine serves as the overarching framework for operations in Iraq. Overlaid on this framework, however, must be localized Iraqi patterns of life. Counterinsurgency operational ideas are not universally applicable. Cultural nuances must be considered by those forces both planning for and conducting counterinsurgency operations. An important question is whether it is too late to inject the Galula methodology now, or have the insurgency's roots grown so deep that trying to follow a Galula-type principle or framework would be for naught?

We believe that it's not too late, but the methodology has to be applied across the spectrum. We cannot afford to duct tape good initiatives only in areas where subordinate commanders are creative and successful, while ignoring other areas where leaders are challenged.

The plan of action has to be equitable. It appears that the right leadership at all levels is now in place, including civilian oversight by Ambassador Crocker.

The leadership team of Crocker and Petraeus continues to study the environment and make recommendations to our nation's senior leadership. The most recent recommendations, made only days before we submitted our manuscript to the publisher, included those given to the Joint Chiefs of Staff. Addressed during the September 2007 congressional testimony and titled "Security while Transitioning: from Leading to Partnering to Overwatch," the report discussed the principles of counterinsurgency doctrine and recognized the importance of developing the ISF.

In the recommendations, Petraeus reflects on the "recognition of the importance of securing the population *and* the imperative of transitioning responsibilities to Iraqi institutions and Iraqi forces as quickly as possible, but without rushing to failure." The report, he adds, "includes substantial support for the continuing development of Iraqi Security Forces. It also stresses the need to continue the counterinsurgency strategy that we have been employing, but with Iraqis gradually shouldering more of the load."[65] It is important to note the considerations Petraeus used to determine those recommendations, both operational and strategic.

Operational considerations:

- The military aspects of the surge have achieved progress and generated momentum.
- The Iraqi Security Forces have continued to grow and have slowly been shouldering more of the security burden in Iraq.
- A mission focus on either population security or transition alone will not be adequate to achieve our objectives.
- Success against Al Qaeda in Iraq and Iranian-supported militia extremists requires conventional forces as well as special operations forces.
- The security and local political situations will enable us to draw down the surge forces.

Strategic considerations:

- Political progress will take place only if sufficient security exists.
- Long-term U.S. ground force viability will benefit from force reductions as the surge runs its course.
- Regional, global, and cyberspace initiatives are critical to success.
- Iraqi leaders understandably want to assume greater sovereignty in their country, although, as they recently announced, they do desire continued presence of coalition forces in Iraq in 2008 under a new UN Security Council resolution. Following that, they want to negotiate a long-term security agreement with the United States and other nations.

Back at home in the United States, training in counterinsurgency principles continues to evolve. Although it's a significant change from training for a conventional fight, it's not a significant departure from counterinsurgency studies of the past. Like all changes, however, it took time to take root. While the operational army had to immediately adapt to this different kind of fight, it took some time for the institutional army to catch up, but it's nearly there. All of the combat training centers have transformed to support the mission rehearsal exercises preparing units to deploy to both Iraq and Afghanistan.

Of note is the Joint Readiness Training Center (JRTC), under the command of Brig. Gen. Dan Bolger, a former 101st Airborne deputy commanding general and combat veteran with the 101st and the MNSTC-I command immediately thereafter. Bolger and the commander of operations group for JRTC, Col. Kevin Owens, a seasoned Ranger Battalion combat veteran and brigade commander with the 173rd Airborne Brigade in Afghanistan, have nearly replicated the fight at these training centers by ensuring that realistic role players and forward operating bases are built into the exercise. This is a testament to the hard work by the forces command and staff under the watch of Gen. Charles "Hondo" Campbell, who now commands operationally the preponderance of all units deploying to the Middle East.

The counterinsurgency framework is further complicated by Iraq's ethnosectarian conflict and terrorist attacks, such as those by Al Qaeda in Iraq. For example, in its original *fatwas* and other statements, Al Qaeda makes no mention of Shiites, condemning only the "Crusaders" and "Jews." But Iraq changed things. Abu Mussab al-Zarqawi, the head of Al Qaeda in Mesopotamia, bore a fierce hatred for Shiites. In a February 2004 letter to Osama bin Laden, he claimed that "the danger from the Shia . . . is greater . . . than the Americans," and that "the only solution is for us to strike the religious, military and other cadres among the Shia with blow after blow until they bend to the Sunnis." If there ever had been a debate between him and bin Laden, Zarqawi won. As a result, an organization that had hoped to rally the entire Muslim world to *jihad* against the West has been dragged instead into a dirty internal war within Islam.[66]

Recognizing that the outcome of this internal fight has major implications on the coalition's success or failure in Iraq has led us to a better understanding of why the reconciliation effort works. Pitting insurgent against insurgent helps the coalition, and therefore the ISF, win over the populace.

Bottom line: It is important to follow the proven counterinsurgency principles, tailoring them to Iraq's current environment. As part of this, we should continue to embrace the "neighborhood watch" type efforts across Iraq and get the government of Iraq involved with them, perhaps establishing a portion of the government to run joint security stations to include the leaders of the local security forces.

ASSIGNING RESPONSIBILITIES

Our plan should be to fight the enemy's strategy, not his forces. If he is seeking the allegiance of a segment of the local population, then we need to co-opt the populace against him. This phenomenon is occurring with the reconciliation effort and the support from the concerned citizens groups throughout Iraq.

A team approach is necessary in order for this effort to succeed. Conventional forces have taken on more of the foreign internal defense role, or the partnership and training of indigenous forces. In the past, this has been a special forces role. The operational environment is changing, however, and the command-and-control structure must also adapt. As Zakaria says, the inclination of the military forces "is to wage conventional war against insurgents."[67] We know this is not the right focus. It is time to delineate who has corps competency for what mission instead of attempting to be all things to all people.

Ten months into this operation, there was no truly trained institution in Iraq called the Iraqi Security Forces. Our conventional forces thought early on that the special forces community would perform the training mission, officially called FID for foreign internal defense. But as noted in *FM 3-24,* "Having reversed course on so many other of Jay Garner's initiatives, Bremer and his subordinates decided to stay with one: to have the Iraqi Security Forces trained not by the Special Forces experts, but rather by defense contractors and some regular Soldiers, including some from the National Guard and the Army Reserve."[68] The defense contractor option did not prove to be successful, however, and the conventional army stepped up to fill the void. This muddled command and control, for training responsibilities added to the complexity of the issue and inevitably slowed down progress.

We're making great strides in delineating who does what to whom. As General Petraeus pointed out in his September 10, 2007, address to Congress: "Al Qaeda is certainly not defeated; however, it is off balance and we are pursuing its leaders and operators aggressively. . . . These gains against Al Qaeda are a result of the synergy of actions by: conventional forces to deny the terrorists sanctuary; intelligence, surveillance, and reconnaissance assets to find the enemy; and special operations elements to conduct targeted raids. A combination of these assets is necessary to prevent the creation of a terrorist safe haven in Iraq."[69]

Bottom line: We need to define the roles of special forces, conventional forces, and special operators. Conventional forces have been doing a little bit of everything since the war has started—direct action, foreign internal defense, security response forces for special operations missions, to name a few. Conventional forces should focus their efforts on training and partnering with the ISF while conducting operations with their partnered Iraqi units and leave the unilateral direct action up to the special elements.

KIT BAG ITEMS

The following are a few ideas and techniques that may help units deploying to the fight. We could write another entire book on lessons learned from our previous counterinsurgency deployments, but noted here are some thoughts to take away with you, whether you're a soldier preparing for deployment or a concerned citizen expanding your awareness on counterinsurgency doctrine.

First, battlefield arrangement is important. Unity of command is key to success; it is a proven principle. We have not done well with this in Iraq. If an asset or element is in a unit's battle space, that unit should own it. No longer should we allow transient forces to operate freely without the BCT commander being empowered to control their mission sets. The Joint Special Operations Command (JSOC), under Lt. Gen. Stan McChrystal, has been incredible in ensuring that its operations, many of which are "black operations," or highly classified, are worked in conjunction with the conventional force in charge of the area of operations. The JSOC may be an anomaly, however, because of increased field experience and the highly formalized senior rank structure. All others, including all forms of the transition teams, should be working for the BCT commander responsible for that battle space. Leaders at all levels have to continue to push to make this effort a reality.

Living among the people and opening smaller forward operating bases strategically established across the Iraqi countryside are the right things to do, regardless of how hard it may be for the tactical commander. If we had followed Galula's principles in the early stages of the war, the Iraqi Security Forces as well as the Iraqi people would have seen more progress across all lines of operation. The directive to follow this doctrine is universally established throughout the Iraqi theater. It has proven successful in most areas and has been especially beneficial to the reconciliation effort. Follow those models to a tee; they have been proven in battle.

Our forces also need cultural, language, and engagement training. While the military tends to concentrate on live-fire exercises, demanding tactical training, and combat-focused physical training, the counterinsurgency fight requires an additional skill set. Interacting with Iraqis is absolutely essential for success. We often thought that if we could speak fluent Arabic, then the majority of challenges would be solved in our engagements with the local population. This is not a realistic expectation, however, and it certainly won't happen for the majority of forces deployed. In fact, as Larry Diamond points out, "The first U.S. civilian administration arrived in Baghdad with virtually no capacity to function in Arabic."[70] We have to find some way to close the communication gap. Cultural training, engagement training with native Iraqis at home stations, and a suite of language skills will help. Counterinsurgency training must occur before, during, and after deployment. It is a constantly evolving process to ensure that lessons learned in the current fight are applied. The training doesn't stop when the aircraft departs for the theater of operations.

The COIN Academy located in Taji, just north of Baghdad, is one area where leaders can refine their counterinsurgency skills. At the academy, leaders are required to attend a forum on counterinsurgency lessons learned. Among the topics are patrol methods, techniques for finding and destroying roadside bombs, and education on the various insurgent factions. In the long term, we hope that the format can be passed on to the new Iraqi Army and ISF. Although the in-theater training shouldn't serve as a "catch-up" period for training missed before deployment, it provides refresher training for those leaders needing additional language, cultural, and counterinsurgency training.

On at least a weekly basis, coalition leaders at all levels must engage with Iraqis leaders in their areas. These engagements are critical to the success of the mission. We have found that rehearsing these meetings, though cumbersome and laborious, makes a difference. Establishing a rapport with local muktars and sheiks will enhance the probability for reconciliation with both leaders and the local population. Rehearsing such meetings is nonnegotiable.

After-action reviews should always be conducted. The term "lessons learned" has become a cliché in recent years, but learning from each other is invaluable. As B. H. Liddell Hart writes, "It should be the duty of every soldier to reflect on the experiences of the past, in the endeavor to discover improvements, in his particular sphere of action, which are practicable in the immediate future."[71] Our leaders need to learn from those who went before, trust in their subordinates, and care for their soldiers and their families. Simple guidance, true, but of paramount importance. The theater of operations may change, as will the lessons learned associated with it. But the importance of our leaders' trust and care of soldiers and their families will never change.

A FINAL WORD

Contrary to what Tom Ricks wrote in his now infamous book on the war in Iraq, this war is not a fiasco. Operation Iraqi Freedom is a complex counterinsurgency brought on by a noble mission to overthrow a tyrant of more than thirty years. As in any other war, mistakes have been made, predictions have been erroneous, and armchair quarterbacks will likely continue to provide opinions in an attempt to build their case against progress. As the senior military leader in Iraq, General Petraeus, said in his opening statement to Congress in September 2007, however, "While noting that the situation in Iraq remains complex, difficult, and sometimes downright frustrating, I also believe that it is possible to achieve our objectives in Iraq over time, though doing so will be neither quick nor easy."

Our armed forces will learn from the past, husband their resources, and continue to make sacrifices so that others may experience the same freedoms they do. Although what "victory" means for this war may be redefined, as it has for most every military conflict in our nation's history, "victory is always possible for the United States."[72]

NOTES

INTRODUCTION

1. David Petraeus, "Transcript: General Petraeus on the Way Ahead in Iraq." *Military Review* (March–April 2007).
2. An example is the Operation Together Forward mission, devised by the then MNC-I (Multi-National Corps-Iraq) and MNF-I commanders in an effort to stop the ethnic strife in Baghdad.
3. Michael R. Gordon, "U.S. Seen in Iraq until at Least '09," *New York Times,* July 24, 2007.
4. Task Force Band of Brothers was an organization built around the 101st Airborne Division (Air Assault) from Fort Campbell, Kentucky, as it assumed Multi-National Force-North Central (MNF-NC) in September 2005, which eventually turned into Multi-National Force-North (MNF-N) in December 2005 with the combination of MNF-N and MNF-NC, essentially combining Ninevah and Dahuk provinces with the four provinces (Al Sulyminiah, Salah ad Din, Kirkuk, and Diyala) under the control of MNF-NC.
5. Faris al-Mehdawi, "Ambush Kills 19 Iraqi Troops North of Baghdad," www.redorbit.com/news/international/320169/ambush_kills_19_iraqi_troops_north_of_baghdad/index.html.
6. The coalition as we know it consists of the following nations: the United States with the preponderance of the force; the United Kingdom, South Korea, Italy, Poland, Georgia, Romania, Australia, Denmark, and El Salvador with respectable participation; and Bulgaria, Azerbaijan, Albania, Latvia, Slovakia, Mongolia, Czech Republic, Lithuania, Armenia, Ukraine, Macedonia, Bosnia-Herzegovina, Estonia, Kazakhstan, Moldova, Japan, Portugal, and Singapore with a token representation in Iraq.
7. Steve Anderson, Briefing on Ten Myths of the War in Iraq, 10–13.
8. Combat operations in Iraq began on March 19, 2003, and ceased with the announcement by President George Bush on May 1, that "major combat operations" in Iraq had ended.
9. Ralph Peters, "Kill, Don't Capture: How to Solve Our Prisoner Problem," *New York Post,* July 10, 2006.
10. We often use terms loosely without concern for their root meanings. Sectarian issues are not relegated only to the Iraqi theater. Any time there is a "bigoted adherence to a factional viewpoint" or a narrow-minded, parochial viewpoint, one can expect a sectarian conflict. In short, it is the friction brought on by two different—at times diabolically different—points of view.
11. Jim Garamone, "Loosely Interpreted Arabic Terms Can Promote Enemy Ideology," American Forces Information Services, June 22, 2006, www.defenselink.mil/news/Jun2006/20060622_5489.html.

12. Wikipedia lists the Five Pillars of Islam as *shahada,* bearing witness that there is nothing worthy of worship but God and that Muhammad is God's messenger; *salat,* performing the prescribed Islamic prayer; *zakat,* almsgiving of a $2^{1}/_{2}$ percent tax on one's assets; *sawm,* fasting from sunrise to sunset during the month of Ramadan; and *hajj,* performing the pilgrimage to Mecca. http://en.wikipedia .org/wiki/Five_Pillars_of_Islam.

13. Most Muslims see the Qur'an as the word of God as received by the prophet Mohammed.

14. Thomas E. Ricks, *Fiasco: The American Military Adventure in Iraq* (New York: Penguin Press, 2006).

CHAPTER 1: FROM EUPHORIA TO COMPLACENCY

1. http://en.wikipedia.org/wiki/2003_invasion_of_Iraq#Bush_declares_.22End_of _major_combat_operations.22_.28May_2003.29.

2. Some think that the current conflict in Iraq takes on the attributes of a guerrilla war, while still others believe it is a string of terrorist attacks with a goal of defeating any success the new Iraqi government may achieve. The common characteristics of an insurgency include protracted warfare, asymmetric violence, ambiguity, dispersal, the use of complex terrain, psychological warfare, and political mobilization, which is the intent to influence the existing distribution of power.

3. Ali A. Allawi, *The Occupation of Iraq: Winning the War, Losing the Peace* (New Haven, CT: Yale University Press, 2007), 1.

4. Doctrine has changed, and "battlefield framework" is now called "operating environment."

5. Ralph Peters, *Wars of Blood and Faith: The Conflicts That Will Shape the Twenty-First Century* (Mechanicsburg, PA: Stackpole Books, 2007), 15.

6. Allawi, *Occupation of Iraq,* 147–62.

7. Ibid.

8. *Peshmerga,* meaning "those who face death," is the term used by Kurds to refer to armed Kurdish fighters from both the Kurdish Democratic Party (KDP) and the Party of Unified Kurdistan (PUK). The *peshmerga* forces of Kurdistan have been around since the advent of the Kurdish independence movement in the early 1920s, following the collapse of the Ottoman and Qajar empires, which had jointly ruled over the area. Michael L. Chyet, *Kurdish-English Dictionary* (New Haven, CT: Yale University Pres, 2003), 452–53, and William Murray and Robert H. Scales, Jr., *The Iraq War: A Military History* (Cambridge, MA: Belknap Press, 2003), 188.

9. Maj. Gen. Turhan Abdurahaman is the deputy chief of police for the city of Kirkuk. In 2003, he was selected by the coalition to lead the establishment of that city's police force.

10. James A. Baker and Lee H. Hamilton, *The Iraq Study Group Report: The Way Forward—A New Approach* (New York: Vintage Books, 2006), 78–83.

11. This is especially true of the Plus Ultra Brigade, under Polish command. http://en.wikipedia.org/wiki/Multinational_force_in_Iraq#_note-3.

12. http://edition.cnn.com/2002/WORLD/europe/11/20/prague.bush.nato/.

13. Liam Anderson and Gareth Stansfield, *The Future of Iraq: Dictatorship, Democracy, or Division?* (New York: Palgrave MacMillan, 2004), 14.

14. Ibid., 8.
15. This was initially stated in frustration by the chief of operations, Lt. Col. R. J. Lillibridge, of Task Force Band of Brothers (101st Airborne Division), stationed at Camp Speicher in Tikrit, Iraq, during 2005–06.
16. Mark Perry, "After Rumsfeld, a New Dawn?" *Asia Times,* June 19, 2007.
17. A "line of operation" is loosely defined in Clausewitzian terms as the directional orientation of a force in relation to the enemy; it is the linkage between a force's objective and its bases of operation. However, Clausewitz discussed LOOs in a purely physical sense, stating that a single line of operation is preferable to multiple lines of operation when available resources are limited, but when resources are adequate, multiple lines of operation can disperse the enemy's efforts. Operating on interior lines (operations that diverge from a central point) benefits a weaker force, whereas operating on exterior lines (operations that converge on the enemy from more than one direction) can benefit a stronger force by offering the opportunity to encircle and annihilate a weaker opponent. LOOs, as proven in this conflict, can include other elements like "governance" which do not relate to the Clausewitzian definition of interior versus exterior examples.
18. John R. S. Batiste and Paul R. Daniels, "The Fight for Samarra: Full-Spectrum Operations in Modern Warfare," *Military Review* (May–June 2005): 15.
19. Todd S. Purdum, *A Time of Our Choosing: America's War in Iraq* (New York: Times Books, 2003), 153–54.
20. The former police commissioner of Philadelphia, Timoney has a reputation for taking harsh action against protesters of any kind. After a brief stint in the private sector, Timoney took the post of Miami police chief as part of Mayor Manny Diaz's efforts to "clean up the department." Jeremy Scahill, "The Miami Model," *Democracy Now!* www.democracynow.org/static/miamimodel.shtml.
21. Rajiv Chandrasekaran, *Imperial Life in the Emerald City: Inside Iraq's Green Zone* (New York: Alfred E. Knopf, 2006), 84.
22. Ibid., 87.
23. George Packer, *The Assassins' Gate: America in Iraq* (New York: Farrar, Straus and Giroux, 2006), 240–41.
24. Greg Jaffe, "A Camp Divided: As U.S. Tries to Give Iraqi Troops More Responsibility, Clash of Two American Colonels Shows Tough Road Ahead," *Wall Street Journal,* June 18, 2006, http://pierretristam.com/Bobst/library/wf-209.html.
25. "Unity of command" refers to the principle that a subordinate should have one and only one superior to whom he or she is directly responsible.
26. Perry, "After Rumsfeld, a New Dawn?"
27. *Joint Publication (JP) 1-02: Department of Defense Dictionary of Military and Associated Terms* (Washington, DC: Government Printing Office, March 22, 2007).
28. Jaffe, "A Camp Divided."
29. For example, to detain an Iraqi female, the force on the ground has to first get approval from the first general officer in the chain of command. To enable the Iraqi Security Forces to pursue a potentially nefarious individual into a mosque, a rigorous and all-encompassing packet needs to be submitted to the multinational corps commander for approval. There is no "turning on a dime" to achieve success, a characteristic for which this army—at least at the battalion level—has been famous in past wars.

30. Larry Diamond, *Squandered Victory: The American Occupation and the Bungled Effort to Bring Democracy to Iraq* (New York: Times Books, 2005), 19–20.
31. Baker and Hamilton, *Iraq Study Group*, 3.
32. Ricks, *Fiasco*, 4.
33. Dominic J. Caraccilo, *Terminating the Ground War in the Persian Gulf: A Clausewitzian Examination*, (Washington, DC: AUSA Land Warfare Papers, September 1997), 10.

CHAPTER 2: CHANGING FACE OF BATTLE: DIAGNOSING AN INSURGENCY

1. *JP 1-02*, 265.
2. Drafted by the coalition-appointed Iraqi Governing Council in a process whose deadline was postponed four times, the text of the proposed constitution was read to the National Assembly on August 28, 2005. In a referendum on October 15 of that year, 78 percent of Iraqis approved the constitution. Two of Iraq's eighteen provinces recorded no votes of more than two-thirds, the threshold for a veto. Had a third province similarly rejected the constitution, the assembly would have been dissolved, fresh elections called, and the constitution redrafted.
3. Kalev I. Sepp, "Best Practices in Counterinsurgency," *Military Review* (May–June 2005): 8.
4. Ibid.
5. The military objectives (tethered well with the strategic goals) in both conflicts were clear. In Operation Just Cause, the goal was to free Panama of Manuel Ortega's rule. In Operation Desert Storm, the goal was to expel Saddam's army from Kuwait after its August 1990 invasion. One could argue that the goal in Operation Iraqi Freedom was similar to the 1989 invasion of Panama: to oust a country of a tyrant through conventional direct action against a definable uniformed enemy. But stage two—the onset of an insurgency—blindsided the Coalition. *Field Manual (FM) 3-24: Counterinsurgency* (Fort Leavenworth, KS: Department of the Army, June 2006), ix.
6. Anthony H. Cordesman, *The Iraq War: Strategy, Tactics, and Military Lessons* (Westport, CT: Praeger, 2003), 160.
7. *FM 3-24*, vii.
8. As explained in the conclusion to *The Threatening Storm*. Kenneth M. Pollack, *The Threatening Storm: The Case for Invading Iraq* (New York: Random House, 2002), 418.
9. Ibid. 422.
10. Alfonso Chardy, "A New Way to Wage War: 'Violent' Peace Keeps Troops Home, *San Jose Mercury News*, October 14, 1986.
11. "Paramilitary" is defined as relating to or being a group of civilians organized in a military fashion, especially to operate in place of or assist regular army troops. *FM 3-24*, 1-1, and *Joint Publication (JP) 3-07.1: Joint Tactics, Techniques, and Procedures for Foreign Internal Defense* (Washington, DC: Government Printing Office, April 30, 2004), GL-6, and definition of *paramilitary* from www.answers.com.
12. *FM 3-24*, ix.
13. Jonathan K. Graff, *United States Counterinsurgency Doctrine and Implementation in Iraq* (Fort Leavenworth, KS: Army Command and General Staff College School of Advanced Military Studies, May 26, 2004), 2.

14. Andrew J. Birtle, *U.S. Army Counterinsurgency and Contingency Operations Doctrine, 1860–1941* (Washington, DC: Center of Military History, United States Army, 2001), 10.

15. Ibid., 11.

16. *Small Wars Manual,* chapter XI, 1–2.

17. Andrew F. Krepinevich, Jr., *The Army and Vietnam* (Baltimore: Johns Hopkins University Press, 1986).

18. Harry G. Summers, *On Strategy: A Critical Analysis of the Vietnam War* (Novato, CA: Presidio Press, 1995), xx.

19. Institute for Foreign Policy Analysis, *American Military Policy in Small Wars: The Case of El Salvador.*

20. *Field Manual (FM) 3-07: Stability Operations and Support Operations* (Fort Leavenworth, KS: Department of the Army, 2004), 3-0.

21. Ibid., 3-7.

22. Ibid., 3-6.

23. Ibid., 3-4.

24. *JP 3-07.1,* viii.

25. Ibid., I-13.

26. Ibid.

27. Since the writing of this joint publication, the term "combatant commander" has changed.

28. *Joint Publication (JP) 5-0: Joint Operations Planning* (Washington, DC: Government Printing Office, December 26, 2004), I-3.

29. Clarence I. Bouchat, "An Introduction to Theater Strategy and Regional Security," *DISAM Journal* (February 2007): 110–11.

30. *Field Manual Interim (FM-I) 3-07.22: Counterinsurgency Operations* (Fort Leavenworth, KS: Department of the Army, 2004), iii.

31. *Field Manual (FM) 90-8: Counterguerrilla Operations* (Fort Leavenworth, KS: Department of the Army, 1986), 1–5.

32. *Fleet Marine Force Manual (FMFM) 8-2: Counterinsurgency Operations* (Quantico, VA: United States Marine Corps, 1980), 3-2.

33. Born in 1967, Dr. David Kilcullen, who holds a doctorate in political anthropology, served for more than twenty years in the Australian Army and retired as a lieutenant colonel. He gained counterinsurgency experience in East Timor and has served as special advisor for irregular warfare to the 2005 U.S. Quadrennial Defense Review, chief strategist in the Office of the Coordinator for Counterterrorism in the U.S. State Department, and senior counterinsurgency advisor to Multi-National Force-Iraq on the staff of Gen. David Petraeus.

34. David Galula, *Pacification in Algeria, 1956–1958,* (Santa Monica, CA: Rand Corporation, 2006), v.

35. David Galula, *Counterinsurgency Warfare: Theory and Practice* (Westport, CT: Praeger Paperback, 2006), 54.

36. Ibid.

37. Ibid., 28.

38. Stephen Vrooman, *A Counterinsurgency Campaign Plan Concept: The Galula Compass* (Fort Leavenworth, KS: Army Command and General Staff College School of Advanced Military Studies, May 26, 2005), 5.

39. An example of the coalition being fixed was when Task Force Band of Brothers assumed MND-NC in November 2005. At that time, it had four combat brigades operating on thirty-five forward operating bases (FOBs), essentially causing the force to man the FOBs and protect the routes in between without having a residual force to conduct combat operations.

40. Galula, *Counterinsurgency Warfare*, 19–21.

41. There are multiple examples of this effort directed by MNC-I in the summer of 2006 in its initial push for Iraqi provincial control. Operation Together Forward was a U.S.-directed mission to surge Iraqi Army (IA) units to Baghdad in an effort to provide the requisite security forces. The result was dismal. In the months preceding this mission, the same effort was taken to move an IA battalion from Ninewah to Ramadi. Col. Sean MacFarland, who commanded 1/1 Armor in Ramadi, made a valiant effort to make this integration work. In the end, the entire IA battalion went AWOL; however, Colonel MacFarland (now known as the hero of Ramadi) was creative enough to use the local tribes to build the security so desperately needed in that anti-Iraqi-government town. Today Ramadi remains calm.

42. Galula, *Counterinsurgency Warfare*, 23–24.

43. Vrooman, *Counterinsurgency Campaign*, 6.

44. Galula, *Counterinsurgency Warfare*, 52–55.

45. Ibid., 52.

46. Ibid, 55.

47. Ibid.

48. Ibid., 57.

49. An example of this is the February 2006 attack on the Golden Mosque in Samarra, which most would agree was a catalyst for sectarian violence in Iraq.

50. *FM 3-24*, 1-21.

51. Galula, *Counterinsurgency Warfare*, 57.

52. *FM 3-24*, 1-21.

53. Galula, *Counterinsurgency Warfare*, 59.

54. Vrooman, *Counterinsurgency Campaign*, 10.

55. Galula, *Counterinsurgency Warfare*, 75–94.

CHAPTER 3: JUST OR UNJUST WAR? A HISTORICAL BRIDGE

1. Clausewitz, Carl von. *On War*, translated and edited by Michael Howard and Peter Paret (Princeton, NJ: Princeton University Press, 1984), 87. Acclaimed author and strategist Ralph Peters writes in his newest book that he believes "Clausewitz had it backwards." Peters goes on to say that the Clausewitzian statement that "war is a continuation of policy by other means" is only partially true. In fact, Peters reverses this, saying that "policy is simply a continuation of war with other means." Peters writes, "Conflict, not peace, is the natural state of human collectives." Ralph Peters, *Wars of Blood and Faith: The Conflicts That Will Shape the Twenty-First Century* (Mechanicsburg, PA: Stackpole Books, 2007).

2. Figures taken from Steve Anderson, Briefing Given by the MNF-I Deputy Chief of Staff for Resources and Sustainment at James Madison University, April 27, 2007.

3. David Espo, "Senate Signals Support for Iraq Timeline," Associated Press, March 27, 2007.

4. Calvin Woodward, "White House Holds Firm on Iraq Strategy," Associated Press, July 15, 2007.
5. *Field Manual (FM) 27-100: Legal Support to Operations,* chapter 8, section 8.2.4.
6. The oath of enlistment is as follows: "I, *(NAME)*, do solemnly swear (or affirm) that I will support and defend the Constitution of the United States against all enemies, foreign and domestic; that I will bear true faith and allegiance to the same; and that I will obey the orders of the President of the United States and the orders of the officers appointed over me, according to regulations and the Uniform Code of Military Justice. So help me God."
7. Martin Van Crevald, *The Art of War: War and Military Thought* (New York: Smithsonian Books, 2005), 37.
8. Baker and Hamilton, *Iraq Study Group,* xvi.
9. Ibid., xiii.
10. Ibid., 9.
11. Radio Iowa talk show, April 3, 2007, www.radioiowa.com.
12. Bushra Juhi, "Iraq PM: Country Can Manage without U.S.," Associated Press, July 14, 2007.
13. We often use terms loosely without concern for their root meaning. Sectarian issues are not relegated only to the Iraqi theater. Any time there is a "bigoted adherence to a factional viewpoint" or a narrow-minded, parochial viewpoint, one can expect a sectarian conflict. In short, it is the friction brought on by two different—at times diabolically different—points of view.
14. "No Safe Way for U.S. to Leave Iraq, Experts Say," CNN, May 3, 2007.
15. Ibid.
16. Ibid.
17. Ibid. We chose to keep this dialogue as it was conveyed on the website, for we agree with the concerns conveyed by both Bergen and Shepperd.
18. United Nations Operation in Somalia II (UNOSOM II) was established in March 1993 to take appropriate action, including enforcement measures, to establish throughout Somalia a secure environment for humanitarian assistance. To that end, UNOSOM II was to complete, through disarmament and reconciliation, the task begun by the Unified Task Force for the restoration of peace, stability, law, and order. UNOSOM II was withdrawn in early March 1995.
19. That warlord, Mohamed Farah Aideed, had orchestrated the murder of United Nations soldiers in June 1993. As the situation escalated in the following months, the United States launched the abortive operation to capture Aideed in October.
20. Casper, "Terror Fall-out."
21. "Peace Operations: Withdrawal of U.S. Troops from Somalia," Government Accounting Office (June 1994): 1–11.
22. *UN Security Council Report: Somalia March 2007,* United Nations Security Council, March 2007.
23. Mohamed Siad Barre (1919–January 2, 1995) was the head of state of Somalia from 1969 to 1991. Prior to his presidency, he was an army commander under the democratic government of Somalia, which had been in place since independence in June 1960.
24. Jackson Mbuvi, "Somalia: U.S. Is About to Pull Out of Country Again: A Mistake," *The Nation* (July 9, 2007).

25. Dominique Orsini, *Multinational Operations in Somalia, Haiti and Bosnia: A Comparative Study* (Montreal, Quebec: McGill University, 1997), 79–80.
26. "Institute on Global Conflict and Cooperation: IGCC Policy Briefs," 2.
27. Amitabh Pal, "Failed Somalia Policy Comes Back to Haunt the U.S.," *Progressive* (June 20, 2006).
28. Alamgir Hussain, "Never Intervene in a Muslim Country," *Global Politician* (May 22, 2007).
29. The Weinberger doctrine asks the following questions: Are vital interests involved? Is there a commitment to victory? Are there clearly defined political and military objectives? Is there a continuous plan to reassess the troop and objective ratio? Does the president intend to mobilize public opinion in support of the operation? And finally, are we using intervention or war as a last resort?
30. Barry R. Posen and Andrew L. Ross, "Competing Visions for U.S. Grand Strategy," in *Strategy and Force Planning*, 2nd ed., ed. Strategy and Force Planning Faculty. (Newport, RI: Naval War College, 1997), 122.
31. Lionel Beehner, "What Are Iraq's Benchmarks?" Council on Foreign Relations (July 16, 2007): xx.
32. Ibid.
33. Ibid.
34. Baker and Hamilton, *Iraq Study Group*, 18–19, 22–26.
35. George W. Bush *Statement on Iraq Strategy*, January 10, 2007.
36. *Iraq Study Group*, 45.
37. Anderson, Briefing, 12.
38. Ibid., 18.
39. Ibid., 18.
40. Beehner, "What Are Iraq's Benchmarks?"
41. Ricks's *Fiasco* intriguingly cites a CIA operative telling Bremer that if he stood down the Iraqi Army, "By nightfall, you'll have driven 30,000 to 50,000 Baathists underground. And in six months you are really going to regret this." 159.
42. Allawi, 150-52.
43. Baker and Hamilton, *Iraq Study Group*, 45.
44. Allawi, *Occupation of Iraq*, 152.
45. Ricks, *Fiasco*, 149.
46. Beehner, "What Are Iraq's Benchmarks?"
47. Baker and Hamilton, *Iraq Study Group*, 45.
48. Ibid., 23.
49. Ibid., 58.
50. Beehner, "What Are Iraq's Benchmarks?"
51. Ibid.
52. Anderson, Briefing, 7.
53. The center of gravity is a concept developed by the Prussian military theorist Carl von Clausewitz in his work *On War*. The definition of center of gravity according to the U.S. Department of Defense is "those characteristics, capabilities, or locations from which a military force derives its freedom of action, physical strength, or will to fight." Thus the center of gravity is usually seen as the source of strength. Accordingly, the army tends to look for a single center of gravity, normally in the principal capability that stands in the way of the accomplishment of its own

mission. In short, the army considers a "friendly" center of gravity as that element—a characteristic, capability, or locality—that enables one's own or allied forces to accomplish their objectives. Conversely, an opponent's center of gravity is that element that prevents friendly forces from accomplishing their objectives.

54. David Kilcullen, "Twenty-Eight Articles: Fundamentals of Company-Level Counterinsurgency," *Small Wars Journal* (March 2006), 5. Full text available at http://smallwarsjournal.com/documents/28articles.pdf.

55. Robert C. Orr, "P-I Focus: Winning the Iraq Peace," *Seattle Post-Intelligencer,* July 28, 2003.

56. Ibid.

57. George McGovern and William R. Polk, *Out of Iraq: A Practical Plan for Withdrawal Now* (New York: Simon & Schuster, 2006), 95.

58. Ricks, *Fiasco,* 115–16.

59. Sepp, "Best Practices in Counterinsurgency," 9.

60. Richard L. Clutterbuck, *The Long, Long War: Counterinsurgency in Malaya and Vietnam* (Westport, CT: Praeger, 1966).

61. Sepp, "Best Practices in Counterinsurgency," 10.

62. *Instruments of Statecraft,* part 1, section 3.

63. Bing West and Owen West, "The Laptop Is Mightier Than the Sword," *New York Times,* June 15, 2007.

64. Chandrasekaran, 158.

65. Diamond, *Squandered Victory,* 20.

66. Daniel L. Byman and Kenneth M. Pollack, "Democracy in Iraq?" *Washington Quarterly* (Summer 2003).

67. Anderson and Stansfield, *The Future of Iraq,* 207.

68. Byman and Pollack, "Democracy in Iraq?"

69. Chandrasekaran, *Imperial Life in the Emerald City,* 283–84.

70. George W. Bush, *Statement on Iraq Strategy,* January 10, 2007.

71. Byman and Pollack, "Democracy in Iraq?"

72. Ali Allawi, "A Real Blueprint for Peace in Iraq," *Independent,* January 9, 2007. www.envirosagainstwar.org/know/read.php?itemid=5079.

73. Everett, Washington, *Herald,* www.heraldnet.com/stories/06/06/17/100wir_a3iraq001.cfm.

74. The definition of anti-Iraqi forces (AIF) has evolved. Clearly Al Qaeda in Iraq (AQIZ), the Sunni arm of the former and disgruntled Baathists, and the Shiite death squads are the most prevalent and most enduring elements of the insurgency. However, each threat arm has evolved over time, and the names change quite frequently as alliances are formed and new groups evolve. What hasn't changed is the motivation behind these groups, none of which want to see an Iraqi government succeed.

75. Galbraith, *End of Iraq,* 211–12.

76. McGovern and Polk, *Out of Iraq,* xiv–xv.

77. Bing West, "Battle of the Narratives."

78. Wade Markel, "Draining the Swamp: The British Strategy of Population Control," *Parameters* (Spring 2006): 35.

CHAPTER 4: THE DECISIVE NATURE OF LEADERSHIP

1. *Marine Corps Doctrinal Publication (MCDP)* 1, 57.
2. To provide the reader a better understanding of what is potentially a cliché in many circles, Clausewitz describes the fog and friction of war as follows on pp. 119–21 of *On War:*

> As long as we have no personal knowledge of war, we cannot conceive where these difficulties lie of which so much is said, and what that genius and those extraordinary mental powers required in a general have really to do. All appears so simple, all the requisite branches of knowledge appear so plain, all the combinations so unimportant, that in comparison with them the easiest problem in higher mathematics impresses us with a certain scientific dignity. But if we have seen war, all becomes intelligible; and still, after all, it is extremely difficult to describe what it is which brings about this change, to specify this invisible and completely efficient factor. Everything is very simple in war, but the *simplest thing is difficult*. These difficulties accumulate and produce a friction which no man can imagine exactly who has not seen war. Suppose now a traveler, who towards evening expects to accomplish the two stages at the end of his day's journey, four or five leagues, with post-horses, on the high road—it is nothing. He arrives now at the last station but one, finds no horses, or very bad ones; then a hilly country, bad roads; it is a dark night, and he is glad when, after a great deal of trouble, he reaches the next station, and finds there some miserable accommodation. So in war, through the influence of an infinity of petty circumstances, which cannot properly be described on paper, things disappoint us, and we fall short of the mark. A powerful iron will overcome this friction; it crushes the obstacles, but certainly the machine along with them. We shall often meet with this result. Like an obelisk towards which the principal streets of a town converge, the strong will of a proud spirit stands prominent and commanding in the middle of the art of war. Friction is the only conception which in a general way corresponds to that which distinguishes real war from war on paper. The military machine, the army and all belonging to it, is in fact simple, and appears on this account easy to manage. But let us reflect that no part of it is in one piece, that it is composed entirely of individuals, each of which keeps up its own friction in all directions. Theoretically all sounds very well: the commander of a battalion is responsible for the execution of the order given; and as the battalion by its discipline is glued together into one piece, and the chief must be a man of acknowledged zeal, the beam turns on an iron pin with little friction. But it is not so in reality, and all that is exaggerated and false in such a conception manifests itself at once in war. The battalion always remains composed of a number of men, of whom, if chance so wills, the most insignificant is able to occasion delay and even irregularity. The danger which war brings with it, the bodily exertions which it requires, augment this evil so much that they may be regarded as the greatest causes of it. This enormous friction, which is not concentrated, as in mechanics, at a few points, is therefore everywhere brought into contact with chance, and thus incidents take place upon

which it was impossible to calculate, their chief origin being chance. As an instance of one such chance take the weather. Here the fog prevents the enemy from being discovered in time, a battery from firing at the right moment, a report from reaching the general; there the rain prevents a battalion from arriving at the right time, because instead of for three it had to march perhaps eight hours; the cavalry from charging effectively because it is stuck fast in heavy ground. These are only a few incidents of detail by way of elucidation, that the reader may be able to follow the author, for whole volumes might be written on these difficulties. To avoid this and still to give a clear conception of the host of small difficulties to be contended with in war, we might go on heaping up illustrations, if we were not afraid of being tiresome. But those who have already comprehended us will permit us to add a few more. Activity in war is movement in a resistant medium. Just as a man immersed in water is unable to perform with ease and regularity the most natural and simplest movement that of walking, so in war, with ordinary powers, one cannot keep even the line of mediocrity. This is the reason that the correct theorist is like a swimming master, who teaches on dry land movements which are required in the water, which must appear grotesque and ludicrous to those who forget about the water. This is also why theorists, who have never plunged in themselves, or who cannot deduce any generalities from their experience, are unpractical and even absurd, because they only teach what everyone knows—how to walk.

3. Liddell Hart, B. H., *Strategy* (New York: New American Library, 1974), 323.
4. Charles F. Hawkins, "Toward a Theory of Military Leadership." www.militaryconflict.org/leader.htm#One.
5. Clausewitz, *On War*, 75.
6. Timothy Williams, "Culture—We Need Some of That! Cultural Knowledge and Army Officer Professional Development" (Carlisle Barracks, PA: U.S. Army War College, March 15, 2006), 6. It is also interesting to explore how others who serve in Iraq define the center of gravity. Some very senior leaders believe that it is, in fact, the ability to convey our message to the American people, because we, the military, derive our power from the acceptance of the American people of our conduct of the war and ability to achieve victory.
7. Fernando Rodriques-Goulart, "Combat Motivation," *Military Review* (November–December 2006): 96.
8. *JP 1-02*, 98.
9. *Field Manual (FM) 6-22: Leadership* (Fort Leavenworth, KS: Department of the Army, October 12, 2006), 1-1–1-2.
10. *Field Manual (FM) 22-100: Command* (Fort Leavenworth, KS: Department of the Army, August 31, 1999), chapter 1.
11. Richard Beckhard, Frances Hesselbein, and Marshall Goldsmith, *The Leader of the Future: New Visions, Strategies and Practices for the Next Era* (San Francisco: Jossey-Bass, 1997), xii.
12. John C. Maxwell and Zig Ziglar, *The 21 Irrefutable Laws of Leadership* (Nashville: Thomas Nelson, 1998), 13.
13. Warren Bennis, *On Becoming a Leader* (New York: Addison Wesley, 1989).

14. Robin Denise Johnson, *Leadership Basics* (self-published, 2003), 3.
15. Clausewitz, *On War*, 189.
16. *FM 3-24*, 7-1.
17. Allawi, *Occupation of Iraq*, 334.
18. "Nuri Kamal al-Maliki," *New York Times*, August 25, 2007, http://topics.nytimes .com/top/reference/timestopics/people/m/nuri_kamal_al-maliki/index.html?in line=nyt-per.
19. Ibid., 180.
20. N. H. Floyd, "The Multi-National Corps-Iraq Partnership:" Interaction and Integration with the Iraqi Army, *Australian Army Journal* 4, no. 1 (Autumn 2007): 145–46.
21. Ibid., 146.
22. Ibid., 146–47.
23. Chandrasekaran, *Imperial Life in the Emerald City*, 30, 70–71.
24. L. Paul Bremer III, *My Year in Iraq: The Struggle to Build a Future of Hope* (New York: Threshold Editions, 2006), 29, 54.
25. Ibid., 74–75.
26. Clausewitz, *On War*, 102.
27. *Field Manual (FM) 3-0: Operations* (Fort Leavenworth, KS: Department of the Army, June 2001), 4-7–4-8.
28. Roby Barrett, briefing on "Iraq: The Way Forward" to the 3rd Brigade Combat Team, 101st Airborne Division (Air Assault), Fort Campbell, Kentucky, August 21, 2007.
29. Ibid.
30. Galula, *Counterinsurgency Warfare*, 75.
31. H. R. McMaster, Interview, *Frontline*, February 2, 2007, www.pbs.org/wgbh/ pages/frontline/endgame/interviews/mcmaster.html
32. Ibid.
33. Ibid.
34. Ibid.
35. *Ready First Combat Team (1/1 Armor) After Action Report*, January 2006–February 2007, 5.
36. Jim Michaels, "Behind Success in Ramadi: An Army Colonel's Gamble," *USA Today*, May 1, 2007.

CHAPTER 5: THE GOOD ENOUGH SOLUTION

1. Jonathan Schell in "How to Get Out of Iraq: A Forum," *The Nation*, www.then-ation.com/doc/20040524/forum.
2. Peters, *Wars of Blood and Faith*, 46.
3. Ibid., 7.
4. *Measuring Stability and Security in Iraq*, Report to Congress in Accordance with the Department of Defense Appropriations Act 2006 (Section 9010), August 29, 2006. The full text of the report is available at www.globalsecurity.org/military/library/ report/2006/iraq-security-stability_aug2006.htm.
5. Ibid., 1.
6. Deborah Amos, "T. E. Lawrence's Middle East Vision." NPR, September 1, 2007, www.npr.org/templates/story/story.php?storyId=4967572.
7. Chandrasekaran, *Imperial Life in the Emerald City*, 90, 227–28.

8. Ibid., 239–40.
9. Ibid., 212–19.
10. Jim Derleth. USAID briefing to the 3rd Brigade, 101st Airborne Division (Air Assault), Fort Campbell, Kentucky, August 31, 2007.
11. Liz Sly, "Some See 'Coup' as Iraq's Best Hope: Ex-Premier Allawi Building Political Bloc to Challenge al-Maliki," *Chicago Tribune,* September 1, 2007.
12. Chandrasekaran, *Imperial Life in the Emerald City,* 90, 227–28.
13. MacFarland, *Behind Success in Ramadi.*
14. Peters, *Wars of Blood and Faith,* 367.
15. Ibid., xii.
16. Ibid.
17. Ibid., xiii.
18. Ibid.
19. Gen. David Petraeus.
20. Joshua Goodman, "Signs of Progress at the Local Level." *Foundation for Defense of Democracies,* August 20, 2007, www.defenddemocracy.org/publications/publications_show.htm?doc_id=516613.
21. Petraeus.
22. Galbraith, *End of Iraq,* dust jacket.
23. Fareed Zakaria, *The Future of Freedom: Illiberal Democracy at Home and Abroad* (New York: W. W. Norton & Company, 2004), 13–14.
24. Ibid., 17, 51.
25. Crocker, xx.
26. Zakaria, *Future of Freedom,* 17–18.
27. Thomas Vail, Interview, August 3, 2007, and Thomas Vail, "Underestimating the Insurgency and the Contemporary Operating Environment in OIF" (unpublished paper), 3.
28. Diamond, *Squandered Victory,* 316.
29. Crocker, xx.
30. Diamond, *Squandered Victory,* 314.
31. Ibid., 316.
32. Thomas Vail, Interview, August 3, 2007.
33. Crocker, xx.
34. Galbraith, *End of Iraq,* 209.
35. Peters, *Wars of Blood and Faith,* 312.
36. Crocker, xx.
37. Ricks, *Fiasco,* 162.
38. Stanton, MR 169 Unit Immersion in Mosul.
39. Kilcullen, "Twenty-Eight Articles," 8. The twenty-eight articles range from "know your turf" and "travel light" to "rank is nothing: talent is everything" and "be prepared for setbacks." He concludes, "Whatever else you do, keep the initiative."
40. James Jones, xx.
41. Diamond, *Squandered Victory,* 5.
42. Barrett briefing.
43. Galbraith, *End of Iraq,* 220.
44. Ibid., 221.
45. Various contributors, "How to Get Out of Iraq: A Forum," *The Nation,* www.thenation.com/doc/20040524/forum.

46. Gordon, "Get Out of Iraq Now? Not So Fast, Experts Say," 1.

47. Ibid.

48. Democratic Presidential Debate hosted by CNN and YouTube, Charleston, South Carolina, on July 23, 2007.

49. Galbraith, *End of Iraq,* 215.

50. Ibid., 216, 218.

51. For an assessment of the benchmarking procedure, see the eMilitary website, www.emilitary.org/article.php?aid=11577.

52. "Hill Report on Iraq Preempts Petraeus," *U.S. News and World Report,* August 31, 2007, www.usnews.com/usnews/politics/bulletin/bulletin_070831.htm.

53. "Analysis of the FY 2007 Supplemental (H.R. 2206) Spending Package Signed by President Bush (P.L. 110-28)," June 7, 2007, www.armscontrolcenter.org/archives/002290.html.

54. "Hill Report on Iraq Preempts Petraeus," *U.S. News and World Report,* August 31, 2007.

55. Ibid.

56. Petraeus, "Multi-National Forces-Iraq Counterinsurgency Guidance," MNF-I Headquarters (June 2007): p. 1.

57. Ibid.

58. Ibid., 1–3.

59. Crocker, xx.

60. "Petraeus, Crocker Talk of Iraq's Fear, Progress: Warn Not to Expect Solid Judgment on U.S. Buildup Now until November," MSNBC, September 5, 2007, www.msnbc.msn.com/id/19844224/.

61. Odierno, "Reconciliation Letter to Soldiers, Sailors, Airmen, and Marines of Multi-National Corps-Iraq."

62. Ibid.

63. Ryan Crocker, testimony to Congress, September 10, 2007.

64. Sepp, "Best Practices in Counterinsurgency," 10.

65. Report to Congress, September 2007.

66. Fareed Zakaria, "We Are Not Losing the War against Radical Islam," *Newsweek,* July 2, 2007, FareedZakaria.com.

67. Ibid.

68. Ricks, *Fiasco,* 328.

69. Petraeus,

70. Diamond, *Squandered Victory,* dust jacket.

71. Liddell Hart, *Strategy.*

72. Peters, *Wars of Blood and Faith,* xv.

BIBLIOGRAPHY

ARTICLES AND MEMORANDUMS

Allawi, Ali. "A Real Blueprint for Peace in Iraq." *Independent,* January 9, 2007. www.envirosagainstwar.org/know/read.php?itemid=5079.

al-Mehdawi, Faris. "Ambush Kills 19 Iraqi Troops North of Baghdad." www.redorbit .com/news/international/320169/ambush_kills_19_iraqi_troops_north_of_baghdad/ index.html.

Amos, Deborah. "T. E. Lawrence's Middle East Vision." NPR, September 1, 2007. www.npr.org/templates/story/story.php?storyId=4967572.

"Analysis of the FY 2007 Supplemental (H.R. 2206) Spending Package Signed by President Bush (P.L. 110-28)." June 7, 2007 www.armscontrolcenter.org/archives/ 002290.html.

Anderson, Joseph, and Gary Volesky. "A Synchronized Approach to Population Control." *Military Review* (July–August 2007): 101-103.

Anderson, Steve. Briefing Given by the MNF-I Deputy Chief of Staff for Resources and Sustainment at James Madison University, April 27, 2007.

Batiste, John R. S., and Paul R. Daniels. "The Fight for Samarra: Full-Spectrum Operations in Modern Warfare." *Military Review* (May-June 2005): 13–21.

Beehner, Lionel. "What Are Iraq's Benchmarks?" Council on Foreign Relations, July 16, 2007.

BeLue, Francis M. "Indigenous Religions: Impacts upon a Unit's Mission." *News from the Front.*

Bouchat, Clarence J. "An Introduction to Theater Strategy and Regional Security." *DISAM Journal* (February 2007): 99–122.

Brinkley, Joel. "The Struggle for Iraq: The Attacks; Despite Positives, More Negatives Are Predicted." *New York Times,* November 3, 2003.

Burns, Robert. "U.S. Warned against Early Pullout: Gains in Iraq Would Be Lost, General Says." *Clarksville Leaf-Chronicle,* July 21, 2007.

Byman, Daniel L., and Kenneth M. Pollack. "Democracy in Iraq?" *Washington Quarterly* (Summer 2003).

Caraccilo, Dominic J. "Measuring Operational Success: Establishing Criteria to Benchmark the Point of Culmination." Naval War College, June 13, 1997.

Chardy, Alfonso. "A New Way to Wage War: 'Violent' Peace Keeps Troops Home." *San Jose Mercury News,* October 14, 1986.

Dreazen, Yochi J. "Discarded Troop Plan Gets a Second Look: Strategy Advocated by General Ousted from Iraq Is Back in Vogue." *Wall Street Journal,* August 23, 2007. http://ebird.afis.mil/ebfiles/e20070823538096.htm.

Espo, David. "Senate Signals Support for Iraq Timeline." Associated Press, March 27, 2007.

Floyd, N. H. "The Multi-National Corps-Iraq Partnership: Interaction and Integration with the Iraqi Army." *Australian Army Journal 4,* no. 1 (Autumn 2007): 145-52.

Garamone, Jim. "Loosely Interpreted Arabic Terms Can Promote Enemy Ideology." Armed Forces Press Service, June 22, 2006, www.defenselink.mil/news/Jun2006/ 20060622_5489.html.

Goodman, Joshua. "Signs of Progress at the Local Level." Foundation for Defense of Democracies, August 20, 2007. www.defenddemocracy.org/publications/publications _show.htm?doc_id=516613.

Gordon, Michael. "U.S. Seen in Iraq until at Least '09." New York Times, July 24, 2007.

Hammes, Thomas X. "Countering Evolved Insurgent Networks." Military Review (July–August 2006): 18-26.

Harper, David. "Targeting the American Will and Other Challenges for 4th-Generation Leadership." Military Review (March–April 2007): 94-104.

Hawkins, Charles F. "Toward a Theory of Military Leadership." www.militaryconflict .org/leader.htm#One.

"Hill Report on Iraq Preempts Petraeus." U.S. News and World Report, August 31, 2007. www.usnews.com/usnews/politics/bulletin/bulletin_070831.htm.

Hoffman, Frank G. "Neo-Classical Counterinsurgency." Parameters (Summer 2007): 71-87.

Hulse, Carl, and Jim Rutenberg. "President Open to Benchmarks in Iraq Measure." New York Times, May 11, 2007.

Hussain, Alamgir. "Never Intervene in a Muslim Country." Global Politician (May 22, 2007).

Lake, David A. "Democratizing Foreign Policy," parts 1–4. IGCC Policy Briefs. San Diego: University of California Institute on Global Conflict and Cooperation, 1997.

Jaffe, Greg. "A Camp Divided: As U.S. Tries to Give Iraqi Troops More Responsibility, Clash of Two American Colonels Shows Tough Road Ahead." Wall Street Journal, June 18, 2006. http://pierretristam.com/Bobst/library/wf-209.html.

Jandora, John W. "Factoring in Culture: Center of Gravity and Asymmetric Conflict." Joint Forces Quarterly 3–9: 78-83.

Juhi, Bushra. "Iraq PM: Country Can Manage without U.S." Associated Press, July 14, 2007.

Kilcullen, David. "Counterinsurgency Redux." Small Wars Journal.

———. "Twenty-Eight Articles: Fundamentals of Company-Level Counterinsurgency." Small Wars Journal (March 2006).

Leighton, Casper. "Terror Fall-out from US Somalia Failure." BBC, October 3, 2003.

Mann, Morgan. "The Power Equation: Using Tribal Politics in Counterinsurgency." Military Review (May–June 2007): 104-8.

Markel, Wade. "Draining the Swamp: The British Strategy of Population Control." Parameters (Spring 2006): 35–48.

Mbuvi, Jackson. "Somalia: U.S. Is About to Pull Out of Country Again—a Mistake." The Nation, July 9, 2007.

Measuring Stability and Security in Iraq. Report to Congress in Accordance with the Department of Defense Appropriations Act 2006 (Section 9010), August 29, 2006.

Michaels, Jim. "Behind Success in Ramadi: An Army Colonel's Gamble." USA Today, May 1, 2007.

Murphy, Dan. "New Commander, New Plan in Iraq." csmonitor.com, February 9, 2007.

"No Safe Way for U.S. to Leave Iraq, Experts Warn." CNN, May 3, 2007.

"Nuri Kamal al-Maliki." *New York Times,* August 25, 2007. http://topics.nytimes.com/top/reference/timestopics/people/m/nuri_kamal_al-maliki/index.html?inline=nyt-per.

Odierno, Raymond. "Reconciliation Letter to Soldiers, Sailors, Airmen, and Marines of Multi-National Corps-Iraq." *MNC-I Headquarters,* June 24, 2007.

Orr, Robert C. "P-I Focus: Winning the Iraq Peace." *Seattle Post-Intelligencer,* July 28, 2003. www.cfr.org/publication/6163/pi_focus.html.

Pal, Amitabh. "Failed Somalia Policy Comes Back to Haunt the U.S." *The Progressive* (June 20, 2006).

"Peace Operations: Withdrawal of U.S. Troops from Somalia." Government Accounting Office (June 1994): 1–11.

Perry, Mark. "After Rumsfeld, A New Dawn." *Asia Times,* June 19, 2007.

Peters, Ralph. "Kill, Don't Capture: How to Solve Our Prisoner Problem." *New York Post,* July 10, 2006.

"Petraeus, Crocker Talk of Iraq's Fear, Progress: Warn Not to Expect Solid Judgment on U.S. Buildup Now until November." MSNBC, September 5, 2007. www.msnbc.msn.com/id/19844224/.

Petraeus, David. "Learning Counterinsurgency: Observations from Soldiering in Iraq." *Military Review* (January–February 2006): 2–12.

———. "Multi-National Forces-Iraq Counterinsurgency Guidance." MNF-I Headquarters (June 2007): 1–3.

———. "Transcript: General Petraeus on the Way Ahead in Iraq." *Military Review* (March–April 2007): 1–4.

Puri, Salil. "Americans Need Patience with Low-Intensity Conflicts like Iraq." *Daily Texan,* April, 25, 2007.

Raghaven, Sudarsan, and Thomas E. Ricks. "Outpost Attack Highlights Troop Vulnerabilities." *Washington Post,* April 25, 2007.

Rodriques-Goulart, Fernando. "Combat Motivation." *Military Review* (November–December 2006): 93–96.

Salmoni, Barak A. "Effective Use of a Translator for U.S. Marine Forces in OIF-2." Naval Postgraduate School, July 30, 2004.

Scahill, Jeremy. "The Miami Model." *Democracy Now!* November 2003. www.democracynow.org/static/miamimodel.shtml.

Sepp, Kalev I. "Best Practices in Counterinsurgency." *Military Review* (May–June 2005): 8–12.

Shanker, Thom. "Civil War Risk in Iraq Rises, U.S. Commander Says." *New York Times,* August 4, 2006.

Sly, Liz. "Some See 'Coup' as Iraq's Best Hope: Ex-Premier Allawi Building Political Bloc to Challenge al-Maliki." *Chicago Tribune,* September 1, 2007.

Tomes, Robert R. "Relearning Counterinsurgency Warfare." *Parameters* (Spring 2004): 22–23.

UN Security Council Report: Somalia March 2007. United Nations Security Council, March 2007.

Vail, Thomas. "Underestimating the Insurgency and the Contemporary Operating Environment in OIF." Unpublished paper.

West, Bing. "Battle of the Narratives." *National Review* (July 30, 2007).

West, Bing, and Owen West. "The Laptop Is Mightier Than the Sword." *New York Times,* June 15, 2007.

Williams, Timothy. "Culture—We Need Some of That! Cultural Knowledge and Army Officer Professional Development." Carlisle Barracks, PA: U.S. Army War College, March 15, 2006.

Woodward, Calvin. "White House Holds Firm on Iraq Strategy." Associated Press, July 15, 2007.

Wunderle, William. "How to Negotiate in the Middle East." *Military Review* (March–April 2007): 33–37.

Zakaria, Fareed. "We Are Not Losing the War against Radical Islam." *Newsweek,* July 2, 2007. FareedZakaria.com.

Zoroya, Gregg. "Troops' 1-Month Breaks Blocked." *USA Today,* June 19, 2007.

BOOKS, FIELD MANUALS, AFTER-ACTION REPORTS (AARS), AND MONOGRAPHS

Allard, Kenneth. *Warheads: Cable News and the Fog of War.* Annapolis, MD: Naval Institute Press, 2006.

Allawi, Ali A. *The Occupation of Iraq: Winning the War, Losing the Peace.* New Haven, CT: Yale University Press, 2007.

Anderson, Liam, and Gareth Stansfield. *The Future of Iraq: Dictatorship, Democracy, or Division?* New York: Palgrave MacMillan, 2004.

Babcok, Robert O. *Operation Iraqi Freedom I: A Year in the Sunni Triangle.* Tuscaloosa, AL: St. John's Press, 2005.

Baker, James A., and Lee H. Hamilton. *The Iraq Study Group Report: The Way Forward—A New Approach.* New York: Vintage Books, 2006.

Bamford, James. *A Pretext for War: 9/11, Iraq, and the Abuse of America's Intelligence Agencies.* New York: Doubleday, 2004.

Becket, Ian F. W. *Modern Insurgencies and Counter-Insurgencies: Guerrillas and Their Opponents since 1750.* New York: Routledge, 2001.

Beckhard, Richard, Frances Hesselbein, and Marshall Goldsmith. *The Leader of the Future: New Visions, Strategies and Practices for the Next Era.* San Francisco: Jossey-Bass, 1997.

Bennis, Warren. *On Becoming a Leader.* New York: Addison Wesley, 1989.

Birtle, Andrew J. *U.S. Army Counterinsurgency and Contingency Operations Doctrine, 1860–1941.* Washington, DC: Center of Military History, United States Army, 2001.

Bogdanos, Matthew. *Thieves of Baghdad: One Marine's Passion to Recover the World's Greatest Stolen Treasures.* New York: Bloomsbury, 2005.

Bremer, L. Paul, III. *My Year in Iraq: The Struggle to Build a Future of Hope.* New York: Threshold Editions, 2006.

Burden, Matthew Currier. *The Blog of War: Front-Line Dispatches from Soldiers in Iraq and Afghanistan.* New York: Simon & Shuster, 2006.

Byers, Michael. *War Law: Understanding International Law and Armed Conflict.* New York: Grove Press, 2005.

Canadian National Defense B-GL-300-003/FP-000 Land Force Command Manual. Kingston, Ontario: Director of Army Doctrine, 1996.

Caraccilo, Dominic J. *Terminating the Ground War in the Persian Gulf: A Clausewitzian Examination.* Washington, DC: AUSA Land Warfare Papers, September 1997.

Carroll, James. *Crusade: Chronicles of an Unjust War.* New York: Metropolitan Books, 2004.

Chandrasekaran, Rajiv. *Imperial Life in the Emerald City: Inside Iraq's Green Zone.* New York: Alfred E. Knopf, 2006.

Chyet, Michael L. *Kurdish-English Dictionary.* New Haven, CT:Yale University Press, 2003.

Clark,Wesley K. *Winning Modern Wars: Iraq, Terrorism, and the American Empire.* New York: PublicAffairs, 2003.

Clausewitz, Carl von. *On War.* Translated and edited by Michael Howard and Peter Paret. Princeton, NJ: Princeton University Press, 1984.

Clutterbuck, Richard L. *The Long, Long War: Counterinsurgency in Malaya and Vietnam.* Westport, CT: Praeger, 1966.

Cordesman, Anthony H. *The Iraq War: Strategy, Tactics, and Military Lessons.* Westport, CT: Praeger, 2003.

DA Pamphlet 550-104: Human Factors Consideration of Undergrounds in Insurgencies.

Diamond, Larry. *Squandered Victory:The American Occupation and the Bungled Effort to Bring Democracy to Iraq.* New York:Times Books, 2005.

Esposito, John L. *The Islamic Threat: Myth or Reality.* New York: Oxford University Press, 1999.

Field Manual (FM) 22-10: Command. Fort Leavenworth, KS: Department of the Army.

Field Manual (FM) 22-100: Leadership. Fort Leavenworth, KS: Department of the Army, August 31, 1999.

Field Manual (FM) 27-100: Legal Support to Operations. Fort Leavenworth, KS: Department of the Army, updated September 1991.

Field Manual (FM) 3-0: Operations. Fort Leavenworth, KS: Department of the Army, June 2001.

Field Manual (FM) 3-07: Stability Operations and Support Operations. Fort Leavenworth, KS: Department of the Army, updated February 11, 2005.

Field Manual Interim (FM-I) 3-07.22: Counterinsurgency Operations. Fort Leavenworth, KS: Department of the Army, 2004.

Field Manual (FM) 3-24: Counterinsurgency. Fort Leavenworth, KS: Department of the Army, June 2006.

Field Manual (FM) 6-22: Leadership. Fort Leavenworth, KS: Department of the Army, October 12, 2006.

Field Manual (FM) 90-8: Counterguerrilla Operations. Fort Leavenworth, KS: Department of the Army, 1986.

Field Manual (FM) 100-20/Air Force Pamphlet (AFP) 3-20: Military Operations in Low Intensity Conflict. Fort Leavenworth, KS: Department of the Army, 1986.

Field Manual (FM) 100-23: Peace Operations. Fort Leavenworth, KS: Department of the Army, 1994.

Fleet Marine Force Manual (FMFM) 8-2: Counterinsurgency Operations. Quantico, VA: United States Marine Corps, 1980.

Fontenot, Gregory. *On Point:The United States Army in Operation Iraqi Freedom.* Annapolis, MD: Naval Institute Press, 2005.

Galbraith, Peter W. *The End of Iraq: How American Incompetence Created a War without End.* New York: Simon & Shuster, 2006.

Galula, David. *Counterinsurgency Warfare:Theory and Practice.* Westport, CT: Praeger Paperback, 2006.

———. *Pacification in Algeria, 1956-1958.* Santa Monica, CA: Rand Corporation, 2006.

Gerges, Fawaz A. *America and Political Islam: Clash of Cultures or Clash of Interests.* New York: Cambridge University Press, 1999.

Gordon, Michael R., and Bernard E.Trainor. *Cobra II:The Inside Story of the Invasion and Occupation of Iraq.* New York: Pantheon Books, 2006.

Graff, Jonathan K. *United States Counterinsurgency Doctrine and Implementation in Iraq.* Fort Leavenworth, KS: Army Command and General Staff College School of Advanced Military Studies, May 26, 2004.

Hart, B. H. Liddell. *Strategy.* New York: New American Library, 1974.

Hersh, Seymour M. *Chain of Command: The Road from 9/11 to Abu Ghraib.* New York: Harper Collins Publishers, 2004.

Joes, Anthony James. *Resisting Rebellion: The History and Politics of Counterinsurgency.* Lexington: University Press of Kentucky, 2004.

Johnson, Robin Denise. *Leadership Basics.* Self-published, 2003.

Joint Publication (JP) 1-02: Department of Defense Dictionary of Military and Associated Terms. Washington, DC: Government Printing Office, March 22, 2007.

Joint Publication (JP) 3-07.1: Joint Tactics, Techniques, and Procedures for Foreign Internal Defense. Washington, DC: Government Printing Office, April 30, 2004.

Joint Publication (JP) 5-0: Joint Operations Planning. Washington, DC: Government Printing Office, December 26, 2004.

Jurgensmeyer, Mark. *Terror in the Mind of God: The Global Rise of Religious Violence.* Berkeley: University of California Press, 2000.

Keegan, John. *The Iraq War.* New York: Alfred E. Knopf, 2004.

Kitson, Frank. *Low Intensity Operations: Subversion, Insurgency, Peace-keeping.* London: Faber, 1971.

Krepinevich, Andrew F., Jr. *The Army and Vietnam.* Baltimore: Johns Hopkins University Press, 1986.

Lacey, Jim. *Takedown: The 3rd Infantry Division's Twenty-One Day Assault on Baghdad.* Annapolis, MD: Naval Institute Press, 2007.

Linn, Brian McAllistar. *The U.S. Army and Counterinsurgency in the Philippine War, 1899-1902.* Chapel Hill: University of North Carolina Press, 1989.

Mackey, Sandra. *The Reckoning: Iraq and the Legacy of Saddam Hussein.* New York: W. W. Norton & Company, 2002.

Mauroni, Al. *Where Are the WMDs? The Reality of Chem-Bio Threats on the Home Front and the Battlefront.* Annapolis, MD: Naval Institute Press, 2006.

Maxwell, John C., and Zig Ziglar. *The 21 Irrefutable Laws of Leadership.* Nashville: Thomas Nelson, 1998.

McCuen, John J. *The Art of Counter-Revolutionary War: Strategy of Counterinsurgency.* St. Petersburg, FL: Hailer, 1966.

McGovern, George, and William R. Polk. *Out of Iraq: A Practical Plan for Withdrawal Now.* New York: Simon & Shuster, 2006.

Murray, Williamson, and Robert H. Scales, Jr. *The Iraq War: A Military History.* Cambridge, MA: Belknap Press, 2003.

Nagl, John A. *Learning to Eat Soup with a Knife.* Chicago: Chicago Press, 2002.

Naftali, Timothy. *Blind Spot: A Secret History of American Counterterrorism.* New York: Basic Books, 2005.

Neven, Tom. *On the Frontline: A Personal Guidebook for the Physical, Emotional, and Spiritual Challenges of Military Life.* Colorado Springs, CO: Waterbrook Press, 2006.

The 9/11 Commission Report: Final Report of the National Commission on Terrorist Attacks upon the United States. New York: W. W. Norton & Company, August 31, 2004.

O'Neill, Bard. *Insurgency and Terrorism: From Revolution to Apocalypse.* Washington, DC: Potomac Books, 2005.

Orsini, Dominique. *Multinational Operations in Somalia, Haiti, and Bosnia: A Comparative Study.* Montreal, Quebec: McGill University, 1997.

Packer, George. *The Assassins' Gate: America in Iraq.* New York: Farrar, Straus and Giroux, 2005.

Parsa, Misagh. *States, Ideologies, and Social Revolutions: A Comparative Analysis of Iran, Nicaragua, and the Philippines.* New York: Cambridge, 2000.

Peters, Ralph. *Beyond Terror.* Mechanicsburg, PA: Stackpole Books, 2002.

———. *Wars of Blood and Faith: The Conflicts That Will Shape the Twenty-First Century.* Mechanicsburg, PA: Stackpole Books, 2007.

Pollack, Kenneth M. *The Threatening Storm: The Case for Invading Iraq.* New York: Random House, 2002.

Posen, Barry R., and Andrew L. Ross. "Competing Visions for U.S. Grand Strategy." In *Strategy and Force Planning,* 2nd ed., edited by Strategy and Force Planning Faculty, 102–43. Newport, RI: Naval War College, 1997.

Prospects for Iraq's Stability: A Challenging Road Ahead. Washington, DC: National Intelligence Estimate, January 2007.

Purdum, Todd S. *A Time of Our Choosing: America's War in Iraq.* New York: Times Books, 2003.

Ready First Combat Team (1/1 Armor) After Action Report. January 2006–February 2007.

Ricks, Thomas E. *Fiasco: The American Military Adventure in Iraq.* New York: Penguin Press, 2006.

Rieckhoff, Paul. *Chasing Ghosts: Failures and Facades in Iraq: A Soldier's Perspective.* New York: NAL Caliber, 2006.

Sageman, Marc. *Understanding Terror Networks.* Philadelphia, PA: University of Pennsylvania Press, 2004.

Shadid, Anthony. *Night Draws Near: Iraq's People in the Shadow of America's War.* New York: Henry Holt and Company, 2005.

Special Text 3.05.206: Counter Urban Insurgency Planning Guide. John F. Kennedy Special Warfare Center and School, 2003.

Stewart, Rory. *The Prince of the Marshes: And Other Occupational Hazards of a Year in Iraq.* Orlando, FL: Harcourt, 2006.

Summers, Harry G. *On Strategy: A Critical Analysis of the Vietnam War.* Novato, CA: Presidio Press, 1995.

Testimony of General Barry R. McCaffrey. West Point, NY: Adjunct Professor of International Affairs, April 17, 2007.

Thompson, Robert. *Defeating Communist Insurgency: The Lessons of Malaya and Vietnam.* New York: Praeger, 1966.

Torchbearer National Security Report: The U.S. Army's Role in Stability Operations. Washington, DC: AUSA, October 2006.

Tucker, Mike. *Hell Is Over: Voices of the Kurds after Saddam.* Guilford, CT: Lyons Press, 2004.

Van Crevald, Martin. *The Art of War: War and Military Thought.* New York: Smithsonian Books, 2005.

Vrooman, Stephen. *A Counterinsurgency Campaign Plan Concept: The Galula Compass.* Fort Leavenworth, KS: Army Command and General Staff College School of Advanced Military Studies, May 26, 2005.

West, Bing. *No True Glory: A Frontline Account of the Battle of Fallujah.* New York: Bantam Books, 2005.

Zakaria, Fareed. *The Future of Freedom: Illiberal Democracy at Home and Abroad.* New York: W. W. Norton & Company, 2004.

SPEECHES AND BRIEFINGS

Barrett, Roby. Briefing on "Iraq: The Way Forward" to the 3rd Brigade Combat Team, 101st Airborne Division (Air Assault). Fort Campbell, Kentucky, August 21, 2007.

Bush, George W. *Statement on Iraq Strategy.* January 10, 2007.

Derleth, Jim. USAID briefing to the 3rd Brigade, 101st Airborne Division (Air Assault). Fort Campbell, Kentucky, August 31, 2007.

Democratic Presidential Debate hosted by CNN and YouTube. Charleston, South Carolina, July 23, 2007.

WEBSITES AND RADIO SHOWS

Answers.com. www.answers.com.

BBC Homepage. http://news.bbc.co.uk/1/hi/world/africa/3158640.stm.

Council on Foreign Relations. www.cfr.org/publication/13333/.

eMilitary. www.emilitary.org/article.php?aid=11577.

"How to Get Out of Iraq: A Forum." *The Nation.* www.thenation.com/doc/20040524/forum.

McMaster, H. R. Interview. *Frontline,* February 2, 2007. www.pbs.org/wgbh/pages/frontline/endgame/interviews/mcmaster.html.

Military Conflict Institute. www.militaryconflict.org/.

Radio Iowa. www.radioiowa.com/.

Small War Center of Excellence. www.smallwar.quantico.usmc.mil.

Small Wars Journal. www.smallwarsjournal.com/documents/kilcullen1.pdf.

U.S. Army Center for Lessons Learned Online. http://call.army.mil.

Vail, Thomas. Interview, August 3, 2007.

Wikipedia. http://en.wikipedia.org/wiki/Main_Page.

ACKNOWLEDGMENTS

This book is dedicated to the brave men and women—and their families—who fight for freedom every day in Iraq and across the globe. To the Screaming Eagle soldiers of the 101st Airborne Division (Air Assault) and their families, you truly are our second family.

And to the Caraccilo and Thompson families, thank you for your love and support. Andrea would also like to dedicate the book, her first, to her parents, Phil and Georgia Hanson, the strongest command team she knows.

INDEX

Sadr, Moqtada, viii, x
Shiites, viii, ix, x, 26, 76, 77, 78,
　80, 90, 95, 110, 124, 138,
　153, 157, 160, 161, 162, 179
　determined to be governing
　majority, 92
Small Wars Manual (1940), 34, 35
Somalia, as historical precedent,
　67–72
Special Text 3.05.206, 44
Summers, Col. Harry, 36
Sunnis, iv, viii, ix, x, 5–6, 27, 76,
　77, 78, 89, 92, 95, 96, 130,
　138, 149, 152, 157, 160, 161,
　162
　fear discrimination, 26
　oppose splitting Iraq into states,
　80
　resent loss of power and pres-
　tige, 5–6, 49
　see Maliki cabinet as Shiite
　puppet, 79
Sun Tzu, 65, 135
Syria, 92

Task Force Band of Brothers,
　xiv, 25, 113, 117, 118, 124,
　125
Task Force Rakkasan, 112–13
theater security cooperation
　program (TSCP), 42–43, 44
Thucydides, 73
"Triangle of Death," vi–vii, 76,
　112, 123, 145
TSCP. *See* theater security coop-
　eration program

Turkey, 92
Turner, Lt. Gen. Tom, 25, 113,
　118, 125, 158
　litmus test for success, xiv

United Nations, 79–80, 178
　in Somalia, 67–70

Vietnam War, insurgency and,
　30–31, 36–37
Vines, Lt. Gen. J. R., 174

Warner, Sen. John, 62
War on Terrorism, xix, 2, 31, 42,
　45, 60, 93, 160, 174
Weinberger, Caspar, 72–73
West, Bing, 96–97
　foreword, iv–xi
withdrawal
　consequences of, 82
　difficulty of, 61
　timeline for, 61–63

U.S. Central Command (CENT-
　COM), 44, 147
　commanders, 10

Yarbrough, Brig. Gen. Jim, 24

Zakaria, Fareed, 150–51, 152,
　180
Zarqawi, Abu Musab al, viii,
　111–12, 179